Journal of ASTM International Selected Technical Papers STP1509

Up Against the Wall: An Examination of Building Envelope Interface Techniques and Systems

JAI Guest Editors:

Charles G. Carll
Barry G. Hardman
Theresa A. Weston

INTERNATIONAL
Standards Worldwide

ASTM International
100 Barr Harbor Drive
PO Box C700
West Conshohocken, PA 19428-2959

Printed in the U.S.A.

ASTM Stock #: STP1509

Library of Congress Cataloging-in-Publication Data
Up against the wall: an examination of building envelope interface / JAI guest editors,
Charlie G. Carll, Barry G. Hardman, Theresa A. Weston.
   p. cm.
   "ASTM Stock #: STP1509."
   Includes bibliographical references and index.
   ISBN 978-0-8031-3417-1 (alk. paper)
1. Exterior walls. 2. Siding (Building materials) 3. Waterproofing. 4. Windows. I. Carll,
Charles. II. Hardman, Barry G., 1940- III. Weston, Theresa A., 1958-
   TH2235.U625 2009
   690'.12--dc22   2009051260

Journal of ASTM International (JAI) Scope
The JAI is a multi-disciplinary forum to serve the international scientific and engineering
community through the timely publication of the results of original research and
critical review articles in the physical and life sciences and engineering technologies.
These peer-reviewed papers cover diverse topics relevant to the science and research that
establish the foundation for standards development within ASTM International.

Photocopy Rights

Peer Review Policy
Each paper published in this volume was evaluated by two peer reviewers and at least
one editor. The authors addressed all of the reviewers' comments to the satisfaction of both
the technical editor(s) and the ASTM International Committee on Publications.

The quality of the papers in this publication reflects not only the obvious efforts of the
authors and the technical editor(s), but also the work of the peer reviewers. In keeping with
long-standing publication practices, ASTM International maintains the anonymity of
the peer reviewers. The ASTM International Committee on Publications acknowledges
with appreciation their dedication and contribution of time and effort on behalf of
ASTM International.

Citation of Papers
When citing papers from this publication, the appropriate citation includes the paper
authors, "paper title", J. ASTM Intl., volume and number, Paper doi, ASTM International,
West Conshohocken, PA, Paper, year listed in the footnote of the paper. A citation is
provided as a footnote on page one of each paper.

Printed in Dayton, OH
January, 2010

Foreword

THIS SPECIAL ISSUE OF *JAI*, Special Technical Publication STP1509, *Up Against the Wall:* An Examination of Building Envelope Interface Techniques and Systems, contains papers presented at the symposium with the same name held in Tampa, FL, November 1, 2007. The symposium was jointly sponsored by ASTM International Committees E06 and E06.51.11.

The symposium co-chairs were Charles G. Carll, USDA Forest Service, Forest Products Laboratory, Madison, WI, USA and Theresa A. Weston, DuPont Nonwovens, Richmond, VA, USA. The lead organizer for the symposium was Barry G. Hardman, National Building Science Corporation, Temecula, CA, USA (deceased).

Dedication

This publication is dedicated to Barry G. Hardman

The Up Against the Wall Symposium was one of the last events to benefit from Barry's passion for innovation and the advancement of the construction industry. Barry was a designer and manufacturer of high-end custom commercial fenestration and installation details. From this platform he reached out to improve industry practices, and became the motive force behind the publication ASTM E2112 *Standard Practice for Installation of Exterior Windows, Doors and Skylights*. He told the group "to never give up" and guided the task-group through the decade long development process. He followed the publication of E2112 by giving his attention to championing innovative installation systems and to educating the industry by organizing workshops for DOE and BETEC and ASTM symposia. Barry was always hands-on and full steam ahead.

Contents

Overview

Up Against the Wall was the second of two symposia for which Barry Hardman served as the principal organizer. The first symposium, entitled Performance and Durability of the Window Wall Interface was held in Salt Lake City, Utah on April 18, 2004.

Barry Hardman was, until 2008, the chair of ASTM Task Group E.06.51.11, on Installation of Windows. Barry, and his wife, Jackie, were the keepers of the document for the series of drafts that would become ASTM E2112-01, -04, and finally -07. Barry had a unique talent for getting industry players to become involved in the effort of developing the Standard. He had intuitive sense regarding what was attainable in the development of an ASTM standard and what was not. Barry was adroit in the use of humor to cajole task group members into acting productively. The effort and competence displayed by Jackie in production and distribution of multiple drafts during development of the three successive versions of E2112 were impressive. Barry and Jackie consistently served as capable and gracious organizers of E06.51.11 activities.

The existence of E2112 has substantially improved window installation practices in residential construction in North America. The contents of E2112 are largely based on what a knowledgeable group of people (of appreciable size) deemed was their best professional judgment. Installation methods that were contrary to that judgment, and that furthermore would be viewed with suspicion by persons having a capacity for analytical reasoning, were nonetheless common prior to the publication of E2112. These poor practices became much less common with the publication of E2112. As pointed out in the lead presentation made at the current symposium however (see the lead manuscript by Mathis and Johnson), the evidentiary basis for what is contained in E2112 (in any of its versions), is modest. The professional judgment of the persons involved in developing the standard is, for the most part, not based on evidence that is quantified, or for which published documentation exists. Such shortage of evidence should be bothersome to persons trained in the natural or the engineering sciences. Although Barry was not formally trained in the sciences, he recognized that there was a shortage of evidence that could be objectively evaluated, and it bothered him a great deal. The purpose of each of the symposia that Barry organized was to serve as forum for the presentation of such evidence.

Actually, meeting this purpose has proven to be a challenge. STP1484 contained manuscripts presented at the April 2004 Symposium in Salt Lake City. Fewer than half of the manuscripts in STP1484 presented data. In planning for the *Up Against the Wall* Symposium, effort was made by the co-chairs (Barry Hardman, Theresa Weston, and I) to assure that presentations made at the symposium would include data. The invitation for submission of abstracts to Against the Wall stated that presentation of data was a requirement for inclusion in the symposium program. The title chosen for the symposium, having law-enforcement overtones, implied that this requirement would be strictly enforced.

ASTM Committee on Publications (COP) made the decision in 2003 that all manuscripts published in ASTM Selected Technical Papers (STPs) would be required to first be published in the Journal of ASTM International (JAI). This meant that manuscripts in STPs would (starting in 2004) be required to meet the standards of a peer-reviewed science and engineering journal. The decision regarding the suitability of a manuscript for publication in JAI is made by the Journal's Associate editor. Under the current policy, one of the symposium co-chairs, entitled the Editorial Board Member (EBM), selects peer reviewers, adjudicates issues of disagreement between reviewers and authors, and for each manuscript, makes a recommendation to the Associate editor. The recommendations that the EBM may make are to reject or accept a manuscript, or to send the manuscript back to the authors for revision. The implication made in the Symposium title regarding the issue of manuscript quality was thus serious; if the Editorial Board Member failed to enforce adequate standards, the Associate Editor would.

Barry Hardman served as the Editorial Board Member for manuscripts published in STP1484. That was the first STP in this field produced subsequent to the COPs 2003 decision requiring that symposia manuscripts be published in JAI. Barry was, as a rule, accommodating to authors. As stated previously, Barry knew the industry; he knew there was a dearth of published information in the field, and he knew that evidentiary standards in this industry are not as stringent as they are, for instance, in the electronics, chemical or aerospace industries. Thus Barry felt that manuscripts with flaws could nonetheless be valuable in filling an information vacuum. This view was not unique to Barry; roughly half the members of ASTM Committee E06 on Performance of Buildings seem to hold this view. This view axiomatically contrasts with that of the editor of any scientific journal (whose responsibility it is to maintain quality standards for the Journal). The publication of STP1484 involved a negotiated process between the EBM and the Associate Editor that considered both the standards of JAI and the norms that prevail in this industry. Insofar as the COPs policy decision regarding STPs was (at that time) recent, this process was deemed appropriate, and it was hoped that STP1484 would serve as a learning experience. The co-chairs for *Up Against the Wall* hoped that the experience associated with the production of STP1484 had indeed been instructive, and thus that the manuscripts submitted by authors for the *Up Against the Wall* symposium would more closely correspond with Journal standards.

Until December of 2007, Barry held the role of Editorial Board Member for manuscripts submitted to JAI for Against the Wall. Barry's health took a drastic downturn after July of 2007. He attended the symposium on November 1, but was obviously suffering. Barry passed away in early February of 2008. In December of 2007, Barry requested that I assume the role of Editorial Board Member. At that stage 21 manuscripts had been submitted (19 of which had been presented at the symposium). Barry had made an Editorial

Board Member recommendation for one manuscript. Editorial Board Member recommendations were thus needed for 20 manuscripts.

Of the 21 manuscripts submitted, twelve are published in this STP. Of the nine manuscripts submitted but not published, most could have been brought up to JAI standards by revision. That they were not revised and re-submitted probably reflects the priorities of the authors. The problems that rendered manuscripts unsuitable for Journal publication were: 1) stated findings, conclusions, or assertions that were not supported by the presentation of evidence, 2) excessive commercial overtones, 3) lack of a clear and coherent manuscript focus, 4) failure to adequately describe test procedures or conditions under which data were obtained, 5) over-extension of the applicability of an otherwise valid concept, 6) use of terminology in unique ways (generally in contrast with that in recognized standards such as ASTM E631), and 7) inaccurate statements regarding the contents of ASTM standards.

I acknowledge the efforts of Leslie Struble of the University of Illinois who served as Associate Editor to JAI. Leslie also served as Editorial Board Member (in my place) for two manuscripts; for each of these, it was appropriate for me to excuse myself from serving as EBM. I also acknowledge Linda Boniello of the American Institute of Physics (AIP) for her coordination of communications between me, the authors, the reviewers, and the Associate Editor. AIP's automated interface did most of the actual coordination, but Linda oversaw the actions taken by the system, cheerfully helped me navigate it when it didn't work in ways that were intuitively logical to me, and interceded in its operation when human intervention was necessary. On some occasions I communicated directly with authors (not through AIP's system). In those communications, it was common for authors to comment that they found Linda to be notably helpful.

The Associate Editor and I were in substantial agreement regarding manuscripts published in this STP. The process of manuscript approval was not negotiated; I studied the Journals standards, and made recommendations to Leslie that aligned with those standards. In no case did I appeal to Leslie to modify the Journals standards to account for industry norms. Most manuscripts published in this STP are thus, in my opinion, more substantive and well-reasoned than the vast majority of published manuscripts in this field. That having been said, it would be fair to note that only about half of the manuscripts included in this STP actually present original data. The manuscripts containing original experimental data are, for the most part, found toward the end of the STP (from manuscript #7 onward).

Finally, I recognize the determination of authors whose manuscripts are published in this STP. Every manuscript published in this STP underwent at least one revision.

Charles G. Carll
acting Editorial Board Member

Reprinted from JAI, Vol. 6, No. 7
doi:10.1520/JAI101242
Available online at www.astm.org/JAI

R. Christopher Mathis[1] and Steve Johnson[2]

What We Do Not Know: Perspectives on Wall-Window Combinations and Performance Assurance We Have yet to Address

ABSTRACT: Collaborative efforts over several years resulted in the development of ASTM E2112, "Standard Practice for the Installation of Exterior Windows, Doors and Skylights". Individuals from the window, sealant, and air barrier industries were involved in the development of the standard. Development of the standard was driven by a desire to reduce water leakage attributed to window installation practices, particularly in residential and light commercial construction. A consensus document addressing the installation of fenestration units in residential and light commercial construction was believed to be needed. While many believe that the development of ASTM E2112 has helped to reduce the prevalence of leaking installations, the Standard, even in its most updated form (ASTM E2112-07), still has significant limitations. This paper addresses some of the limitations of the Standard and is intended to provoke the further development and documentation of installation techniques for a wide array of wall-window combinations that are not yet addressed in ASTM E2112.

KEYWORDS: windows, walls, performance, risk, energy efficiency, durability, water performance, design loads, glass, structural performance, code compliance, builder training, durability, sustainability

The Basics of ASTM E2112

The most basic premise of ASTM E2112 [1] is that fenestration units must be adequately integrated with adjacent water-shedding surfaces and systems of the building envelope. The document recognizes that there are two general types of

Manuscript received May 17, 2007; accepted for publication May 28, 2009; published online July 2009.

[1] MC2 Mathis Consulting Co., Asheville, NC 28801.

[2] Andersen Corporation, Bayport, MN, 55003.

Cite as: Mathis, R. C. and Johnson, S., "What We Do Not Know: Perspectives on Wall-Window Combinations and Performance Assurance We Have yet to Address," *J. ASTM Intl.*, Vol. 6, No. 7. doi:10.1520/JAI101242.

1

wall systems: barrier wall systems (in which water is managed at the exterior surface) and membrane drainage walls (which employ a concealed weather-resistive barrier and provide means for managing water that penetrates past the exterior surface). ASTM E2266, "Standard Guide for Design and Construction of Low-Rise Frame Building Wall Systems to Resist Water Intrusion" [2], limits its scope to walls that contain sheathing and a weather-resistive barrier. E2266 reflects that the exterior walls of light-frame buildings are predominantly constructed as membrane drainage walls and that most incorporate sheathing panels. As will be discussed in greater detail later in this paper, ASTM E2112 contains extensive recommendations and instructions relating to installations in light-frame walls that incorporate wood-based sheathing and meager guidance relating to installations in walls of other constructions.

ASTM E2112 addresses two general types of windows: (a) windows with perimeter mounting flanges (nail fins) and (b) windows without perimeter mounting flanges (which it terms "non-finned," "block frame," or "box frame" windows). Standard E2112 makes an assumption that the flanges of windows with mounting flanges form a watertight seal with the frame of the window. Inasmuch as this feature is not present in non-finned windows, installed non-finned windows are assumed to be more prone to water penetration around their perimeters—between the window frame and the (factory-applied or site-installed) exterior casings or trim. The combinations of wall and window types recognized by ASTM E2112 can be represented as a 2×2 matrix, as shown in Table 1.

The document provides four sets of explicit steps for installation of fin type windows in newly constructed membrane drainage walls of one particular type. That type is a typical wood stud-frame wall that incorporates wood-based (plywood or oriented strand board) sheathing. The four sets of installation steps differ from each other based on sequencing of the window installation relative to installation of the weather-resistive barrier membrane and on the order of installation of flexible jamb flashing sheets relative to insertion of the window into the rough opening. Standard E2112 also provides one set of less-explicit steps for installation of block frame windows in newly constructed membrane drainage walls of the same type (a stud-frame wall incorporating wood-based sheathing).

Standard E2112 also provides recommendations relating to installation of replacement windows. It addresses partial replacement (in which the frames of the existing windows are left in place) and complete replacement (in which the units in their entirety—including frames—are removed and replaced). The recommendations relating to the replacement of existing windows are (in the case of partial replacement) organized with regard to window type (finned or non-finned) but are not organized with regard to wall type. Only general recommendations are provided—not explicit sets of installation protocols or instructions. The section of Standard E2112 that introduces the subject of replacement installations specifically states that "Many combinations of construction detail variables exist for this type of installation."

Continued efforts to further define and expand these generic installation recommendations to specific wall and window combinations have identified clear limits in our window installation and water management knowledge

TABLE 1—*Generic window and wall combinations in ASTM E2112-07.*

	Barrier Wall System	Membrane/Drainage System
Fin-type window (assumes that the fin/frame junction of the window is, or can be made, watertight.)		
Non-fin-type/block frame window		

base—even with common wall construction systems. These limitations are made even more glaring when viewed in the context of an expanding array of wall systems (with different degrees of water tolerance) combined with different window types. These limitations are further magnified when viewed in terms of builder risk—due to water exposure, wind loads, structural considerations, and skilled labor availability.

This paper attempts to help clarify and quantify what we do not (yet) know about the delivered performance assurance of the vast array of wall-window combinations, the loads to which they are exposed, and the need for additional window installation guidance. Ideally this paper will provide builders and other users with an understanding that ASTM E2112 provides generic guidance based on consensus efforts to date and that its recommendations must still be viewed in the context of the specific wall-window combination system being considered for a specific application. It will also help identify window +wall/risk combinations for which no data has yet been published assessing the application of these generic principles to specific systems. Where such specifics have not yet been addressed by these standards, this paper will also provide builders with a clear indication of risk due to a limited knowledge base.

This paper should also serve to encourage others in the window, wall, design, or building industries and to provide data for known wall-window combinations where such a knowledge base may be available. Hopefully readers of this paper will be provoked into providing further guidance and examples of proven window installation techniques for wall-window combinations that are not addressed in ASTM E2112. In addition, specific guidance is sought to address known regional variations (due to construction techniques, wind loads, water loads, labor issues, etc.) that impact final, delivered window and wall performance.

Specific Limitations of ASTM E2112

ASTM E2112 does not attempt to address the wide array of wall-window combinations that can be found in contemporary construction, nor does it attempt to address the possible range of environmental loadings to which a given wall-window combination may be exposed over its service life. Most of the recommendations made in this Standard are based primarily on professional judgment with little peer-reviewed, substantiating data with which to back up or otherwise defend the veracity of the recommendations.

An industry association provided a limited set of experimental test data applicable to the four sets of steps given in ASTM E2112 for installation of windows with nailing fins in light-frame walls incorporating wood-based sheathing and a weather-resistive barrier. Because walls of this construction predominate residential construction in North America, the choice of wall on which the testing was based was logical. The wall type is, although most prominent, only one of a variety of possible wall constructions that are currently used in new residential construction in North America.

The testing mentioned in the previous paragraph was performed on an installed window with integral flanges. ASTM E2112 recognizes that window flanges may be structural or non-structural and integral or applied. Applied flanges are not, by themselves, anticipated to form a watertight seal with the window frame. The Standard assumes that watertight seals can be formed between the applied flanges and the window frame by use of a sealant. Whether this can in fact be done with consistency under field conditions has not been ascertained.

Performance-related issues in these wall-window combinations are further multiplied by the other risk factors faced by builders attempting to address the proper techniques needed for a given project in a given location. These additional risk factors might include seismic forces, snow loads, likelihood of high wind events and wind-driven precipitation, sand and other wind-driven abrasives, environmental salinity, and other environmental considerations. These environmental variables require important builder decisions concerning "boundary conditions" and "design conditions." Is a builder to provide for water management to withstand a design condition that might be expected once per year, once every 10 years, or for the building's expected life? Is the installation technique to provide 95 % confidence against a design event? If a design event occurs, is the building's water tolerance sufficient to the amount of potential water intrusion?

For example, an installation method for a particular wall-window combination that performs admirably at one location may not perform adequately when subjected to the wind-driven rain loads on a building just a few miles away. Wind speeds during a rainstorm at coastal locations may be substantially higher than wind speeds during the same rainstorm at locations 10 or 15 miles inland. In addition, there is not as yet consensus regarding how to characterize a design storm with regard to rain-control design [3]. A design storm would be more intense than an average rainstorm but would be less intense than the most severe storm that could be anticipated over the life of the building. A storm as intense as the design storm would occur infrequently but may occur multiple times over the life of the building. A 10-year return period has been suggested as appropriate for rain-control design [4]. The (recently adopted) ASHRAE Criteria for Moisture-Control Design Analysis in Buildings [5] does not explicitly address the selection of return period for a design rainstorm, although it specifies that at least ten consecutive years of weather data be used when performing analyses; this implies recognition of a 10-year return period. been proposed [6] for relating historic weather data to simulation of design storms, with the ultimate goal of using such data in selecting appropriate levels of water spray rate and differential air pressure in laboratory spray testing. Based on the state of the knowledge at the time of document development, it is understandable that the recommendations and procedures of E2112 are not referenced to any specified level of wind-driven rain exposure and do not address regional or local variations in wind-driven rain exposure. In summary, ASTM E2112 does not attempt to quantify the level of resistance to water intrusion that is required of a given window installation.

These are just a few of the questions to be considered when deciding on which wall-window combination is being considered for a particular location and set of loads. This multitude of variables is compounded further by the availability of skilled labor to ultimately deliver the performance durability (and risk management) desired for a given project.

Writers' Perspective

We believe that future refinement and development of ASTM E2112 are needed, and should be based on documented experimentation and testing (with robust data sets), and on documented professional experience. In the absence of documented experimental data and experiential knowledge, we are left to "history" and "professional judgment" as the guiding principles behind any recommendations we might make.

As efforts continue at ASTM (and elsewhere) to provide guidance on best practices for addressing the wall-window interface in various building types, we are well-advised to recognize the limitations of our knowledge. We must clearly define the limits of both our experiential and experimental knowledge. Finally, we should invite (and challenge) others to bring their knowledge, data, and understanding to the task of refining Standard E2112.

What We Do Not Yet Know

As stated previously, there are many different wall constructions currently being used in North America. Some of the various types are typically constructed as barrier walls as defined in ASTM E2112. Others are typically constructed as membrane drainage walls as defined in ASTM E2112. Still others can hypothetically be constructed as either barrier or membrane drainage walls.

Table 2 provides a starting point for discussions addressing what we do not (yet) know about the many varied types of wall-window interfaces and the installation techniques necessary to ensure good building water management. This table shows combinations for which ASTM E2112 provides installation instructions and where those recommendations are supported with experimental test data.

For the combination of an integral flange window in a light-frame wall with wood-based sheathing, ASTM E2112 provides installation instructions that are based on limited experimental data. For applied-flange windows installed in this type of wall, ASTM E2112 provides installation instructions based on experimental data for integral flange windows. For block frame windows (with or without factory-applied exterior casings) installed in this type of wall, ASTM E2112 provides installation instructions that are based on conceptual logic but not that are supported by experimental data (at least not with data that has been shared with the writers or the standards development task group). These two cells of the table are marked with "ND," (indicating "no data"). Most other cells in the table are marked with "NA" (indicating "not addressed by ASTM E2112").

The table also shows some wall-window combinations where testing or standards are currently known to be under development.

The combinations of windows and wall systems shown in Table 2 are not

TABLE 2—An expanded listing of wall-window combinations.

Wall Type (Based on Structural Elements and Integration Surface)	Window Type (Based on Integration Interface)				
	Integral flange; frontal location (like some aluminum windows)	Integral flange; non-frontal location (like some clad-wood and vinyl windows)	Applied flange; non-frontal location (like many clad-wood windows)	Block frame with factory-applied ext. casings ("brick mold") (like many wood windows)	Block frame without factory-applied casings
Wood frame with wood-based sheathing	NA	ASTM E2112	ND, but methods for integral flange windows are assumed to apply	ND	ND
Wood frame with rigid foam insulating sheathing	NA	NA	NA	NA	NA
Wood frame with wood sheathing and rigid foam insulating sheathing	NA	NA	NA	NA	NA
Wood frame with no sheathing (California wall)	NA	NA	NA	NA	NA
Structural insulated panels (SIPs)	NA	NA, but E2112 may apply	NA	NA	NA
Concrete masonry units with stucco applied directly (Florida wall)	Developed by FMA/AAMA [7]	NA	NA	NA	NA
Concrete masonry unit with grade D paper, lath, and stucco	NA	NA	NA	NA	NA
Concrete masonry unit with brick veneer	NA	NA	NA	NA	NA
Poured concrete with applied waterproofing (basement wall)	NA	NA	NA	NA	NA
Poured concrete with applied waterproofing and exterior insulating sheathing	NA	NA	NA	NA	NA
Poured concrete with foam insulation on interior and exterior [insulating concrete forms (ICFs)]	NA	NA	NA	NA	NA
Poured concrete with foam insulation in the center	NA	NA	NA	NA	NA
Steel frame with gypsum and/or rigid fiberglass insulating sheathing	NA	NA, but E2112 may apply	NA	NA	NA
Log (stacked timber)	NA	NA	NA	NA	NA
Autoclaved aerated concrete	NA	NA	NA	NA	NA

TABLE 2— (Continued.)

Wall Type (Based on Structural Elements and Integration Surface)	Window Type (Based on Integration Interface)				
	Integral flange; frontal location (like some aluminum windows)	Integral flange; non-frontal location (like some clad-wood and vinyl windows)	Applied flange; non-frontal location (like many clad-wood windows)	Block frame with factory-applied ext. casings ("brick mold") (like many wood windows)	Block frame without factory-applied casings
Rammed earth or adobe	NA	NA	NA	NA	NA
Straw bale	NA	NA	NA	NA	NA

Note: ND indicates "no data"; NA indicates "not addressed by ASTM E2112".

exhaustive. The table is, instead, provided to emphasize the scope of additional test data needed to "prove" the generic recommendations of Standard E2112. There are certainly other combinations and variables not included in the table. We can only say "good building water management" because that only helps to further define the boundary conditions and limitations of our current and future recommendations. Cells in the table that show ND or NA indicate areas where future research, testing, and standards recommendation development efforts are needed.

Topics for Additional Research, Testing, and Investigation

While Table 2 may seem disheartening to those wishing to apply ASTM E2112 principles to their specific window installation and water management objectives, the good news is that many of the guiding principles in ASTM E2112 can be applied to every project. In fact, new standards development efforts are underway to specifically define these guiding principles in such a way as to be applicable to almost any project.

Another reason for optimism in the face of these expanding myriad wall-window performance combinations is that more laboratory and field-scale testing is now underway. For example, industry associations have begun to conduct testing and to draft procedures intended to expand the knowledge base of proper installation techniques. While ASTM has not (yet) developed a laboratory or field test for assessing installed window performance, efforts toward those ends are also underway. These tests are extremely important when making decisions about design events and boundary conditions on specific recommendations.

There is an increasing interest in addressing the issue of "installed performance." The challenge will be defining a reasonable prescriptive procedure that covers most of the anticipated jobsite and environmental conditions versus how to measure actual installed performance for a specific field application and wall-window combination.

Another area of needed research is on the subject of "performance equivalence." Laboratory tests in a controlled and steady-state environment may yield one set of results, while the same test in the field (with more uncontrolled variables) may yield what might appear as very different results. Should the laboratory test method be adjusted? Is the field test too severe or not severe enough? What defines essentially equivalent performance when installed performance is not consistently defined?

These questions—and many more like them—suggest the need to re-look at establishing some performance standards.

In the absence of "performance" being clearly defined, building industry participants are left to the chaos of marketing claims, non-comparable test methods, and increased liability exposure. We must ask ourselves as standards writers, flashing providers, wall designers, window manufacturers, testing specialists, and building industry leaders if we are content to let installed performance be solely defined in the courtroom.

Acknowledgments

The writers would like to acknowledge the editorial support and assistance of Charles Carll in the review and improvement of this paper.

References

[1]   ASTM E2112-07, 2007, "Standard Practice for Installation of Exterior Windows, Doors, and Skylights," *Annual Book of ASTM Standards*, Vol. 04.12, ASTM International, West Conshohocken, PA, 87 pp.

[2]   ASTM E2266-04, 2004, "Standard Guide for Design and Construction of Low-Rise Frame Building Wall Systems to Resist Water Intrusion," *Annual Book of ASTM Standards*, Vol. 04.12, ASTM International, West Conshohocken, PA, 15 pp.

[3]   Carll, C., "Rainwater Intrusion in Light-Frame Buildings," *Proceedings of the PATH Second Annual Conference on Durability and Disaster Mitigation in Wood-frame Buildings*, Nov. 6–8, 2000, Forest Products Society, Madison, WI, 2001.

[4]   Saunders, C., "Environmental Conditions," Final Report, Vol. 2, Task 2, IEA Annex 24, International Energy Agency, Leuven, Belgium, 1996.

[5]   ANSI/ASHRAE Standard 160-2009, 2009, "Criteria for Moisture-Control Design Analysis in Buildings," American Society of Heating Refrigerating and Air-Conditioning Engineers, Atlanta, GA, 14 pp.

[6]   Cornick, S. M. and Lacasse, M. A., "An Investigation of Climate Loads on Building Facades for Selected Locations in the United States," *J. ASTM Int.*, Vol. 6, No. 2, 2009, Paper ID JAI101210.

[7]   FMA-AAMA 200-XX, Draft, 2007, "Standard Practice for the Installation of Windows with Frontal Flanges for Surface Barrier Masonry Construction," www.f-mausaonline.org.

Erratum for JAI101242, Journal of ASTM International

What We Don't Know: Perspectives on Wall-Window Combinations and Performance Assurance We Have Yet To Address, R. Mathis and S. Johnson; published JAI Volume 6, Issue 7, (July, 2009) and STP1509, Up Against the Wall: An Examination of Building Envelope Interface.

Page 3, Line 30, should read: "…Only recently has a methodology been proposed [6] for relating historic weather data to simulation of design storms,"

Reprinted from JAI, Vol. 6, No. 2
doi:10.1520/JAI101210
Available online at www.astm.org/JAI

S. M. Cornick[1] and M. A. Lacasse[1]

An Investigation of Climate Loads on Building Façades for Selected Locations in the United States

ABSTRACT: The ability of a wall assembly to manage rainwater and control rain penetration depends on the assembly configuration, including interface details for penetrations, and on the rain loads to which the wall is subjected. There are a variety different protocols for evaluating the ability wall systems to resist water intrusion. Generally they involve spraying varying amounts of water while maintaining a pressure difference across the specimen. Across the conterminous United States hourly weather data for extended periods (climatic data) is available for many locations. From this climatic data estimates of wind-driven rain loads can be determined. We answer the question of how often these combinations of rainfall intensities and pressure are likely to present a problem with respect to moisture management of the assembly and how often these are likely to occur over the expected life of the wall assembly. Climate information related to rainfall and wind-driven rain for Boston, Miami, Minneapolis, Philadelphia, and Seattle are provided. A methodology for generating rates of water spray impinging on and pressure differences acting across the wall assembly is also developed. Although the methodology was primarily developed to select the proper testing criteria and test conditions to mimic real events, it can also be used by designers and practitioners to: (i) determine the response of the wall assembly to the effects of wind-driven rain; (ii) estimate design loads below which adverse effects on the assembly are minimized; (iii) assess the likelihood and degree of dam-

Manuscript received May 3, 2007; accepted for publication November 18, 2008; published online January 2009.

[1] Institute for Research in Construction, National Research Council Canada, 1200 Montreal Road, Building M24, Ottawa, ON, K1A 0R6, E-mail: Steven.Cornick@nrc-cnrc.gc.ca

Cite as: Cornick, S. M. and Lacasse, M. A., "An Investigation of Climate Loads on Building Façades for Selected Locations in the United States," J. ASTM Intl., Vol. 6, No. 2. doi:10.1520/JAI101210.

age to the assembly when design loads are exceeded; (iv) estimate the long-term performance of the wall assembly based on watertightness and moisture management the wall assembly.

KEYWORDS: rainwater entry, rain penetration, wall performance testing, water intrusion, wind-driven rain, extreme value analysis

Nomenclature

Greek Symbols

$$\alpha = \text{Weibull distribution scale parameter}$$
$$\delta, \delta_{met} = \text{Boundary layer thickness at the site and at the met. Station, m}$$
$$\gamma = \text{Weibull distribution shape parameter}$$
$$\pi = \text{Pi}$$
$$\theta = \text{Angle of wind to the outward wall normal, }°$$
$$\rho_{air} = \text{Density of air, 1.22 kg/m}^3$$
$$\sigma = \text{Unbiased standard deviation}$$
$$\Phi_{pred} = \text{Raindrop diameter, mm}$$
$$\Gamma(\ ) = \text{Gamma function}$$

Latin Symbols

$$a, amet = \text{Factors for wind height correction}$$
$$f_{drf} = \text{DRF time averaging factor}$$
$$f_p = \text{Wind pressure factor}$$
$$f_{rain} = \text{Rain time averaging factor}$$
$$f_t = \text{Wind terrain factor}$$
$$h = \text{Height of interest, m}$$
$$p = \text{Cumulative probability of an event}$$
$$r_t = \text{Equivalent rainfall intensity } t \text{ averaging period, mm/h}$$
$$r_h = \text{Hourly rainfall intensity, mm/h}$$
$$s = \text{Standard extremal variate}$$
$$t = \text{Time}$$
$$x_n = \text{Expected value at } T$$
$$DRF = \text{Driving-rain factor, s/m}$$
$$DRF_t = \text{Driving-rain factor for t averaging period, s/m}$$
$$DRF_{60} = \text{Driving-rain factor 60-min averaging period, s/m}$$
$$DRWP = \text{Driving-rain wind pressure, Pa}$$
$$H_{met} = \text{Reference height, m}$$
$$RDF = \text{Rain Deposition Factor}$$
$$T = \text{Return period, } y$$

$T_{WDR(\text{Direction})}$, = Return period for the extreme WDR and DRWP in a given
$T_{DRWP(\text{Direction})}$ direction, years
$V(h)$ = Wind speed at height, h
V_t = Terminal velocity of raindrops, m/s
WDR = Wind-Driven Rain, L/m²-h
$\bar{X}$ = Sample set mean

Introduction

Weather may cause physical damage to building envelopes or result in moisture intrusion either as a result of deficiencies in the envelope or weather related damage. The extent to which singular climate events, such as tropical cyclones, tornadoes, and thunderstorms, cause damage to the built infrastructure is well known; building destruction or significant physical damage can accrue from high winds, lightning, hail, and flooding. Apart from the risk to catastrophic damage should structural design limits be exceeded, there is also interest in climatic conditions up to the design limit as these offer a significant risk for water intrusion. A building may be subjected to a severe climatic event and indeed survive structurally, but to what extent does it remain serviceable if it is not watertight and thus susceptible to water intrusion? The consequences of loss in watertightness are not insignificant although the costs of damages due to water intrusion are difficult to assess since the effects might be delayed and damages hidden from view within the structure of the envelope.

The fact that such events occur and cause damage does not essentially provide the type of information required to aid in the performance assessment of building façades and their related components, nor assist in establishing useful design criteria to manage the watertightness of wall assemblies. Of importance is obtaining knowledge of the wind-driven rain loads that occur over the course of such events; in essence, determining the magnitude and occurrence of wind-driven rain loads impinging on the surface of the façade. Information on the likely recurrence of key climatic events and the expected level at which these occur in a given time period helps provide a measure of the possible response of the wall. That is, understanding the level and recurrence of loads permits assessing the potential risk of inadequate performance of the wall assembly over time. A methodology for determining the magnitude and occurrence of wind-driven rain loads is required for selection of proper test conditions and testing criteria to replicate the basic climatic features of pluvial events. Acquiring information on the magnitude and occurrence of driving-rain loads allows designers and practitioners to: (i) determine the response of the wall assembly to the effects of wind-driven rain; (ii) estimate design loads below which adverse effects on the assembly are minimized; (iii) assess the likelihood and degree of damage to the assembly when design loads are exceeded; (iv) estimate the long-term performance of the wall assembly based on watertightness and moisture management the wall assembly. An applied methodology could in addition to the above be used in conjunction with hygrothermal, energy, and combined hygrothermal and energy models to assess a variety of performance factors such as energy use and moisture related damage. Finally, the methodology is proposed for use in the development of related test standards that could eventually be referenced in building codes.

Several studies have been completed in respect to assessing wind-driven rain on a geographical scale [1], the first of which were completed by Hoppestad in 1955 for Norway [2] and thereafter by Lacy [3] and others for the British Isles in the 60s and late 70s [4,5]. An extensive list of countries for which driving-rain maps have been produced in the manner suggested by Lacy can be found in Ref. [1], including work more recently carried out by Underwood [6] for the conterminous United States.

The work carried out by Underwood [6] was based on data obtained from the Solar and Meteorological Surface Observation Network (SAMSON) and the Hourly United States Weather Observations data set, compiled by the United States, National Climatic Data Center (NCDC); the information represents data extracted from 1961 to 1995 and from 182 stations across the United States.

Underwood's work is highly useful; it provides a measure of the wind-driven rain intensity normals[2] on an average annual basis as well as estimates of the seasonal variation (spring, summer, autumnal and winter) of intensities for the conterminous United States. Additionally, annual and seasonal WDR event duration normals (h/event) are provided. Underwood also reports the annual and seasonal WDR frequency normals in terms of hours of wind-driven rain as well as the total receipt of wind-driven rain (mm) and the directional characteristics for 20 selected locations. Useful but generalized information is provided about what might be expected on average to occur for different locations across the conterminous United States.

What is missing from the work carried out by Underwood is some measure of the expected recurrence of specific events, in particular the recurrence interval or return period,[3] T, for the different locations and a systematic means of arriving at these numbers consistent with properly derived statistical measures for determining wind-driven rain. This information is crucial, especially with regards to designing, monitoring, and testing wall systems for moisture management. When designing and testing walls, mean or averaged data are useful in generating first approximations and estimating the performance of designs. Prudent design, however, requires that assemblies function acceptably when subjected to loads well beyond mean or average conditions. Generally the magnitude of peak or extreme loads is determined by statistical analysis, usually extreme value analysis (EVA). When designing for peak or extreme loads, the actual values are based on the return period for the geographical location of

---

[2]A normal, as defined by the World Meteorological Organization, is an average of a particular climate variable, generally determined over a 30-year period.
[3]A recurrence interval or return period is an estimate of the interval of time between events

interest to the designer. Higher peaks and greater extreme loads are evidently obtained over longer return periods, but if designing to meet performance requirements at greater loads, this would typically entail more costly measures to ensure that the wall assembly has the necessary performance attributes to achieve the design requirements. Hence depending on the expected life of the assembly, a compromise is made between the overall cost of the wall assembly and the expected benefits of uninterrupted serviceability and of reduced risk of premature failure. Selecting the design period is of some importance if one considers the risk of failure of the system, the resulting loss in watertightness, and the ensuing consequences in terms of costs due to loss of service, or the cost to repair or replace wall components or indeed the entire wall system. Hence designing wall assemblies and selecting appropriate components for buildings in climates having severe storms that often recur requires an expectation of the load extremes, the recurrence of these extremes and knowledge of approaches that can mitigate the effects of these loads on the wall assembly and manage moisture intrusion to the assembly.

It is also necessary to assess the performance of wall assemblies to the expected in-service loads. In respect to the water management performance of cladding systems several testing protocols have been developed. For example, there are seven ASTM standard test methods for water penetration of walls or wall components a list of which is provided in Table 1.

As well, there is a similar set of test methods available in ISO and related European (EN) standards. Additionally, derivatives of standard methods are sometimes used in experimental tests [7,8].

It is clear that water tightness testing is a fundamental requirement to help ensure adequate management of water entry into, migration within and drainage from the wall assembly. Assurance of adequate watertightness of the envelope and components incorporated within the envelope helps ensure the long-term performance of the wall assembly [9].

All such test protocols simulate wind-driven rain conditions. Most of these protocols involve spraying water and applying a pressure difference across a wall specimen in a test chamber. The protocols use various combinations of water spray rates, pressure differences, and dwell times. In the test protocols, the combinations of levels of spray rate and pressures difference, and dwell times would ideally be related to some statistical analysis of climate data. Examples of protocols based on statistical analysis are given by Cornick [10] and Lacasse [11]. The Canadian standard CSA A440 for window specification [12] refers to ASTM E547, but states that the pressure settings must follow a stepwise progression that is outlined in the (CSA) standard. The water penetration performance of the windows are then related back to climate-maps and tables that present the "1 in 5" and "1 in 10" values for driving-rain wind pressure.

Objectives

The work described in this manuscript had two objectives. The first involved a comparison of the default spray rate of 3.4 L/min-m^2 in standards ASTM E331 and ASTM E547 with calculated wind-driven rain values derived from a sto-

TABLE 1—*List of ASTM standard test methods for water penetration of wall or wall components.*

ASTM Standard Designations[a]	Title
E331-00	Standard Test Method for Water Penetration of Exterior Windows, Skylights, Doors, and Curtain Walls by Uniform Static Air Pressure Difference
E514-08	Standard Test Method for Water Penetration and Leakage Through Masonry
E547-00	Standard Test Method for Water Penetration of Exterior Windows, Skylights, Doors, and Curtain Walls by Cyclic Static Air Pressure Difference
E1105-00	Standard Test Method for Field Determination of Water Penetration of Installed Exterior Windows, Skylights, Doors, and Curtain Walls, by Uniform or Cyclic Static Air Pressure Difference
C1601-06	Standard Test Method for Field Determination of Water Penetration of Masonry Wall Surfaces
E2140-01	Standard Test Method for Water Penetration of Metal Roof Panel Systems by Static Water Pressure Head
E2268-04	Standard Test Method for Water Penetration of Exterior Windows, Skylights, and Doors by Rapid Pulsed Air Pressure Difference

[a]*Annual Book of ASTM Standards*, ASTM International, West Conshohocken, PA, 2008.

chastic evaluation of climatic weather data for various locations in the conterminous United States. The default spray rate in E331 and E547 is the rate most commonly selected in test protocols in North America.

The second objective was to create a methodology where testing protocols can be developed that are based on, or related to, the likelihood of occurrence of specific weather or climatic events. The methodology involved estimation of the intensity of driving rain and of wind pressure during rain over specified return intervals. These values logically relate to water spray rate and differential pressure respectively across test specimens. The methodology was intended to permit development of test protocols for specific locations, assuming that climatological data was available for the location. The (alternative) intent was that the methodology be applicable to a range of different locations.

Generating the necessary information to produce weather-based test protocols would ideally be developed from a rainfall and wind speed dataset that provides data every minute. Indeed, rainfall data for durations shorter than one hour do exist; however, the length of serial strings of concurrent rainfall and wind data for durations shorter than one hour are generally limited. Hence, given the current limitation on the availability of weather data, the scope of this study is limited to hourly events.

Wind-Driven Rain and Driving-Rain Wind Pressure Sets

The SAMSON[4] [13] and HUSWO[5] [14] hourly datasets were used as a basis to create a combined dataset on which were subsequently conducted statistical analysis of hourly wind and rain data for five locations in the United States. These were: Boston, MA, Miami, FL, Minneapolis-St. Paul, MN, Philadelphia, PA, and Seattle, WA. Each of these datasets consisted of at least 35 years of hourly data, or a total for each city of about 300 000 hours of data. Extracting the wind speed and wind direction data from the source was straightforward as both sets provide average hourly wind data concurrent with precipitation data. Precipitation is a general term that includes both liquid and solid forms (e.g., snow, hail, ice pellets, and sleet). Solid precipitation is not of interest for water penetration studies. In the hourly datasets, observation codes reporting precipitation type are listed and precipitation amounts are recorded as a single number as liquid equivalent regardless of whether the precipitation fell as solid, or liquid, or a mix. To obtain hourly rainfall data, the following extraction procedure was devised:

1. If snow was indicated and liquid precipitation was not, then the hourly precipitation was set to zero regardless of the amount reported.
2. If liquid precipitation was indicated and snow was not the entire hourly precipitation amount reported was used. Freezing liquid precipitation (freezing rain or drizzle) was not included.
3. If the hourly weather observation indicated that both snow and liquid precipitation occurred a prorated estimate for rainfall was made according to the following procedure:
   • If the reported intensities of snow and liquid were the same, the liquid (rainfall) amount was assumed to be 50 % of the precipitation amount recorded.
   • If the reported intensity for snow exceeded that for liquid precipitation, the liquid amount was assumed to be 33 % of the precipitation amount recorded.

---

[4]Covering the period 1961–1990.
[5]Covering the period 1990–1995.

- If the observed intensity for snow was less than that for liquid precipitation, the liquid amount was assumed to be 67 % of the precipitation amount recorded.

In the published climate normal datasets, snowfall amounts (expressed as solid depths) are reported. The climate normal datasets thus provide information against which hourly rainfall estimates, made from hourly precipitation amounts and hourly observation codes, might be compared for winter months in cold climates. The climate normal datasets provide no similar opportunity for comparison during warm months, when solid precipitation as hail or ice pellets may occur.

It was fairly common that the hourly rainfall estimates, (using the procedure described above), when summed over monthly periods, yielded monthly average rainfall estimates that differed moderately from monthly average rainfall estimates derived from climate normal data for the same period of record. The first two rows in Table 2 show the climate normal data for precipitation and for snowfall for Philadelphia. The third row in the table shows an estimate of the climate normal rainfall, calculated as total precipitation minus the snowfall (assuming that the snowfall equivalent liquid amount is one-tenth the reported snowfall depth amount). Note that in the summer months the total precipitation is the same as the rainfall. The fourth row shows the estimated total precipitation determined from the hourly data. The values are the same as the published climate normal data; as they should be since the climate normal data was derived from the SAMSOM set. The fifth row shows the amount of rainfall estimated from the hourly data using the procedure outlined above. There appears to be a considerable underestimation of rainfall in summer months compared to the estimate from the climate normal data (sixth and seventh rows in Table 2). For the summer months there should be no difference given that there was no observed snowfall during the summer. The difference can be explained partly by the incorrect assumption in estimating rainfall from the climate normal data, namely that all solid precipitation was snow implying that the difference between the precipitation and snowfall was all liquid precipitation. In fact solid precipitation, apart from being registered as snow, may also be reported as, for example, ices pellets or hail. Row eight in Table 2 shows the mean of all the other forms of solid precipitation excluding snow calculated using the hourly files. When these amounts were added back to the mean long-term rainfall estimate derived from the hourly datasets the resulting total precipitation estimates for summer months correspond well with the total climate normal precipitation reported in row one of Table 2. The difference is reported in rows eight and nine.

Hence, the method for extracting liquid precipitation amounts from the SAMSON and HUSWO datasets used in this work seems to be adequate in generating plausible rainfall amounts. When compared to long term data, this overall procedure for extracting rain from precipitation data was accurate to within a few percent. It should also be noted that simply subtracting the

TABLE 2—*Climate normal precipitation data for Philadelphia, PA and estimated rainfall from NCDC hourly data.*

		Years	Jan	Feb	Mar	Apr	May	Jun	Jul	Aug	Sep	Oct	Nov	Dec	Annual
1	Climate normal precipitation	30	81.5	70.9	87.9	91.9	95.3	95.0	108.7	96.5	86.9	66.5	84.8	85.9	1051.8
2	[a]Climate normal snowfall	56	15.2	16.8	9.1	0.8	0.0	0.0	0.0	0.0	0.0	0.0	1.8	8.1	51.8
3	Normal rainfall estimate (Line 1 − Line 2)	30	66.3	54.1	78.7	91.2	95.3	95.0	108.7	96.5	86.9	66.5	83.1	77.7	1000.0
4	SAMSON mean precipitation	30	81.5	70.9	87.6	91.9	95.3	95.0	108.7	96.5	86.9	66.5	84.8	85.9	1051.8
5	SAMSON rain estimated by extraction	30	56.6	48.8	74.4	85.1	88.4	86.4	95.3	85.3	79.8	62.0	78.2	72.1	912.4
6	Difference (Line 5 − Line 3)		−9.7	−5.3	−4.3	−6.1	−6.9	−8.6	−13.5	−11.2	−7.1	−4.6	−4.8	−5.6	−87.6
7	% Difference		−14.6	−9.9	−5.5	−6.7	−7.2	−9.1	−12.4	−11.6	−8.2	−6.9	−5.8	−7.2	−8.8
8	SAMSON Solid precipitation (excluding snow)	30	2.3	2.5	3.8	5.1	6.9	9.4	13.5	11.7	7.1	4.3	4.6	3.0	72.4
9	SAMSON rain plus solid precipitation (Line5 + Line 8)	30	58.9	51.3	78.2	90.2	95.3	95.8	108.7	97.0	86.9	66.3	82.8	75.2	984.8
10	Difference, (Line 9−Line 3)		−7.4	−2.8	−0.5	−1.0	0.0	0.8	0.0	0.5	0.0	−0.3	−0.3	−2.5	−15.2
11	% Difference		−11.1	−5.2	−0.6	−1.1	0.0	0.8	0.0	0.5	0.0	−0.4	−0.3	−3.3	−1.5

[a]Snowfall is reported in terms of liquid amounts assuming a 10:1 ratio of snowfall volume to rainfall volume.

equivalent liquid snowfall amount from the total precipitation will most likely yield an over estimate of the actual rainfall when using climate normal data.

Wind-Driven Rain

Wind-driven rain (WDR) was calculated using a method recommended by Straube and Burnett [15] (Eq 1). The driving rain factor, *DRF* is inversely proportional to the terminal velocity of raindrops (Eq 2).

$$WDR = RDF\ DRF(r_h)V(h)r_h\ cos(\theta) \tag{1}$$

$$DRF(r_h) = 1/V_t(\Phi_{pred}) \tag{2}$$

Raindrop terminal velocity (V_t) is according to Dingle and Lee [16] (Eq 3). The size of raindrops, dependent on the horizontal rainfall intensity, can be calculated from the drop size distribution suggested by Best [17]. For this work the predominant raindrop size (Φ_{pred}), the drop size that produces the greatest volume of water was used. The predominant raindrop size was determined from Eq 4.

$$V_t(\Phi) = -0.16603 + 4.91884 * \Phi - 0.888016 * \Phi^2 + 0.054888 * \Phi^3 \tag{3}$$

where: V_t =9.20 m/s

$$\Phi_{pred} = (1.30r_h^{0.232}) * ((2.25 - 1)/2.25)^{1/2.25} \tag{4}$$

Equation 1 assumes that horizontal raindrop velocity is equal to wind speed. Choi [18] found that this assumption is not necessarily valid close to the ground. Choi also found that in thunderstorms (short-term intense rainfall) the drop size distribution differs from that assumed by Best with the result that the driving rain factor (DRF) during these storms may be under estimated when the assumptions implicit in Eqs 3 and 4 are made. Finally, Blocken and Carmeliet [19] have shown that the cosine assumption in Eq 1, relating to the angle of the wind with relation to the outward wall normal, is not necessarily valid, and can lead to significant errors in estimating WDR. They, however, do not recommend an alternative method other than using modeling to examine the effect of glancing winds. In summary, although Eq 1 is recognized as being imperfect, it is the best algorithm available for estimating WDR, particularly for use with hourly data.

The following assumptions were used in the analysis:
1. *RDF* is assumed= 1.0. This is the equivalent to free wind-driven rain, i.e., without aerodynamic obstruction.
2. The wind direction is assumed to be normal to the wall. In other words, θ was assumed to be 0° and hence $cos(\theta) = 1$.
3. Height, h, is assumed to be 10 m, the standard World Meteorological Organization (WMO) anemometer height.These assumptions, relative to alternative assumptions, yield estimates of wind driven rain of relatively large magnitude. They counteract the effects mentioned in the previous paragraph, which would tend to result in under-estimation of WDR.

Mean annual wind-driven rain rosette, L/m²

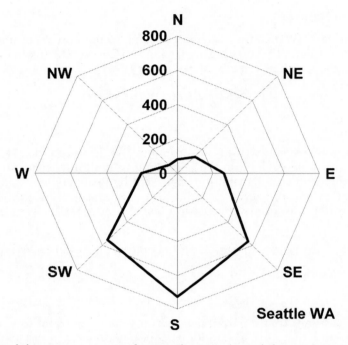

FIG. 1—*Wind-driven rain rosette for Seattle, WA, derived from mean annual wind-driven rain for eight directions over a period of* 26 *years.*

Driving-Rain Wind Pressure

In order to analyze the characteristics of driving-rain wind pressure (DRWP) all the wind records occurring coincidentally with measurable rainfall events were extracted from the SAMSON [13] and HUSWO [14] datasets. The DRWP was defined as the pressure exerted on a surface normal to the wind direction during rain and calculated using Eq 5.

$$DRWP = 1/2\rho_{air}[V(h)]^2 \tag{5}$$

Directionality

Two types of analysis were considered: one that considered the direction of the impinging WDR; the other did not. Hence for the omni-directional analysis, wind direction was ignored and the wall was assumed to always be perpendicular to the wind direction. This assumption provided the maximum WDR for the

TABLE 3—*Correlation coefficients between rainfall parameters and wind speed parameters. The period of record was 1961–1995.*

City	BOS	MIA	MIN	PHL	SEA
Correlation Coefficient[a]					
Rain and wind during rain	0.13	0.08	0.04	0.07	0.06
WDR and DRWP	0.55	0.45	0.32	0.42	0.47
Annual max. WDR and annual max. DRWP	0.48	0.63	0.43	0.29	0.48

[a]The correlation coefficient is the covariance between x and y divided by the product of σ_x and σ_y.

location. However, this type of analysis precluded the availability of any information regarding the direction of the impinging WDR being available.

The directional analysis was performed such that eight rain corridors were evenly delineated about the compass, each sweeping a sector of 45°. An imaginary vertical surface was assumed to be normal to each of these directions. All wind within a corridor was assumed to be normal to the wall. An example of a typical wind-driven rain rosette is shown in Fig. 1.

Wind and Rain

An important assumption made in the analysis was that the probability of occurrence of rain intensity and the probability of occurrence of wind speed are statistically independent. In general this would be expected since the physical processes involved in precipitation and the forces generating wind are different. Table 3 shows the correlation coefficients between the rain intensity and wind speeds *during rain* and derivatives of the two climatic parameters. In this study the concurrent wind speeds and rainfall intensities from the NCDC sources [13,14] were compared. The correlation coefficients seem to show that there is no relation between rainfall intensity and wind speeds for the locations considered. However, there does seem to be some correlation between wind-driven rain and driving-rain wind pressure. This would be expected inasmuch as wind speed is a factor in both WDR and DRWP (Eqs 1 and 5). The correlation coefficients, while much higher than those between wind and rain, still are somewhat low. WDR and DWRP thus seem to be neither independent, nor highly dependent. For the purposes of this analysis the assumption of statistical independence seems to be valid. A more detailed analysis would consider the relation of wind speed and rainfall intensity while considering storm type. Although this information is available in the form of a qualitative weather observation code a detailed analysis would require a higher resolution dataset. The source data included an hourly precipitation total (i.e., the total precipitation at the end of the hour) and an hourly wind speed, usually estimated from 1- or 2-minute spot readings at the top of the hour. Given the nature of the data (which has an hourly resolution), independence (or non-independence) of wind and rain over a time scale similar to that of a laboratory spray test protocol cannot really be determined.

The independence assumption is important to the proposed method. If

Seattle WA Wind-driven rain contour plot, L/m2-h

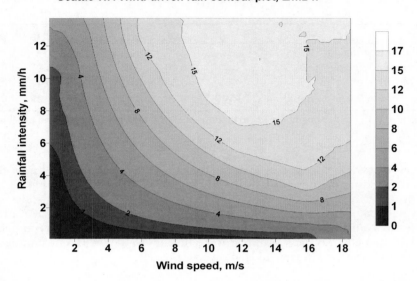

FIG. 2—*Contour plot of WDR, wind speed, and rainfall intensity for Seattle, WA; the period of record is* 26 *years.*

wind-driven rain and driving-rain wind pressure were conditionally dependent and positively correlated then it would be expected that the highest levels of wind-driven rain would occur concurrently with the highest wind pressures. Test protocols in that case would logically be focused on maximum pressures and spray rates. As discussed in the previous paragraph, a weak correlation apparently exists between WDR and DRWP. The likelihood of concurrent occurrence of extreme WDR and extreme DRWP can be estimated (although imperfectly) as the product of the respective probabilities of occurrence. This must be qualified however; in regions where topography plays a large role in generating precipitation, it often also has a pronounced effect on wind patterns. In these regions (for example, mountainous terrain) a moderate to strong correlation between WDR and DRWP may be expected, and the likelihood of concurrent occurrence of extreme WDR and DRWP will thus be higher.

Figures 1 and 2 show some WDR data for Seattle, WA. Figure 1 shows the mean annual wind-driven rain for eight sectors each tending an angle of 45°. The mean values were calculated by averaging the total catch of wind-driven rain over the period of record. In the first figure it is apparent that there is a strong correlation between wind direction and WDR; clearly the bulk of the wind-driven rain producing events are associated with southerly winds. While this figure does not relate to the independence of wind and rain it shows clearly that, for this location, the loads are different for different orientations. The second figure shows a contour plot of WDR with wind speed and rainfall intensity in which a correlation between WDR and either wind speed or rainfall intensity is evident. Recall that by definition WDR is a product of wind speed and rainfall intensity, thus some positive correlation between the parameters would be expected. Theoretically an infinite number of combinations of wind speed and rainfall can be used to produce a given WDR intensity. Physical processes, however, limit the values for wind speed and rainfall. For high intensities of WDR there is a limited range of combinations for wind speed and rainfall (see Fig. 2). For low intensities of WDR, which constitute the bulk of WDR events, a wide range of combinations is possible and likely.

Extreme Value Analysis

Extreme value analysis (EVA) was used to analyze the datasets for the purpose of estimating the magnitude of an event that corresponds to a given return period or recurrence interval. The two-parameter Gumbel distribution was used to estimate the return period of WDR intensities and the magnitudes of DRWP. The procedure was straightforward: for a given set of hourly wind speed and corresponding rainfall intensity data a subsequent set of information was constructed that provided the annual maximum values for WDR and DRWP. These sets of maximums can be assumed to have a Type I generalized extreme value (GEV) distribution (i.e., Gumbel) [20–22]. If the underlying distribution is not a Type I but a Type III distribution, the more general case, the expected values for a given return period should be over estimated and thus the assumption is conservative [23]. In other words the intensity of an event for a given return period will be overestimated. Cook [24] suggested that when composing a GEV, at least 20 maxima should be used to obtain reliable results and the method should not be used when the period of record is less than ten years.

If the data can reliably be assumed to have a Type I GEV distribution then the expected values, x_n (for either WDR or DRWP), for a given return period, T, can be calculated directly from sample set statistics given in Eqs 6 and 7.

$$x_n = \bar{X} + K(T)\sigma \qquad (6)$$

Values of $K(T)$ for various return periods were calculated using Eq 7.

$$K(T) = -\frac{\sqrt{6}}{\pi}\left[0.5772 + \ln\ln\left(\frac{T}{T-1}\right)\right] \qquad (7)$$

The standard extremal variate, s, is a function of the return period (Eq 8). For example, for a return period of ten years the value of s is 2.25. For 50 years the value of s is 3.9.

$$s = -\ln\left(\ln\left(\frac{T}{T-1}\right)\right) \qquad (8)$$

Using these relations, the extreme values for WDR (L/m^2-h) and DRWP (Pa) for the selected U.S. locations in relation to the return period are given in Table 4. Figure 3 shows a typical Gumbel plot of extreme WDR intensities and the corresponding return periods. The 95 % confidence bands are also shown.

For Miami, the distribution of yearly maximum values does not appear to follow the assumed GEV Type I plot (see Fig. 4). The most extreme outlier in the

TABLE 4—*Summary of extreme one-hour values of WDR.*

Location	BOS		MIA		MSP		PHL		SEA	
Return Period	WDR, L/m²-h	DRWP, Pa	WDR, L/m²-h	DRWP, Pa	WDR, L/m²-h	DRWP, Pa	WDR, L/m²-h	DRWP, Pa	WDR, L/m²-h	DRWP, Pa
2	24	197	47	105	27	105	28	122	10	109
5	29	247	62	140	38	134	36	172	12	137
10	33	280	72	163	46	153	42	206	14	156
20	37	311	206	490	53	171	47	238	16	174
30	39	329	271	642	57	182	51	256	16	185
50	42	352	351	833	62	195	54	279	18	198
100	45	383	460	1090	69	212	60	310	19	216

BOS=Boston, MA, MIA=Miami, FL, MSP=Minneapolis, MN, PHL=Philadelphia, PA, SEA=Seattle, WA.

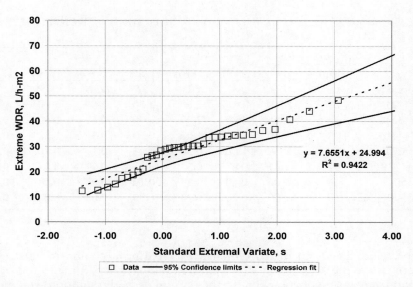

FIG. 3—*Expected extreme values versus extremes from the dataset for Philadelphia, PA.*

graph occurred during hurricane Andrew (1992). The standard EVA technique, linear regression, overestimates the WDR for shorter return periods (i.e., T = 10 to 20 years), and underestimates the WDR over longer return periods. This is typical of so-called mixed climates, climates in which cyclonic storms sometimes occur. Gomes and Vickery [25] proposed a solution to estimating

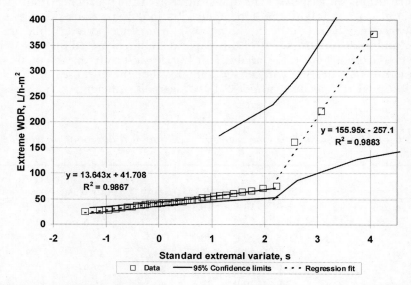

FIG. 4—*Expected extreme values versus extremes from the dataset for Miami, FL, an example of a mixed climate.*

TABLE 5—*Table of likelihood in % of annual extreme events of WDR and DRWP for Philadelphia PA.*

Likelihood	DRWP, Pa WDR, L/m²-h	50 % (1/2) 122	20 % (1/5) 172	10 % (1/10) 206	5 % (1/20) 238	3.3 % (1/30) 256	2 % (1/50) 279	1 % (1/100) 310
50 % (1/2)	28	25.00	10.00	5.00	2.50	1.67	1.00	0.50
20 % (1/5)	36	10.00	4.00	2.00	1.00	0.67	0.40	0.20
10 % (1/10)	42	5.00	2.00	1.00	0.50	0.33	0.20	0.10
5 % (1/20)	47	2.50	1.00	0.50	0.25	0.17	0.10	0.05
3.3 % (1/30)	51	1.67	0.67	0.33	0.17	0.11	0.07	0.03
2% (1/50)	54	1.00	0.40	0.20	0.10	0.07	0.04	0.02
1% (1/100)	60	0.50	0.20	0.10	0.05	0.03	0.02	0.01

extreme wind speeds in mixed climates by creating a composite gust speed diagram where the set maxima are separated into sets according to the significant wind generating phenomena. In the present case, the solution would be to break the set of extremes into two distributions: one set of extremes for the noncyclonic wind data and a second comprised of wind data generated by tropical cyclones.

Cook [25,26] has revised the methodology for estimating extreme wind speeds in mixed climates to take advantage of improvements in methodology and the increased availability of data. Cook suggests that the problem may revert to a single dominant mechanism thus making the generation of composite distributions unnecessary. The appearance (that the yearly maximum values for Miami do not follow the Type I distribution) is perhaps deceptive. The appearance may be might be due to a long convergence period. While analysis of this kind is beyond the scope of this paper it should be noted there is an issue with standard extreme value analysis in hurricane prone areas but there do exist methods for dealing with mixed climates. For the purposes of this study, the traditional composite method [27] was deemed sufficient.

TABLE 6—*Table of expected extreme values of WDR for eight directions for Philadelphia, PA.*

WDR, L/h-m²	North	North East	East	South East	South	South West	West	North West
2 year return	12.9	15.3	14.5	10.1	13.0	13.1	12.2	15.2
5	19.3	24.4	19.4	16.1	21.8	20.6	18.9	25.6
10	23.6	30.5	22.6	20.2	27.7	25.5	23.5	32.4
20	27.6	36.3	25.7	23.9	33.3	30.2	27.8	39.0
30	29.9	39.7	27.5	26.2	36.5	32.9	30.2	42.8
50	32.9	43.9	29.9	28.9	40.5	36.3	33.3	47.5
100	36.9	49.5	32.7	32.7	45.9	40.9	37.5	53.9

Wind-Driven Rain and Driving-Rain Wind Pressure Pairs

The goal of the preceding analysis was to estimate the likelihood of various combinations of WDR and DRWP impinging on a wall. Each combination of WDR and DRWP can be assigned a likelihood related to the climate data analyzed. As indicated previously, the occurrence of concurrent levels of WDR *and* DRWP can be estimated (although imperfectly) as the product of the respective probabilities. For Philadelphia, this is shown in the Table 5.

Directional Analysis

It was of interest to further develop the WDR dataset to account for directionality. This information could be used to determine whether the wind-driven rain load of a particular orientation is significantly different than any other. Eight datasets of annual maximum WDR and DRWP were created, one for each corridor (45 degrees). An EVA similar to that previously described was completed and expected values for each of the eight directions were calculated for different return periods, T, ranging from 2 to 100 years. Table 6 gives the directional extreme values of WDR and Table 7 of DRWP for Philadelphia.

A table of spray rates and DRWP pairs can readily be generated similar to the table listed above by simply referring to the appropriate corridor. The top rows represent the expected DRWP and the columns the expected WDR spray rates. The annual likelihood of occurrence of a pair can be estimated as the product of the return periods, this based on the imperfect assumption of statistical independence (Eq 9).

$$Likelihood(Direction) = (1/T_{WDR(Direction)})(1/T_{DRWP(Direction)}) \qquad (9)$$

In-Service Conditions for Wind and Rain

Extreme value analysis gives an estimate of the maximum or extreme loads or events that might possibly occur for a certain probability, generally expressed as the return period. These loads do not represent typical in-service conditions. To obtain typical in-service conditions it was necessary to examine the WDR and DRWP datasets using a different statistical approach.

The first task was to fit a probability density function (PDF) or statistical distribution to rain events and coincident wind events. The first step in this task was to construct a histogram of wind events by allotting rain events of specific magnitudes into bins. A PDF was then fitted to each of the histograms using a Weibull distribution.

Such types of distributions have been shown to be useful in fitting climate or weather data for engineering purposes [20–22]. For example, Justus [28] discussed the applicability of the Weibull distribution for estimating wind frequency distributions especially the advantage of projecting the distribution to other wind speed heights. Much of the reported work on fitting Weibull distributions to wind speed data speed is related to the estimation of parameters for

TABLE 7—*Table of expected extreme values of DRWP for eight directions for Philadelphia, PA.*

DRWP, Pa	North	North East	East	South East	South	South West	West	North West
2 year return	60.4	85.4	84.3	46.3	74.5	53.8	69.5	77.4
5	84.1	128	123	63.9	106	74.1	98.2	127
10	99.9	157	149	75.6	127	87.6	117	160
20	115	184	174	86.8	148	100	136	192
30	124	199	188	93.3	159	108	146	209
50	134	219	206	101	174	117	159	233
100	149	246	229	112	193	129	177	263

assessing wind power [29,30]. The general consensus is that the Weibull distribution is appropriate for modeling wind data [31–34].

In respect to using a Weibull distribution for categorizing rain events, Wilks [35] and Testa [36,37] have demonstrated the fit of short-term rain data using a Weibull distribution. Hence, there are useful examples on the use of this type of distribution for categorizing both rain and wind events.

Figure 5 shows the cumulative probability function (CDF) for wind speeds and rainfall intensities for Seattle, WA. The CDFs derived from the sample data and the Weibull estimates are shown, as well as the root mean squared error.

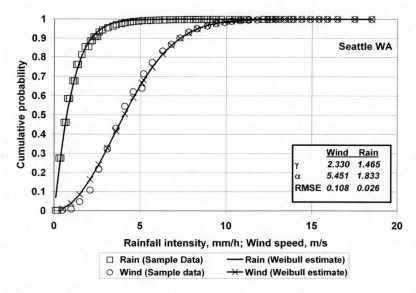

FIG. 5—*Cumulative distribution functions for rainfall intensity (mm/h) and wind speed (m/s) for Seattle, WA, and corresponding Weibull estimates. The shape and scale parameters as well as the root mean squared error between the actual and assumed distributions are given. The period of record was 26 years.*

TABLE 8—*Basic statistics and formulas for the two-parameter Weibull distribution.*

Statistic	Formula
Mean	$\alpha\Gamma\left(\dfrac{\gamma+1}{\gamma}\right)$
Median	$\alpha\ln(2)^{1/\gamma}$
Mode	$\alpha\left(1-\dfrac{1}{\gamma}\right)^{1/\gamma}\dots\gamma>1$
	$0\dots\gamma\le1$
Standard Deviation	$\alpha\sqrt{\Gamma\left(\dfrac{2+\gamma}{\gamma}\right)-\left(\Gamma\left(\dfrac{1+\gamma}{\gamma}\right)\right)^2}$
Percent point function	$G(p)=\alpha(-\ln(1-p))^{1/\gamma}$

Having determined the basic distribution parameters it was then possible to estimate, using the percentage point function, the magnitude of the wind speed for a given likelihood of occurrence of an event. Common statistics for the two-parameter Weibull distribution are given in Table 8 whereas in Table 9, the corresponding WDR intensities and DRWPs for various likelihoods of occurrence obtained from the cumulative distribution function are provided.

Given the magnitudes of rainfall intensity and DRWP at various probabilities of occurrence, a table of rainfall and wind speed pairs was then constructed for Philadelphia, as given in Table 10. Pairs for the other cities surveyed in this study are in given in the Appendix. The values provided in Table 10 assume statistical independence between the occurrence of rainfall and the DRWP. However, as previously noted, this assumption is imperfect, and is particularly in doubt in mountainous terrain.

Modifying the Loads

This section presents methods for modifying the two basic load parameters, i.e., *WDR* and *DRWP*, to suit specific conditions. Both loads depend on one or two of the basic input parameters, specifically rainfall intensity and wind speed. Two general classes of modifiers are considered: (i) modifiers for aerodynamic effects, and (ii) those that account for shorter time-averaging periods. It is useful to recall the two basic load-generating Eqs 1 and 5, when reviewing the following sections.

Aerodynamic Effects

Rain Deposition Factor—The *RDF* accounts for the aerodynamic effects caused by the building on the flow field around the building. The flow field is either slowed near the center of the building or accelerated near the edges. As is evident in Eq 1, the *RDF* is a scalar factor in the calculation of *WDR*. To

TABLE 9—*DRWPs (Pa) and WDR intensities (L/m²-h) for various likelihoods from the Cumulative Distribution Functions. The period of record was 1961–1995.*

Location	BOS		MIA		MSP		PHL		SEA	
Cumulative Probability	DRWP	WDR	DRWP	WDR	DRWP	WDR	DRWP	WDR	DRWP	WDR
0.5	23	1.44	15	1.69	21	1.21	14	1.23	13	0.93
0.9	71	7.82	55	16.5	47	6.14	48	7.28	38	3.71
0.95	91	11.4	74	27.4	56	8.80	63	10.8	47	5.03
0.99	136	21.1	118	63.4	74	15.9	98	20.6	68	8.25
0.995	155	25.8	138	83.7	82	19.4	114	25.4	77	9.72
1[a]	492	159	548	1060	190	113	420	171.3	225	41.7

[a]–0.99999 probability.

TABLE 10—*Hourly pairs of in-service conditions for wind driven-rain (WDR) and driving rain wind pressure (DRWP) for Philadelphia, PA. The likelihood is an estimate of the cumulative probability that the WDR and DRWP pair will occur.*

Cumulative Probability	0.5				0.9			0.95		
	Wind Speed, m/s									
	4.68				8.77			10.06		
	Rainfall, mm/h	WDR, l/m²-h	DRWP, Pa	Likelihood, %	WDR, l/m²-h	DRWP, Pa	Likelihood, %	WDR, l/m²-h	DRWP, Pa	Likelihood, %
0.1	0.12	0.22	14	5.00	0.40	48	9.00	0.46	63	9.50
0.2	0.28	0.43	14	10.00	0.80	48	18.00	0.92	63	19.00
0.3	0.48	0.66	14	15.00	1.24	48	27.00	1.43	63	28.50
0.4	0.73	0.93	14	20.00	1.74	48	36.00	1.99	63	38.00
0.5	1.04	1.24	14	25.00	2.31	48	45.00	2.66	63	47.50
0.6	1.45	1.61	14	30.00	3.01	48	54.00	3.46	63	57.00
0.7	1.99	2.08	14	35.00	3.91	48	63.00	4.48	63	66.50
0.8	2.80	2.75	14	40.00	5.16	48	72.00	5.92	63	76.00
0.9	4.26	3.88	14	45.00	7.28	48	81.00	8.35	63	85.50
0.95	5.80	5.01	14	47.50	9.39	48	85.50	10.78	63	90.25
0.975	7.40	6.14	14	48.75	11.51	48	87.75	13.21	63	92.63
0.99	9.59	7.64	14	49.50	14.31	48	89.10	16.42	63	94.05
0.995	11.31	8.77	14	49.75	16.43	48	89.55	18.86	63	94.53
0.998	13.63	10.27	14	49.90	19.24	48	89.82	22.08	63	94.81
1	48.64	30.81	14	50.00	57.74	48	90.00	66.27	63	95.00

Note: The likelihood of X given Y is the likelihood of X. The likelihood of X and Y is product of the likelihoods. Each rainfall intensity wind speed pair produces a corresponding WDR and DRWP pair.

TABLE 11—*Parameters for standard terrain classifications* [38].

Terrain	a	δ	Description
1	0.33	400	Large city centers
2	0.22	370	Urban and sub urban areas, wooded areas etc.
3	0.14	270	Open terrain with scattered obstructions
4	0.10	210	Flat unobstructed areas

calculate loads at various points of interest on the building, the free wind-driven rain, that is, the rain field in absence of a building downstream is multiplied by the appropriate *RDF*. Straube and Burnett [15] have obtained typical values of *RDFs* measured for simple buildings by measurement.

Wind Speed Correction—The variation in the mean wind speed with height is most commonly approximated by a power law representation [38]. The generalized equation (Eq 10) for the wind factor, f_t, is used to adjust the wind speed from the height at the measurement site, H_{met}, such as a meteorological station to the height of interest at a specific building, h. Typical exponents, a, and boundary layer thicknesses δ are given in Table 11.

$$f_t = \left(\frac{\delta_{met}}{H_{met}}\right)^{amet} \left(\frac{h}{\delta}\right)^{a} \tag{10}$$

The effect of wind on *WDR* is scalar. To modify the loads for the effect of height and terrain the wind speed multiply by the appropriate wind terrain factor, f_t. The effect of wind on *DRWP* is also scalar. To modify the loads for the effect of height and terrain the wind speed multiply by the square of the appropriate wind terrain factor, f_t.

Time Averaging

Wind Speed—For events having durations shorter than one hour the rainfall intensities may be greater and the wind speeds higher. Factors, f_s and f_p, that relate wind speed and wind pressure, respectively, for converting hourly wind speeds to averages over 1, 3, 5, 10, and 15 minutes have been extracted the ASCE Standard, Minimum Design Loads for Buildings [39].

Ro's work [33] suggests that assuming a Weibull distribution for wind speeds is robust over different averaging periods for wind speed datasets collected over long periods of time. For shorter study periods, e.g., five days in Ro's

TABLE 12—*Wind speed and pressure factors for shorter averaging times* [39].

Averaging Time	15 minutes	10 minutes	5 minutes	3 minutes	1 minute
Factor on speed, f_s	1.04	1.07	1.11	1.14	1.25
Factor on pressure, f_p	1.08	1.14	1.23	1.30	1.56

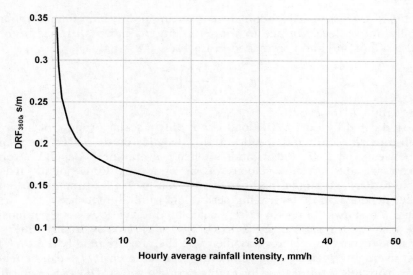

FIG. 6—*Chart for estimating the* DRF_{60} *for hourly average rainfall, mm/h.*

study, wind speed data does not seem to fit a Weibull distribution.

The wind speed and wind pressure adjustment factors are given in Table 12. To increase the WDR and DRWP loads simply multiply the loads by the appropriate speed or pressure factor.

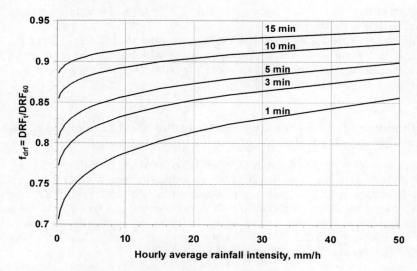

FIG. 7—*Chart for estimating the driving-rain factor modifier,* f_{drf}, *for shorter averaging periods using hourly average rainfall,* r_h, *mm/h as input.*

Rainfall Intensity—The factor for converting hourly rain intensities falling vertically onto a level surface to shorter averaging periods, r_t, has been suggested by Choi [40] and is provided in Eq 11.

$$r_t = r_h \left(\frac{3600}{t} \right)^{0.42} \tag{11}$$

where t, time, is in seconds.

As indicated by Eq 1 WDR load is not only a scalar product of horizontal rainfall intensity and wind speed but also depends on the *DRF*. The relationship between the DRF and rainfall intensity is nonlinear, depending on the raindrop size and terminal velocity of the raindrops. Consequently it is not possible to derive a single modifier for a given averaging time given that the modifier depends on the averaging period and rainfall intensity.

Figure 6 shows values for DRF_{60} calculated for various hourly intensities. Figure 7 shows the ratio of DRT_t to DRF_{60} for various averaging times. This ratio is the driving-rain factor modifier, f_{drf}. Therefore to modify the *DRF* for a shorter averaging period at a given hourly rainfall intensity f_{drf} can be read off directly from Fig. 7 for desired averaging period given r_h. DRF_{60} is read off Fig. 6. The product of DRF_{60} and f_{drf} yields the appropriate *DRF*. Alternatively the *DRF* can be calculated directly from Eqs 2–4 using a modified intensity for shorter averaging periods, r_t, or read off from Fig. 6 directly given, r_t.

For example, suppose the 1 in 2 (the 50 % or median value) 15 minute WDR intensity is of interest. The median value for rainfall intensity in Philadelphia is 1.04 mm/h. The 15 minute value, r_t, is $1.04 *(3600/900)^{0.42}$ = 1.04*1.79 1.86 mm/h. The *DRF* from Eqs 2–4 or Fig. 6 is 0.226 s/m. Alternatively if using the unmodified median value, 1.04 mm/h, DRF_{60} is 0.25 (from Fig. 6) and from Fig. 7 f_{drf} is 0.89. The product of terms is 0.223 s/m, as before. Examples of f_{rain} and f_{drf} are shown in Table 13 for several common measures of the Weibull distribution.

The most conservative assumption is to assume that the *DRF* modifier, f_{drf}, is 1. This is the recommended approach for modifying extreme loads. For in-service conditions assuming a value of 1 for the *DRF* modifier, f_{drf}, is also a conservative assumption.

A Methodology for Determining the Magnitude and Likelihood of Wind-Driven Rain Loads on Building Facades

The methodology outlined in this paper is to be used to determine the wind driven-rain and driving rain wind pressure loads for North American locations and the corresponding probability of occurrence. This method can be applied to most locations; however, caution should be exercised when it is suspected that the qualifying assumptions may not hold, as might be the case for mountainous terrain or coastal regions. In such regions a more detailed analysis is required. The general process is as follows:

Step 1—Obtain historical climate data for the location of interest. A minimum record length of ten years is suggested. A maximum averaging time of

TABLE 13—*Rain and driving rain factor, DRF, for shorter averaging times for in-service conditions for Philadelphia, PA.*

Averaging Time	r_h	15 minutes	10 minutes	5 minutes	3 minutes	1 minute
Factor on rain, f_{rain}	n/a	1.79	2.12	2.84	3.52	5.58
DRF modifier, mode, f_{drf}	0.09	0.88	0.85	0.80	0.76	0.69
DRF modifier, mean, f_{drf}	0.74	0.90	0.87	0.83	0.80	0.74
DRF modifier, median, f_{drf}	1.04	0.89	0.87	0.82	0.79	0.73
DRF modifier, 90th %, f_{drf}	4.26	0.91	0.88	0.84	0.81	0.76

1 hour is also recommended. The required data fields are: rainfall,[6] concurrent wind speed and wind direction data. Useful but optional fields are: temperature (to calculate air density), atmospheric moisture (wet bulb, dew point or RH to calculate air density) and station pressure (to calculate air density). The measurement station should also provide basic information such as longitude, latitude, and elevation.

Step 2—From the historical data produce a new dataset containing hourly rainfall, wind speed and direction, wind driven-rain, and driving rain wind pressure (Eqs 1 and 5).

Step 3—If the qualifying assumption of statistical independence between rainfall intensity and wind speed holds, produce two subsets of the annual maximum WDR and DRWP loads. If the location is in a mixed climate then perform an EVA. Otherwise, assuming a TYPE I GEV, compute the expected values for given return periods using Eqs 6 and 7 for both WDR and DRWP, from the sample set statistics, (i.e., sample mean and unbiased standard deviation).

Step 4—For each pair of WDR and DRWP estimate the likelihood of occurrence. The probability of a certain WDR load given a certain DRWP load is simply the probability of the WDR and vice versa, assuming statistical independence. The probability of both events occurring is the product of both probabilities. Using this approach a table of likelihoods for various pairs of extreme WDR and DRWP loads can be produced.

Step 5—If directional information is required, repeat Steps 3 and 4 with the exception that the dataset be broken into individual rain corridors (minimum of eight corridors). Steps 3 and 4 are then repeated for each corridor.

Step 6—For in-service loads (i.e., nonextreme), fit rainfall intensity and wind speed to a two-parameter Weibull distribution. The distribution parameters can then be estimated using many different methods. One of the easiest methods is to linearize the cumulative distribution function and regress on the resultant dataset to estimate the distribution parameters.

Step 7—Once the distribution parameters have been estimated, for in-service loads use the percent point function to estimate the likelihood of occurrence of certain rainfall intensities or wind speeds. The percent point function,

---

[6]Rainfall data are required. If precipitation data are available, rainfall should be separated from solid precipitation. A present weather observation is useful in this respect. Ideally rain gage data, such as tipping bucket data, would be best. Radar and satellite data are also available; however, the assessment of the reliability of these data was beyond the scope of this study.

also commonly referred to as the inverse distribution function, is the inverse of the cumulative distribution function.

Step 8—For in-service loads (nonextreme), calculate for each pair of rainfall intensity and wind speed, the *WDR* and *DRWP* load. For each pair of *WDR* and *DRWP* estimate the likelihood of occurrence. The probability of a certain *WDR* given a certain *DRWP* load is simply the probability of the *WDR* and vice versa, assuming statistical independence. The probability of both events occurring is the product of both probabilities. Using this approach a table of likelihoods for various pairs of in-service WDR and DRWP loads can be produced.

Step 9—If directional information on in-service loads is required the dataset should be broken into individual rain corridors, a minimum of eight. Steps 6, 7, and 8 are then repeated for each corridor.

Step 10—Modify the loads to suit particular circumstances using the appropriate modifying factors.

Summary and Recommendations

The work described here primarily relates to water penetration and water leakage of building façades. The objectives of the work were to: (i) investigate the basis for the spray rates prescribed in various standards; (ii) relate the water spray rates and applied pressure differences applied to test specimens to the likelihood of occurrence, and (iii) develop a methodology for determining spray rates and applied pressure differences for a given likelihood of occurrence. Test protocols can be developed for specific locations or a standard test protocol can be related to specific locations using the methodology.

Five cities in the United States were examined: Boston, Miami, Minneapolis-St. Paul, Philadelphia, and Seattle. Given the small number of stations examined, five out of the several hundred in the SAMSON and HUSWO datasets, any conclusions regarding the results must be guarded. Generally there were no oddities in the probably distributions derived from the data with one exception. The extreme value data for Miami clearly shows that there are two sets of data–"normal" extremes and those due to hurricanes. This is typical of mixed climates where a longer period of record might be required for convergence of GEV Type I distributions. The traditional approach is to create a composite chart categorizing the events according to the underlying synoptic phenomena. There are other approaches, however, and a more detailed study of mixed climates is warranted.

The 3.4 L/min-m² (204 L/h-m²), the base spray rate used in the ASTM E331 and E547 methods, is high for most cases especially for hour-long durations. In all the locations included in this evaluation, this spray rate exceeds typical annual maximum values for WDR, never mind typical in-service values for WDR. However, if shorter duration episodes are considered, e.g.,

15 minutes or shorter, the 204 L/h-m² mark may be reasonable. Miami was exceptional with regard to the distribution of annual maximum WDR values. In Miami, where hurricanes sometimes occur, there seems to be a reasonable chance, 1 in 30, of that the maximum annual WDR value will be equivalent to 3.4 L/min-m² with a duration of an hour. The study also indicates that the extreme driving-rain wind pressures in the order of 500 Pa can occur. Thus the 700 Pa level found in some protocols is clearly justified. What is not clear, however, is the likelihood of both extreme driving-rain and extreme driving-rain wind pressure occurring simultaneously. In Miami, FL, the higher values for WDR do not necessarily occur during the windiest events. The most extreme hourly wind-driven rain event in the record set, 378 L/h-m², occurred with an hourly wind speed of 92.7 m/s just below the hurricane storm threshold. The next most extreme hourly wind-driven rain event in the record set, 221 L/h-m², occurred with an hourly wind speed of 11.2 m/s well below the tropical storm threshold. Thus the combined spray rates and pressure differences used in most protocols and standards appear to be a bit higher than warranted given that the probability of occurrence for these events is low; they occur very rarely, even during unusually strong storms. Their probability of occurrence is even lower when the dataset used to determine probability incorporates all in-service rain events (not just the more extreme events).

Despite the limited number of locations analyzed in this study, the observations made for four of the five locations suggest that the methodology is probably applicable to most locations within the conterminous United States. Analyzing wind-driven rain data in this manner is useful for understanding the variances in the rain loading on building façades in terms of both extreme events and of more typical in-service conditions. The methodology builds upon the work previously carried out by Underwood and others. It could be used as the basis for a comprehensive wind-driven rain atlas and serve as a basis for standards and codes development.

Although our investigations suggest that the methodology can be applied to most locations, caution should be exercised when it is suspected that qualifying assumptions may not apply, as might be the case for mountainous terrain or coastal regions. In such regions a more detailed analysis is probably required.

In conclusion, a methodology that attempts to derive appropriate testing levels on a statistical analysis of climatic or weather-based related to likelihoods of occurrence has been described. The limitations of the study are: (i) the small number of locations used in the analysis; (ii) the lack of analysis of events of duration less than one hour; (iii) the assumption of statistical independence between wind speed and rainfall intensity, and (iv) the need for a more detailed analysis of mixed climates. The first limitation can be remedied through continued work. The other limitations cannot be solved until finer grained datasets become available.

Appendix: Rainfall and wind speed pairs for Boston, Miami, Minneapolis, and Seattle are given in Tables A1–A4.

TABLE A1—*Hourly pairs of in-service conditions for wind driven-rain (WDR) and driving rain wind pressure (DRWP) for Boston, MA. The likelihood is an estimate of the cumulative probability that the WDR and DRWP pair will occur.*

| | | 0.5 | | | 0.9 | | | 0.95 | | |
| | | 6.15 | | | 10.73 | | | 12.13 | | |
Cumulative Probability	Rainfall, mm/h	WDR, l/m²-h	DRWP, Pa	Likelihood, %	WDR, l/m²-h	DRWP, Pa	Likelihood, %	WDR, l/m²-h	DRWP, Pa	Likelihood, %
	Wind speed, m/s									
0.1	0.10	0.26	23	5.00	0.45	71	9.00	0.50	91	9.50
0.2	0.24	0.51	23	10.00	0.88	71	18.00	1.00	91	19.00
0.3	0.42	0.78	23	15.00	1.36	71	27.00	1.54	91	28.50
0.4	0.63	1.09	23	20.00	1.89	71	36.00	2.14	91	38.00
0.5	0.90	1.44	23	25.00	2.52	71	45.00	2.84	91	47.50
0.6	1.25	1.87	23	30.00	3.27	71	54.00	3.69	91	57.00
0.7	1.71	2.42	23	35.00	4.22	71	63.00	4.77	91	66.50
0.8	2.40	3.18	23	40.00	5.56	71	72.00	6.28	91	76.00
0.9	3.64	4.48	23	45.00	7.82	71	81.00	8.83	91	85.50
0.95	4.94	5.76	23	47.50	10.06	71	85.50	11.37	91	90.25
0.975	6.29	7.05	23	48.75	12.30	71	87.75	13.90	91	92.63
0.99	8.14	8.74	23	49.50	15.26	71	89.10	17.24	91	94.05
0.995	9.58	10.02	23	49.75	17.49	71	89.55	19.77	91	94.53
0.998	11.53	11.71	23	49.90	20.45	71	89.82	23.11	91	94.81
1	40.77	34.67	23	50.00	60.53	71	90.00	68.39	91	95.00

TABLE A2—Hourly pairs of in-service conditions for wind driven-rain (WDR) and driving rain wind pressure (DRWP) for Miami, FL. The likelihood is an estimate of the cumulative probability that the WDR and DRWP pair will occur.

Cumulative Probability	Wind speed, m/s	Rainfall, mm/h	0.5 / 4.85			0.9 / 9.42			0.95 / 10.90		
			WDR, l/m²-h	DRWP, Pa	Likelihood, %	WDR, l/m²-h	DRWP, Pa	Likelihood, %	WDR, l/m²-h	DRWP, Pa	Likelihood, %
0.1		0.07	0.15	15	5.00	0.29	55	9.00	0.33	74	9.50
0.2		0.23	0.39	15	10.00	0.75	55	18.00	0.87	74	19.00
0.3		0.50	0.71	15	15.00	1.38	55	27.00	1.59	74	28.50
0.4		0.90	1.13	15	20.00	2.20	55	36.00	2.54	74	38.00
0.5		1.47	1.69	15	25.00	3.28	55	45.00	3.80	74	47.50
0.6		2.32	2.45	15	30.00	4.75	55	54.00	5.50	74	57.00
0.7		3.62	3.52	15	35.00	6.84	55	63.00	7.91	74	66.50
0.8		5.82	5.21	15	40.00	10.12	55	72.00	11.70	74	76.00
0.9		10.42	8.49	15	45.00	16.48	55	81.00	19.07	74	85.50
0.95		16.00	12.21	15	47.50	23.70	55	85.50	27.41	74	90.25
0.975		22.46	16.32	15	48.75	31.68	55	87.75	36.64	74	92.63
0.99		32.24	22.30	15	49.50	43.30	55	89.10	50.08	74	94.05
0.995		40.52	27.22	15	49.75	52.84	55	89.55	61.12	74	94.53
0.998		52.54	34.20	15	49.90	66.41	55	89.82	76.80	74	94.81
1		308.47	171.93	15	50.00	333.81	55	90.00	386.06	74	95.00

TABLE A3—*Hourly pairs of in-service conditions for wind driven-rain (WDR) and driving rain wind pressure (DRWP) for Minneapolis, MN. The likelihood is an estimate of the cumulative probability that the WDR and DRWP pair will occur.*

| | 0.5 | | | | 0.9 | | | 0.95 | | |
| | Wind speed, m/s 5.77 | | | | 8.66 | | | 9.47 | | |
Cumulative Probability	Rainfall, mm/h	WDR, l/m²-h	DRWP, Pa	Likelihood, %	WDR, l/m²-h	DRWP, Pa	Likelihood, %	WDR, l/m²-h	DRWP, Pa	Likelihood, %
0.1	0.07	0.19	21	5.00	0.28	47	9.00	0.31	56	9.50
0.2	0.19	0.39	21	10.00	0.59	47	18.00	0.64	56	19.00
0.3	0.34	0.62	21	15.00	0.93	47	27.00	1.02	56	28.50
0.4	0.53	0.89	21	20.00	1.33	47	36.00	1.45	56	38.00
0.5	0.78	1.21	21	25.00	1.81	47	45.00	1.98	56	47.50
0.6	1.11	1.60	21	30.00	2.39	47	54.00	2.62	56	57.00
0.7	1.56	2.11	21	35.00	3.16	47	63.00	3.45	56	66.50
0.8	2.24	2.83	21	40.00	4.25	47	72.00	4.64	56	76.00
0.9	3.52	4.09	21	45.00	6.14	47	81.00	6.71	56	85.50
0.95	4.89	5.37	21	47.50	8.06	47	85.50	8.80	56	90.25
0.975	6.35	6.67	21	48.75	10.01	47	87.75	10.94	56	92.63
0.99	8.39	8.42	21	49.50	12.63	47	89.10	13.80	56	94.05
0.995	10.00	9.76	21	49.75	14.64	47	89.55	16.00	56	94.53
0.998	12.22	11.55	21	49.90	17.33	47	89.82	18.94	56	94.81
1	47.77	37.43	21	50.00	56.15	47	90.00	61.37	56	95.00

TABLE A4—Hourly pairs of in-service conditions for wind driven-rain (WDR) and driving rain wind pressure (DRWP) for Seattle, WA. The likelihood is an estimate of the cumulative probability that the WDR and DRWP pair will occur.

Cumulative Probability	Wind speed, m/s		0.5 4.66			0.9 7.80			0.95 8.73		
	Rainfall, mm/h	WDR, l/m²-h	DRWP, Pa	Likelihood, %	WDR, l/m²-h	DRWP, Pa	Likelihood, %	WDR, l/m²-h	DRWP, Pa	Likelihood, %
0.1	0.14	0.25	13	5.00	0.42	38	9.00	0.47	47	9.50
0.2	0.27	0.42	13	10.00	0.71	38	18.00	0.79	47	19.00
0.3	0.41	0.59	13	15.00	0.98	38	27.00	1.10	47	28.50
0.4	0.57	0.76	13	20.00	1.26	38	36.00	1.42	47	38.00
0.5	0.74	0.93	13	25.00	1.57	38	45.00	1.76	47	47.50
0.6	0.95	1.14	13	30.00	1.91	38	54.00	2.14	47	57.00
0.7	1.21	1.39	13	35.00	2.33	38	63.00	2.60	47	66.50
0.8	1.57	1.71	13	40.00	2.86	38	72.00	3.20	47	76.00
0.9	2.16	2.21	13	45.00	3.71	38	81.00	4.15	47	85.50
0.95	2.73	2.68	13	47.50	4.48	38	85.50	5.03	47	90.25
0.975	3.28	3.11	13	48.75	5.21	38	87.75	5.84	47	92.63
0.99	3.99	3.66	13	49.50	6.13	38	89.10	6.86	47	94.05
0.995	4.52	4.06	13	49.75	6.79	38	89.55	7.60	47	94.53
0.998	5.20	4.56	13	49.90	7.64	38	89.82	8.55	47	94.81
1	13.63	10.22	13	50.00	17.12	38	90.00	19.16	47	95.00

References

[1] Blocken, B. and Carmeliet, J., "A Review of Wind-Driven Rain Research in Building Science," *J. Wind. Eng. Ind. Aerodyn.*, Vol. 92, No. 13, 2004, pp. 1079–1130.

[2] Hoppestad, S., Slagregn i Norge (in Norwegian), Norwegian Building Research Institute, Report No. 13, Oslo, 1955.

[3] Lacy, R. E., "Climate and Building in Britain," Building Research Establishment Report, London, UK: Department of the Environment, Her Majesty's Stationary, Office, 1977.

[4] Lacy, R. E. and Shellard, H. C., "An Index of Driving Rain," *Meteorol. Mag.*, Vol. 91, 1962, pp. 177–184.

[5] Lacy, R. E., "An Index of Exposure to Driving Rain," *Building Research Station Digest*, Vol. 127, Garston, UK, 1971.

[6] Underwood, S. J. and Meentemeyer, V., "Climatology of Wind-Driven Rain for the Contiguous United States for the Period 1971 to 1995," *Phys. Geogr.*, Vol. 19, No. 6, 1998, pp. 445–462.

[7] Leslie, N. P., "Laboratory Evaluation of Residential Window Installation Methods in Stucco Wall Assemblies," *ASHRAE Trans.*, Vol. 113, Part 1, 2007, pp. 296–305.

[8] Teasdale-St-Hilaire, A. and Derome, D., "Methodology and Application of Simulated Wind-Driven Rain Infiltration in Building Envelope Experimental Testing," *ASHRAE Trans.*, Vol. 112, Part 2, 2006, pp. 656–670.

[9] Lacasse, M. A., Durability and Performance of Building Envelopes," *BSI 2003 Proceedings*, Oct. 2003, pp. 1–6 (NRCC-46888).

[10] Cornick, S. M. and Lacasse, M. A., "A Review of Climate Loads Relevant to Assessing the Watertightness Performance of Walls, Windows and Wall-Window Interfaces," *J. ASTM Int.*, Vol. 2, No. 10, 2005, pp. 1–16.

[11] Lacasse, M. A., O'Connor, T., Nunes, S. C., and Beaulieu, P., Report from Task 6 of MEWS Project: Experimental Assessment of Water Penetration and Entry into Wood-Frame Wall Specimens—Final Report, Research Report, Institute for Research in Construction, National Research Council Canada, (IRC-RR-133), 2003.

[12] CSA, Canadian Supplement to AAMA/WDMA/CSA 101/I. S.2/A440-05, "Standard/ Specification for Windows, Doors, and Unit Skylights," Canadian Standards Association, Mississauga, Ontario, Canada, 128 pp.

[13] National Oceanic and Atmospheric Administration, Solar and Meteorological Surface Observational Network 1961–1990 Version 1.0, Sep. 1993. National Climatic Data Center Federal Building, 151 Patton Avenue, Asheville, NC 28801-5001.

[14] National Oceanic and Atmospheric Administration, Hourly United States Weather Observations, 1990–1995, Oct. 1997, National Climatic Data Center Federal Building, 151 Patton Avenue, Asheville, NC 28801-5001.

[15] Straube, J. F. and Burnett, E. F. P., *Building Science for Building Enclosures*, Chapter 12, Building Science Press, Westford, MA, 2005, 549 pp.

[16] Dingle, A. N. and Lee, Y., "Terminal Fall Speeds of Raindrops," *J. Appl. Meteorol.*, Vol. 11, Aug. 1972, pp. 877–879.

[17] Best, A. C., "The Size Distribution of Raindrops," *Q. J. R. Meteorol. Soc.*, Vol. 76, 1950, pp. 16–36.

[18] Choi, E. C. C., "Wind-Driven Rain and Driving Rain Coefficient During Thunderstorms and Non-Thunderstorms," *J. Wind. Eng. Ind. Aerodyn.*, Vol. 89, 2001, pp. 293–308.

[19] Blocken, B. and Carmeliet, J., "On the Validity of the Cosine Projection in Wind-Driven Rain Calculations on Buildings," *Build. Environ.*, Vol. 41, No. 9, 2006, pp.

1182–1189.

[20] Ang, A. H. S., and Tang, W. H., *Probability Concepts in Engineering Planning and Design—Vol. 1, Basic Principles*, John Wiley & Sons, NY, 2001, 424 pp.

[21] Bras, R. L., *Hydrology: An Introduction to Hydrologic Science*, Addison Wesley, Boston, MA, 1990, 643 pp.

[22] Hahn, G. J. and Shapiro, S. S., *Statistical Models in Engineering*, John Wiley & Sons, New York, 1968, 355 pp.

[23] Palutikof, J. P., Bradcock, B. B., Lister, D. H., and Adcock, S. T., "A Review of Methods to Calculate Extreme Wind Speeds," *Meteorological Applications*, Vol. 6, No. 2, 1999, pp. 119–132.

[24] Cook, N. J., *The Designer's Guide to Wind Loading of Building Structures. Part 1: Background, Damage Survey, Wind Data and Structural Classification*, Building Research Establishment, Garston, and Butterworths, London, 1985, 371 pp.

[25] Cook, N. J., Harris, R. I., and Whiting, R., "Extreme Wind Speeds in Mixed Climates Revisited," *J. Wind. Eng. Ind. Aerodyn.*, Vol. 91, No. 3, 2003, pp. 403–422.

[26] Cook, N. J., "Confidence Limits for Extreme Wind Speeds in Mixed Climates," *J. Wind. Eng. Ind. Aerodyn.*, Vol. 92, No. 1, 2004, pp. 41–51.

[27] Gomes, L. and Vickery, B. J., "Extreme Wind Speeds in Mixed Wind Climates," *J. Wind. Eng. Ind. Aerodyn.*, Vol. 2, No. 4, 1978, pp. 331–344.

[28] Justus, C. G., Hargraves, W. R., Mikhail, A., and Graber, D., "Methods for Estimating Wind Speed Frequency Distributions," *J. Appl. Meteorol.*, Vol. 17, No. 3, 1978, pp. 350–353.

[29] Stevens, M. J. M. and Smulders, P. T., "Estimation of the Parameters of the Weibull Wind Speed Distribution for Wind Energy Utilization Purposes," *Wind Eng.*, Vol. 3, No. 2, 1979, pp. 132–145.

[30] Seguro, J. V. and Lambert, T. W., "Modern Estimation of the Parameters of the Weibull Wind Speed Distribution for Wind Energy Analysis," *J. Wind. Eng. Ind. Aerodyn.*, Vol. 85, No. 1, 2000, pp. 75–84.

[31] Tuller, S. E. and Brett, A. C., "The Characteristics of Wind Velocity that Favor the Fitting of a Weibull Distribution in Wind Speed Analysis," *J. Appl. Meteorol.*, Vol. 23, No. 1, 1984, pp. 124–134.

[32] Deaves, D. M. and Lines, I. G., "On the Fitting of Low Mean Wind Speed Data to the Weibull Distribution," *J. Wind. Eng. Ind. Aerodyn.*, Vol. 66, No. 3, 1997, pp. 169–178.

[33] Ro, K. S. and Hunt, P. G., "Characteristic Wind Speed Distributions and Reliability of the Logarithmic Wind Profile," *J. Environ. Eng.*, Vol. 133, No. 3, 2007, pp. 313–318.

[34] Celik, A. N., "Weibull Representative Compressed Wind Speed Data for Energy and Performance Calculations of Wind Energy Systems," *Energy Convers. Manage.*, Vol. 44, No. 19, 2003, pp. 3057–3072.

[35] Wilks, D. S., Rainfall Intensity, the Weibull Distribution, and Estimation of Daily Surface Runoff," *J. Appl. Meteorol.*, Vol. 28, No. 1, 1989, pp. 52–58.

[36] Testa, O., Colacino, M., Lavagnini, A., and Malvestuto, V., "A Study of Rainfall in the Roman Area in the Years 1951–2000," *Nuovo Cimento Soc. Ital. Fis., C*, Vol. 29C, No. 2, 2006, pp. 191–213.

[37] Testa, O., Lavagnini, A., Malvestuto, V., Diodato, L. D., and Abramo, F., "A Detailed Study of Rainfall in the Roman Area in the Decade 1992–2001," *Nuovo Cimento Soc. Ital. Fis., C*, Vol. 29C, No. 6, 2006, pp. 623–640.

[38] American Society of Heating Refrigeration and Air-Conditioning Engineers. *ASHRAE 2005 Handbook of Fundamentals*, Atlanta, GA, p. 16.3.

[39] ASCE 7-95 "Minimum Design Loads for Buildings and Other Structures," Ameri-

can Society of Civil Engineers, 345 East 47th Street New York, NY 10017-2398, p. 155.

[40]   Choi, E. C. C., "Criteria for Water Penetration Testing," *Water Leakage Through Building Facades, ASTM STP 1314*, ASTM International, West Conshohocken, PA, 1998, 12 pp.

Reprinted from JAI, Vol. 6, No. 10
doi:10.1520/JAI101455
Available online at www.astm.org/JAI

Achilles N. Karagiozis[1] *and Hartwig M. Kuenzel*[2]

The Effect of Air Cavity Convection on the Wetting and Drying Behavior of Wood-Frame Walls Using a Multi-Physics Approach

ABSTRACT: The moisture performance of building envelope systems are strongly dependent on the materials used, the workmanship, and the exposure loads from the interior and exterior environments. The authors have long recognized the need to include the effects of exterior cladding ventilation in the predictive capability of software tools used for hygrothermal analysis. Exterior cladding ventilation has been studied, but no conclusive recommendations have been generated until recently (Burnett, E., Straube, J., and Karagiozis, A., "Synthesis Report and Guidelines," *ASHRAE TRP-1091 Report No. 12*, Nov. 2004). While the physics describing the thermal and moisture transport in the presence of air convection is understood, the pressure dynamics is still somewhat qualitatively known. With the addition of new literature data and available field generated monitored data, a simplified model for the wall air cavity ventilation was developed. The scientific approach followed initially included the benchmarking of multi-dimensional advanced hygrothermal model with laboratory and field data. The flow was understood for a wide range of exterior loadings, and once this was completed, an attempt to reduce the complex three-dimensional air flow characteristics into a simple one-dimensional analogue was made. The paper describes how this important feature was included into the WUFI-4.1 software. The paper also describes how users may employ this feature in hygrothermal designs to investigate the advantages and disadvantages of cavity ventilation. Results are also presented on the hygrothermal performance of two

Manuscript received October 12, 2007; accepted for publication September 2, 2009; published online November 2009.

[1] Distinguished Research and Development Staff, Oak Ridge National Laboratory, 1 Bethel Valley Rd., Oak Ridge, TN 37831-6070.

[2] Director of Hygrothermics, Fraunhofer-Institut in Bauphysik, Holzkirchen, 83626 Valley, Germany.

Cite as: Karagiozis, A. N. and Kuenzel, H. M., "The Effect of Air Cavity Convection on the Wetting and Drying Behavior of Wood-Frame Walls Using a Multi-Physics Approach," *J. ASTM Intl.*, Vol. 6, No. 10. doi:10.1520/JAI101455.

walls, one ventilated and the other is unvented. Results show that major differences were predicted and the wall with the ventilation cavity dried out nearly five times faster than the wall without the ventilation. Field monitored stucco wall systems with and without cavity ventilation are also included compared to the prediction provided by the hygrothermal model. Good agreement is shown between the field and WUFI 4.1 model.

KEYWORDS: air convection, ventilation, moisture performance, hygrothermal performance, simulations

Introduction

In many parts of the United States, damage caused by uncontrolled moisture accumulation in building enclosures is of great concern to the construction and energy conservation communities. Concern about moisture accumulation has caused the building industry to be skeptical of new energy efficient construction methods and has slowed the adoption of new energy efficient building envelopes. This can hinder the adoption of energy efficient building envelope systems with high levels of insulation. The Department of Energy through the Building America Program and the Building Emerging Technology has been working towards the next generation of high performance envelope systems that are to be included in the 2020 net zero-energy buildings. In a recent DOE funded project on interior vapor retarder strategies, Karagiozis et al. [1,2] determined that a well ventilated exterior cladding negated the impact of solar driven moisture transport for all International Energy Conservation Code (IECC) climate zones. As one insulates the envelope walls with higher thermal resistance, parts of the wall will become warmer, but at the same time other parts will be much colder. Temperature differences in the wall affect the flow and redistribution of moisture in the wall, a dynamic moisture transport process in both vapor and liquid phases. The amount of free energy that is available to assist in the drying transport of moisture stored in the envelope is reduced by increasing the thermal value of the envelope. Special care and attention are required when selecting material and control layers in envelope systems in high thermal performance applications.

Indeed, cladding ventilation was found to be so critical that even the impact of interior vapor retarders could be relaxed. An IECC code submission by Lstiburek [3] based on the scientific work performed by Karagiozis et al. [1,2] included accommodations for cladding cavity air ventilation in wall systems. In that study, it was found that wall systems with exterior cladding ventilation may have a drying potential significant enough to minimize the impact of the interior vapor retarder. Air cavity ventilation drying was found to be many times (10–100) greater in strength than diffusion alone.

The paper by Salonvaara et al. [4], Ventilated Air Cavities Behind Claddings—What Have We Learned?—provides an excellent state-of-the-art review of exterior air cavity ventilation. The authors demonstrated that wall cavity ventilation is generally beneficial for almost all wall structures, allowing them to dry out from incidental moisture leakage into the wall cavity. At times, cavity ventilation was found to help bring moisture into the wall. In an ideal world, a perfectly air, water, and water vapor tight wall would remain dry even in wet and humid conditions. If this ideal wall is suddenly ventilated, the ventilation will bring in humid outdoor air and thus increase the moisture content of the materials in the wall. However, in the real world we have to be prepared to dry out incidental water leakage that is introduced into the wall. Therefore, wall cavity ventilation is primarily beneficial with occasional minor drawbacks. Wall cavity ventilation is especially important for walls with high water absorptive claddings, such as bricks and stucco claddings.

However, the authors found that the combination of water vapor permeances of the sheathing, insulation, and exterior cladding dictated the benefits of the exterior ventilation. As such generalized cladding guidelines do not exist. This makes the selection of the building envelope design choices by architects or building envelope specialists a difficult task. The only way to make these choices correctly requires a hygrothermal design tool that includes the capability to handle cavity ventilation scenarios.

Current Understanding

Any building envelope requires a number of basic elements present to operate satisfactory. The overall hygrothermal performance of the building envelope will depend on the performance of each of these elements and the combination of the elements. For example, the presence of insulation provides the specified thermal control. The vapor retarder provides the element that controls the flow of vapor from either the interior or exterior. The sheathings, both interior and exterior, provide the structural and sound control. In addition to these basic elements, other elements may be included in the design of the building envelope that enhances the performance of the buildings. In this category, the exterior coatings (penetrant or non-penetrant), drainage elements, phase change materials included in either the insulation or other elements of the envelope, and air ventilation cavities can be included, which further include additional functionality in the performance of the building envelope system.

In retrospect, air ventilation cavities provide a multitude of additional function [5–9]. For example, an air cavity can provide a (1) capillary break for water penetration into the wall cavity, (2) an effective drainage space, (3) a reduction in direct moisture bridges, and (4) a passive mechanism to remove moisture that might have penetrated the cladding and (5) can potentially permit pressure equalization of the system to prevent water infiltration through the inner Wythe and into the inner structure.

Indeed, air ventilation cavities can be propelled by mechanically induced fans or by passive forces such as the presence of wind pressures and buoyancy forces due to the density gradients caused by moisture concentration or temperature differences. For the majority of the building envelope applications, the use of passive systems is most desirable as long as the particular envelope design has large enough drying potential or high levels of forgiveness. Many of the next generation of highly insulated building envelope structures within the DOE zero net energy building program will need to encompass passive approaches to reduce the amount of moisture accumulating in these structures. The use of air cavity ventilation is expected to enhance the drying performances of a number of highly energy efficient structures. In general the classification of the types of air cavity ventilation strategies can be grouped into three categories.

(1) Full ventilated cavities (ventilated strategies) where opening are intentionally designed into the envelope that are open at the bottom and top of the wall or roof system. These types of air cavity ventilation strategies maximize the amount of air convention occurring. Typically the openings span the full length or are present frequently.

(2) Vented cavities that are open only one side, most frequently at the bottom of the structure.

(3) Unvented cavities that do not have intentional opening either at the bottom or top of the envelope system.

There are systems such as vinyl cladding that allows a certain number of air exchanges based on the assembly. In other words, for most of the installed vinyl claddings where no intentional cavities or opening are designed into the wall system, ventilation occurs due the rather leaky openings at the joints of the vinyl cladding. Even for some applications of brick work where one would assume minimal leakage, up to 40 % contribution of leakage is present at the joints between the mortar and joints, as measured by Van Straaten [10]. These two above systems can be classified as vented systems.

The ventilation air space behind the exterior cladding with the exterior air movement offers a few benefits.

(1) The flow of relatively dry outside air promotes convective drying of the inside face of wet cladding and the outside face of the wall layer facing into the cavity.

(2) Water vapor diffusing through the inner wall layers can bypass the vapor diffusion resistance of the cladding and be carried directly to the outside of the wall system.

Ventilation has, in theory, the ability to increase the drying potential of semi and absorptive ventilated wall systems, allowing these cladding to behave close to non absorptive claddings with low vapor resistance. In vented and ventilated wall systems, ventilation air will be driven through the air cavity by one or the combination of two motive forces: Either a wind-induced air pressure differential or thermal buoyancy (stack effect). The direction of airflow through the air cavity could be from the lower vents to the upper vents or reversed, depending on the combination of the driving forces. In some cases, lateral airflow can also occur in some wall systems, such as those with horizontal siding.

Simplification of the Physics

The physics involved in the movement of heat and air through a ventilated air cavity is complex. The air transport is definitively a three-dimensional flow with stagnation boundary layers forming at each of the corners of the air cavity. In the air cavity, depending on the activity exterior loading, the flow may be either laminar, transitioning, or even turbulent. The flow inside these air cavities is strongly dependent on the effects of the wind, which is very unsteady in nature, with large bursts and fluctuation present. Further analysis showed that air

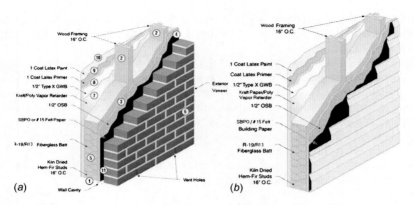

FIG. 1—(a) A vented brick veneer wall. (b) A vented vinyl wall.

flows through ventilation spaces due to the combined effects of wind pressure, thermal buoyancy, and moisture concentration buoyancy. Other issues further complicating the physics are pertinent to the actual geometry of the air cavity. The effect of discrete rough elements, such as protruding mortar joints, vent arrangements, cavity openings, mortar bridging/blockage, makes the analysis a challenge. In Figs. 1 and 2 the velocity distribution is depicted for a ventilated brick veneer air cavity. The cross sectional flow is shown for the full height of the wall, and the air entrance and exit regions are along with the two openings. To solve the flow a conjugate heat and mass transfer computational fluid dynamics (CFD) model is needed. In most cases, CFD models are commercially

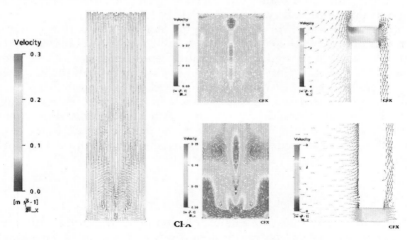

FIG. 2—(Clockwise, starting at left, all from case S7) Velocity field midway between the brick and building paper surfaces of the cavity, mirrored about the plane of symmetry; close-up view near the top ventilation slot; close-up side view near the top ventilation slot; close-up side view near the bottom ventilation slot; and close-up view near the bottom ventilation slot [11].

available to assist to investigate the combined heat and air flow transport in building envelope systems. Stovall and Karagiozis [11], using a CFD model, CFX, were able to investigate the complex flow developed for a number of discreet conditions. This extensive study permitted the CFD results to be benchmarked via comparison to the then available empirical data; the results were then correlated with weather parameters and construction details in order to supplement these broader hygrothermal analysis tools. The outcome was to deduce a number of simple equations sets (multi-regression analysis) to permit good prediction of the air cavity ventilation strength. The air flow was characterized by the pressure drops through the inlet and outlet ventilation slots, the pressure variation within the cavity, the flow rate of air through the cavity, and the flow patterns within the cavity. These factors were examined using the matrix of case models. This matrix permitted an examination of the individual contribution of each parameter, covering five wind speeds, two outdoor air temperatures, three levels of solar radiation, two slot heights, and two cavity depths. The resulting analysis demonstrated the ability of simplifying the complex flow conditions to one-dimensional analogs with lumped contributions for flow coefficients.

Air Cavity Ventilation

A comprehensive compilation of the air cavity ventilation has been presented in a report to ASHRAE TRP1091 by Straube et al. [12] and Burnett et al. [13]. The authors summarized the research performed to date on cavity ventilation. In 1973, Schwarz instrumented an 18-storey apartment building in Hamburg, Germany, with a 1.25×1.35 m^2 open-jointed panel cladding system to measure the velocity of the air flow in the cavity. The researchers from the Institut für Bauphysik measured velocities of 0.2–0.6 m/s under a range of wind speeds of 0–8 m/s. They found little relationship between building height and cavity ventilation velocity. It was also found that although lower velocities in the cavity were measured for the lee side than the windward side, the velocity on the lee side was usually stable at around 0.2 m/s for the normal range of wind velocities. From the measured velocities the air change rate (ACH) would be several hundred exchanges per hour, and vapor diffusion through the cladding therefore played a completely insignificant role in the transfer of vapor from inside to outside. This is depicted in Fig. 3 where the leeward and windward sides velocities in the air cavity are depicted. A series of field and laboratory studies conducted in Belgium showed that ventilation had an insignificant effect on heat transmission within the air space [9]. In the same study, it was found that quantifying the benefit of ventilation in relation to moisture performance (i.e., moisture removal rate) was difficult. Contradictory results were reported by Fraunhofer-Institut for Building Physics [15], indicating that the presence of an air space had no effect on the moisture content of the brick veneer. These findings highlighted a significant dilemma and questioned the benefits of cavity ventilation in brick clad walls.

Similar research has also been performed on walls with other types of cladding, sheathing, and insulation. Pressure gradient measurements within the air cavity of a wood-framed siding-clad wall filled with low density fibrous

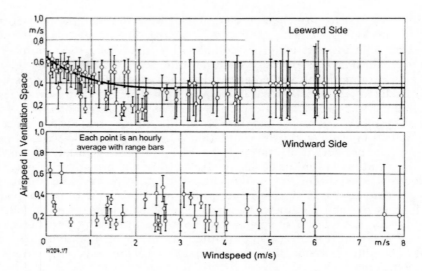

FIG. 3—*Ventilation space velocity measurements versus wind speed for the lee (top) and windward side (bottom) of a ventilated panel system [14].*

insulation were performed by Norwegian Research Institute [16]. The results indicated that a wind barrier installed on the exterior side of the insulation was necessary to reduce convective heat losses. It was also found that the mean pressure gradient behind the siding correlated with the wind speed and wind direction. Average pressure gradients measured range between 0.1 and 0.5 Pa/m.

The Fraunhofer-Institut für Bauphysik has conducted field monitoring of ventilation flow and drying effectiveness for different types of panel cladding during several projects. One project measured the ventilation velocity and air exchange rate behind asbestos cement and wood siding with various types of cavities and venting arrangements [17]. The cladding was installed over initially wet aerated concrete block work, and the moisture content (and hence drying rate) of these blocks was monitored over a period of 2 years. It was clear the drying rate was much faster when the cladding was ventilated (case 2 in Fig. 4), although even venting (small openings through the cladding without a clear airflow space behind) considerably improved the drying rate compared to the situation where the cladding was glued directly to the block work (case 1 in Fig. 4).

Hansen, et al. [7] performed field experiments with 12 wall assemblies. The constructed assemblies included different cladding, sheathing, and air barrier types and were either ventilated, non-ventilated, or had no cavity. Moisture contents of wood dowels mounted behind the air barrier showed greater moisture in assemblies with ventilated cavities than in non-ventilated cavities. Accounting for the time lag, changes in moisture content correlated well with the outdoor relative humidity.

The Canada Mortgage and Housing Corporation (CMHC) supported a study of ventilation of enclosure walls by the Building Engineering Group at

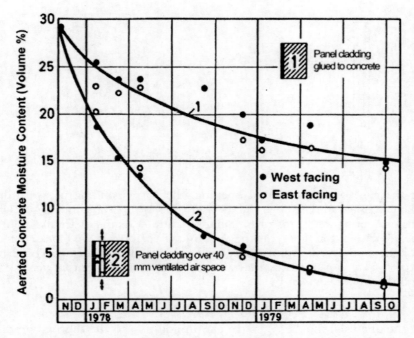

FIG. 4—*Ventilation drying observed in full-scale field research [17].*

the University of Waterloo [18]. The report concluded that ventilation could provide a significant drying potential and bypassed the vapor resistance of cladding such as metal panels and vinyl siding. A subsequent full-scale field study by Building Envelope Group (BEG) [5] investigated the role of air spaces in ventilation drying and pressure moderation. This study demonstrated that ventilation could be useful as a means to control inward vapor drives behind brick veneers. It also presented and compared measurements of air moisture contents behind brick veneers and vinyl siding.

Derivation of Transport Equations

Air Transport—The total pressure drop through the ventilation cavity is comprised by the entrance pressure drop (ΔP_{AB} or ΔP_{in}), the channel pressure drop (ΔP_{BC} or ΔP_{cavity}), and the exit pressure drop (ΔP_{CD} or ΔP_{exit}). This is depicted in the following Fig. 5.

For a full slotted opening at the bottom and top, the following pressure drop equation is developed:

$$\Delta P_{total} = \Delta P_{in} + \Delta P_{cavity} + \Delta P_{exit} \tag{1}$$

$$\Delta P_{total} = C_{in} \cdot 0.5 \ \rho v^2 + \frac{32 k_f \cdot v \cdot \mu \cdot L}{\gamma \cdot D_h^2} + C_{exit} \cdot 0.5 \ \rho v^2 \tag{2}$$

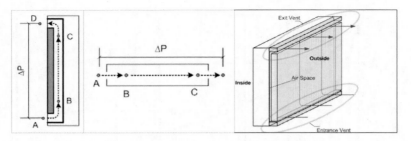

FIG. 5—*Cavity air ventilation diagram (figures from Ref 12).*

In the case of a non-slotted opening, the corresponding pressure drops would be included in the above equations for the ΔP_{total}, ΔP_{in}, and ΔP_{exit}, where k_f is the correction factor for rectangular conduit, D_h is the hydraulic diameter, ν is the velocity of the flow, μ is the dynamic viscosity, γ is the blockage factor, L is length of the ventilation cavity, and ρ is the density of air. The driving potential for air movement by the two resulting pressures that induce the flow through the cavity is given by

$$\Delta P_{\text{total}} = \Delta P_{\text{wind}} + \Delta P_{\text{stack}} \tag{3}$$

In the analysis, the ΔP_{stack} term can in addition to the thermal gradients include the effect of moisture buoyancy, especially as this term can contribute a significant amount of body pressure. The ΔP_{wind} depends on the environmental conditions (wind and wind orientation), and the wind pressure coefficients C_{in} and C_{exit} will depend on the type (shape) of the building, the location, and type of vent size and opening. From the solution of the above equations (ΔP_{total}), the air cavity velocity is calculated and is used to provide the sources and sinks in the enthalpy and moisture governing equations.

Thermal Transport—The law of continuity applies to heat as well as to moisture, i.e., the change in enthalpy or moisture in a volume element is determined by the divergence of heat or moisture flows through the surface of the element and the heat or moisture sources or sinks in the element. As far as heat is concerned, this results in the following balance equation:

$$\frac{\partial H}{\partial t} = -\nabla \cdot q + S_h \tag{4}$$

where:
  H = total enthalpy (J/m^3),
  Q = heat flux density (W/m^2), and
  S_h = heat source or heat sink (W/m^3).
  The total enthalpy of a building component layer consists of the enthalpy of the dry building material and the enthalpy of the water contained therein,

$$H = H_s + H_w \tag{5}$$

where:

H_s = enthalpy of the dry building material (J/m^3) and
H_w = enthalpy of building material moisture (J/m^3).

The heat flux density is proportional to the thermal conductivity of the moist building material and the temperature gradient,

$$q = -\lambda \nabla \vartheta \tag{6}$$

where:
q = heat flux density (W/m^2),
λ = thermal conductivity of the moist building material (W/mK), and
ϑ = temperature (°C).

The enthalpy flows through moisture movement and phase transition can be taken into account in the form of source terms in the heat balance equation. In addition the enthalpy flow associated with the air cavity ventilation also needs to be included. The contribution is the difference in the enthalpies entering and exiting the air cavity. The total source term is given by taking into account the vapor diffusion with simultaneous phase transition and the contribution due to air flow in the cavity. The following relation results for the source term:

$$S_h = h_v \nabla g_v + Q_{\text{vair}} \cdot \rho \cdot (h_{\text{ext}} - h_{\text{cavity}}) + Q_s \tag{7}$$

where:
S_h = heat source/heat sink through condensation/evaporation $(J/m^3 \text{ s})$,
h_v = latent heat of phase change (J/kg),
g_v = vapor diffusion flux density $(kg/m^2 \text{ s})$,
Q_{vair} = air flow per volume of ventilation cavity $(m^3/s \text{ m}^3)$,
h_{ext} = enthalpy of air in cavity at entrance (J/kg),
h_{cavity} = enthalpy of air at exit (J/kg), and
Q_s = additional heat source/sink $(J/m^3 \text{ s})$.

Moisture Transport—The moisture transport is calculated with the moisture balance equation. The moisture balance equation includes the contributions of both the liquid and vapor flows. The equation describing the balance is analogous to the heat balance equation and can be expressed as follows:

$$\frac{\partial w}{\partial t} = -\nabla \cdot (g_w + g_v) + S_w \tag{8}$$

where:
w = water content of the building material layer (kg/m^3),
g_w = liquid transport flux density $(kg/m^2 \text{ s})$,
g_v = vapor diffusion flux density $(kg/m^2 \text{ s})$, and
S_w = moisture source or moisture sink $(kg/m^3 \text{ s})$.

In the new version 4.1 of WUFI the moisture source or sink term S_w includes the contribution for the 1 % water penetration required by the ASHRAE SPC 160 and the contributions due to the amount of moisture deposited or withdrawn from the envelope part due to air convection. The equation with moisture sources or sinks due to the presence of air cavity ventilation (with exterior air only) is given by

$$S_w = Q_{\text{vair}} \cdot (\rho_{\text{ext}} - \rho_{\text{cavity}}) + Q_{\text{penetration}} \tag{9}$$

where:

ρ_{ext} = vapor density at inlet of ventilation cavity (exterior) (kg/m³),

ρ_{cavity} = vapor density at exit of ventilation cavity (at cavity exit) (kg/m³),

Q_{vair} = air flow per volume of ventilation cavity (m³/s m³), and

$Q_{\text{penetration}}$ = water penetration source (i.e., 1 % ASHRAE SPC 160P) (kg/m³s).

The liquid transport flux density g_w depends on the gradient of the relative humidity

$$g_w = D_\varphi \nabla \varphi \tag{10}$$

where:

D_φ = liquid conduction coefficient (kg/ms),

φ = relative humidity.

The vapor diffusion flux density g_v can be determined as follows according to section

$$g_v = \delta_p \nabla (p_v) = \delta_p \nabla (\varphi p_{\text{sat}}) \tag{11}$$

where:

p_{sat} = water vapor saturation pressure (Pa),

δ_p = water vapor permeability of building material (kg/ms Pa), and

p_v = water vapor partial pressure (Pa).

Assembly of Governing Equations for Combined Heat and Moisture Transport

The following two governing equations (heat conservation and moisture conservation), with the closure equation provided by the water vapor saturation pressure, allow the determination of a unique solution to the partial differential equations:

$$\frac{dH}{d\vartheta} \cdot \frac{\partial \vartheta}{\partial t} = \nabla \cdot (\lambda \nabla \vartheta) + h_v \nabla \cdot (\delta_p \nabla (\varphi p_{\text{sat}})) + S_h \tag{12}$$

$$\frac{dw}{d\varphi} \cdot \frac{\partial \varphi}{\partial t} = \nabla \cdot (D_\varphi \nabla \varphi + \delta_p \nabla (\varphi p_{\text{sat}})) + S_w \tag{13}$$

The water vapor saturation pressure can be calculated by means of an empirical relationship as a function of temperature

$$p_{\text{sat}} = 611 \cdot \exp\left(\frac{a \cdot \vartheta}{\vartheta_0 + \vartheta}\right) \tag{14}$$

with

$$a = 22{,}44, \quad \vartheta_0 = 272{,}44 \,^\circ\text{C}, \quad \vartheta < 0 \,^\circ\text{C} \tag{15}$$

$$a = 17{,}08, \quad \vartheta_0 = 234{,}18 \,^\circ\text{C}, \quad \vartheta \geq 0 \,^\circ\text{C} \tag{16}$$

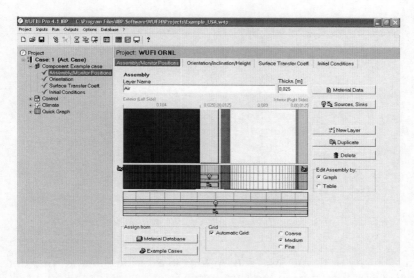

FIG. 6—*Assigning the air cavity to be modified by clicking the air layer first and then the Sources and Sink option control.*

Analysis of Ventilated Air Cavities Using Numerical Models

Currently the WUFI 4.1 software [19,20] includes the capability to include the impact of exterior air cavity ventilation and water penetration. These new features have been incorporated so that the user of the software only enters the cavity ventilation exchange (i.e., how many air changes per hour occur in the cavity) as a function of time and the heat and moisture sources per hour.

To include the ventilation, thermal, or moisture sources, the user needs to perform three steps. In the first step the user clicks the layer for which the source is to be prescribed. In Fig. 6 the user has selected the air layer to be ventilated. The user has already developed an American Standard Code for Information Interchange (ASCII) file with information on the cavity ventilation specifying the hour (hour 1 is first hour in January) and the cavity air exchange rate (air changes per hour) using a procedure similar to the one presented above. This is repeated for all 8760 h of the year, each hour in separate lines. In this particular ventilated brick cavity case, a file named vent.dat was created. Next the user clicks on Sources, Sinks and, as shown in Fig. 7, selects the option New Air Change Source. The software then launches another screen where the user enters the file name for the hourly ventilation exchange rate as shown in Fig. 8. At the end of these three steps, the user has modified the stagnant unvented air layer into a ventilated air layer.

Example Case to Demonstrate the Importance of Wall Cavity Ventilation

The WUFI Oak Ridge National Loaboratory (ORNL) 4.1 version is used to investigate the drying potential of a brick veneer wall system. Two cases were developed, one with an unvented wall cavity and the other with a ventilated

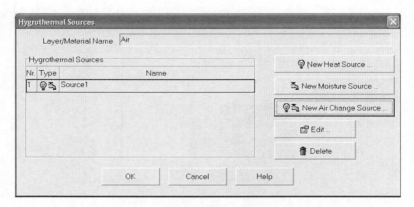

FIG. 7—*Assigning the layer with cavity ventilation properties.*

system. The city of Seattle was chosen for the exterior climatic conditions. All materials were chosen from the North American database, and the brick layer was very absorptive low temperature fired clay brick (old brick). In Fig. 9, the wall make-up is given for the example case investigated for the unvented and ventilated brick wall. The material layer dimensions and wall component assembly are displayed in Fig. 9. A 1 year time period was chosen for these wall cases, and all elements of the wall were initially in equilibrium with 80 % RH, except the oriented strand board (OSB) layer that was in equilibrium with 95 %

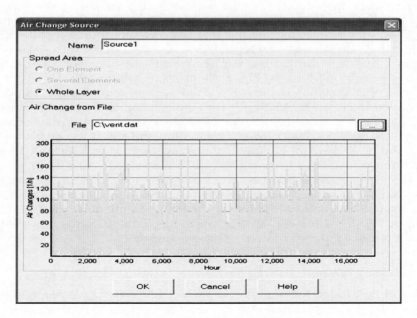

FIG. 8—*Read in the hourly air changes per hour.*

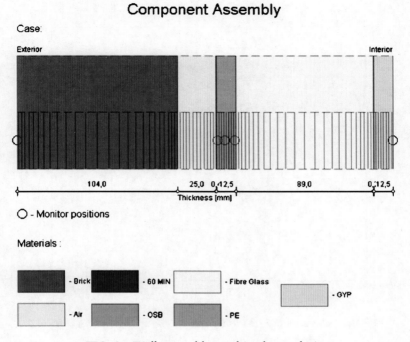

FIG. 9—*Wall assembly used in the analysis.*

relative humidity (RH). These values are typical initial moisture construction values for buildings in the Northwest Pacific United States.

Simulation Study Results

In Fig. 10, the unvented moisture content of the OSB is shown as a function of time for a period of 1 year. The simulations are started out in October, and the OSB is initially wet. It is clear that for a substantial period of time, 9 months, the OSB did not dry out below 80 %. On the right axis, the mass percent is plotted out, indicating that the panel does dry out during the Summer months but rather slowly until the driving force kicks in during Summer. In Fig. 11, the effectiveness of air cavity ventilation is clearly depicted showing substantial drying out performance for the OSB. Figures 12 and 13 plot out the temperature and relative humidity at the exterior most elements in the OSB (1 mm from the exterior). It is evident again that the substantial improvement in the brick wall is due to the presence of cavity ventilation.

Calculation of Wall Performance with and without Ventilation in Comparison with Experimental Data

In 2002 DOE funded a research project entitled "Developing Innovative Wall Systems that Improve Hygrothermal Performance of Residential Buildings" for

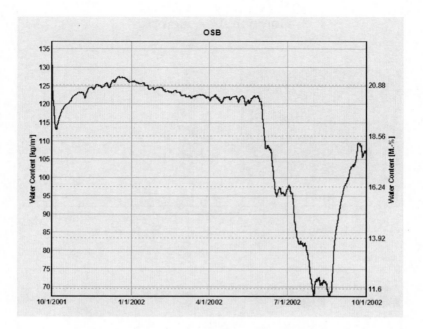

FIG. 10—*Unvented OSB moisture content as a function of time.*

the Northwest. This study was developed jointly by Washington State University (WSU) and ORNL staff and was located in Puyallup, WA. The study focused on addressing a number of hygrothermal issues such as impact of the higher insulation values, impact of the placement of insulation (interior or exterior), impact of cladding ventilation (unvented, vented, and ventilated), and the impact of various interior vapor retarder strategies (see reports by Tichy and Murray [21] and Karagiozis et al. [1,2] for more details).

A specially designed test facility was built that housed 12 walls on each side of the building. Figure 14 shows the southern façade of this test building. Most of the wall sections where stucco-clad 2×6 in.² (140 mm) wood frame structures, a few were stucco-clad 2×4 in.² (89 mm), and a number were cementitious siding.

The particular facility was ideal to validate the new features of the WUFI 4.1 model. For the validation case, wall 4 was selected. The wall basically is typical for the Northwest and includes starting from the exterior to the interior a 7/8 (22 mm) in. three coat stucco with the exterior coating being cementitious, an air space of 25 mm, two layers of 60 min building paper, an OSB 12.5 mm sheathing, 140 mm fiberglass insulation, a four-mil polyethylene vapor retarder, and a gypsum drywall with a 35 perm paint. The microclimate in a ventilated air cavity is different from the conditions in cavity with stagnant air because the vapor concentration is diluted by the incoming outdoor air. The reduction in vapor pressure in the air gap enhances the drying potential of the adjacent materials layers. The validation would allow us to investigate whether WUFI 4.1 with the simplified air cavity ventilation model could capture this

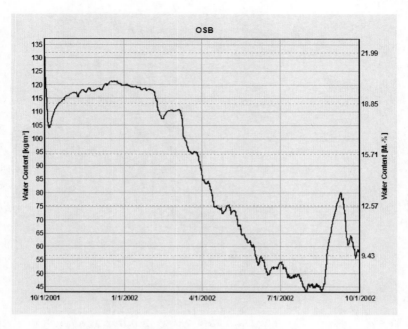

FIG. 11—*Ventilated OSB moisture content as a function of time.*

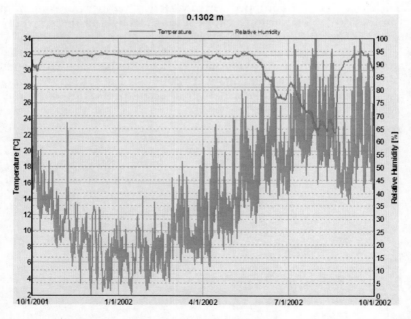

FIG. 12—*Unvented OSB relative humidity and temperature as a function of time.*

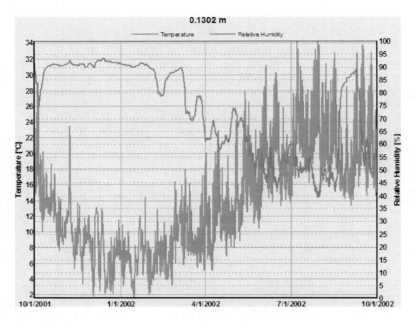

FIG. 13—*Ventilated OSB relative humidity and temperature as a function of time.*

effect in order to predict the overall hygrothermal performance of the building assembly.

The test sections were equipped with a variety of temperature and humidity sensors in the air gap and at different positions throughout the assembly. The tests began in October 2003, and measurement went on for a period of 1 year. During the whole period the indoor air conditions were kept between 68 and 72°F, and the relative humidity was allow to fluctuate between 50 % and 60 % RH. At the same time measurements were conducted at ORNL by Karagiozis and Wilkes to determine the material hygrothermal properties and these have

FIG. 14—*WSU outdoor test building with weather station on top of the roof.*

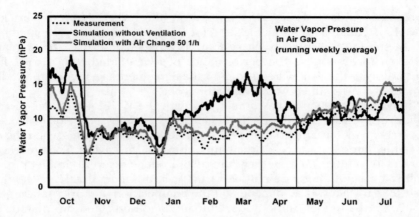

FIG. 15—*Vapor pressure in the air cavity simulated with stagnant air (no ventilation) and with a constant ACH in the cavity of* 50 h^{-1} *compared to the conditions recorded in the air cavity of wall section 4.*

been reported by Karagiozis [1,2]. The exterior climate dates were hourly recorded onsite by a small weather station on top of the test building's roof. The short wave absorptivity a_s of the brown colored stucco has not been determined in the laboratory. It was selected by comparing the measured and simulated surface temperatures. The best fit was obtained by $a_s = 0.9$, which appears a little higher than expected at first sight. However, this rather high value compensates the lack of solar reflection from the ground, which is not captured by the horizontally positioned solarimeter at the weather station on the roof.

In Fig. 15, the predictions from WUFI 4.1 were compared against the hourly measured values in wall 4. Results are shown for the water vapor pressure as a function of time for both the model predictions and the field data. While there is a rather good fit in vapor pressure conditions in the air cavity between experiment and simulations when a constant ventilation ACH of 50 h^{-1} is assumed, the calculated vapor pressure assuming an unvented air cavity is too high especially during winter period. This value was chosen from the ASHRAE 1091 project [12] as average condition in the ventilated stucco cases. Since Seattle experiences most of its precipitation during the same period, the water content of the stucco is responsible for the high vapor pressure in the air gap, which prevails in the cavity as long as it is not diluted or carried away by air convection through cavity ventilation. It is expected that further improvement between the WUFI 4.1 predictions and measured field data can be achieved if an hourly changing air cavity ventilation model as presented in this paper is used.

Conclusions

This paper offers a simplified approach to calculate the ventilation present in a wall cavity. This simplified approach seems to be effective at capturing the bulk performance and gives rather good agreement with field data. The authors investigated the impact of air cavity ventilation in a rather absorptive brick veneer wall system. Results show the superior performance of the ventilated brick cavity versus the unvented brick system. The paper describes the validation undertaken to investigate the performance of a ventilated stucco wall. Field data monitoring the wall were used, and the agreement even when the ventilation model was simplified was remarkably good.

While in the particular cases analyzed with the WUFI 4.1 model one may conclude that cavity ventilation is beneficial, in some scenarios the performance may be inconsequential or even detrimental (in rare cases when the dew point of the outdoor air exceeds the temperature in the cavity). The presence of the air cavity ventilation may therefore also produce a severe problem for the durability of a building assembly. Alas there is no general rule of thumb to assess the real stakes. It all depends on the composition and orientation of the assembly, on the indoor and outdoor climate conditions, and on the moisture sensitivity of the employed building materials. Therefore the availability of easy to use simulation tools like WUFI 4.1 is critical, and these tools must be able to handle the effects of ventilation along with other potential loads properly in order to assist designers and building envelope engineers.

References

[1]   Karagiozis, A. N., Lstiburek, J., and Desjarlais, A. O., "Scientific Analysis of Vapor Retarder Recommendations for Wall Systems Constructed in the North America," *Thermal Performance of the Exterior Envelopes of Whole Buildings X International Conference*, Clearwater Beach, FL, December 2–7, 2007, ASHRAE Special Publication.

[2]   Karagiozis, A. N., "Developing Innovative Wall Systems That Improve Hygrothermal Performance of Residential Buildings, Part B," *Report No.* NETL DE-FC26-02NT41498, Department of Energy, Washington, D.C., May 2007.

[3]   Lstiburek, J., "IECC Submission on Vapor Retarders," Personal communication, 2007.

[4]   Salonvaara, M. H., Karagiozis, A. N., Pazera, M., and Miller, W., "Air Cavities Behind Claddings—What Have We Learned?" *Thermal Performance of the Exterior Envelopes of Whole Buildings Tenth International Conference*, Clearwater Beach, FL, December 2–7, 2007, ASHRAE Special Publications.

[5]   Straube, J. F. and Burnett, E. F. P., "Drainage, Ventilation Drying and Enclosure Performance," *Thermal Performance of the Exterior Envelopes of Buildings VII*, Clearwater Beach, FL, 1998, ASHRAE Special Publication, p. 189.

[6]   Salonvaara, M. H., Ojanen, T., Kokko, E., and Karagiozis, A. N., "Drying Capabilities of Wood Frame Walls with Wood Siding," *Thermal Performance of the Exterior Envelopes of Buildings VII*, Clearwater Beach, FL, 1998, ASHRAE Special Publication, pp. 165–177.

[7]   Hansen, M., Nicolajsen, A., and Stang, B., "On the Influence of Ventilation on Moisture Content in Timber Framed Walls," *Building Physics—Sixth Nordic Symposium*, June 17-19, 2002, Trondheim, Norway.

[8]   TenWolde, A. and Carll, C. G., "Effect of Cavity Ventilation on Moisture in Walls and Roofs," *Proceedings of the Thermal Performance of the Exterior Envelopes of Buildings V*, Clearwater Beach, FL, December 1992, ASHRAE Special Publication,

pp. 555–562.

[9]   Hens, H., *Bouwfysica 1: Warme-En Massatransport*, Boek, Leuven, Belgium, 1992.

[10] Van Straaten, R., 2004, "Ventilation of Enclosure Wall Assemblies," M.A.Sc. thesis, Civil Engineering Department, University of Waterloo, Canada.

[11] Stovall, T. K. and Karagiozis, A. N., "Airflow in the Ventilation Space Behind a Rain Screen Wall," *Exterior Envelopes of Whole Buildings Ninth International Conference*, Clearwater, FL, 2004, ASHRAE Special Publication.

[12] Straube, J. F., VanStraaten, R., Burnett, E. F., and Schumacher, C., "Review of Literature and Theory," *Report No. 1, ASHRAE 1091 Report*, University of Waterloo, Canada, 2004.

[13] Burnett, E., Straube, J., and Karagiozis, A., "Synthesis Report and Guidelines," *ASHRAE TRP-1091 Report No. 12*, Nov. 2004.

[14] Schwarz, B., "Witterungsbeansphruchung von Hochhausfassaden," *HLH*, Vol. 24(12), 1973, pp. 376–384.

[15] Kuenzel, H. and Mayer, E., *Untersuchung über die Notwendige Hinterlüftung an Außenwandbekeidung aus Großformatigen Bauteilen*, Schriftenreihe Bundesminister für Raumordnung, Bauwesen, und Städtebau, 1983.

[16] Uvslokk, S., "The Importance of Wind Barriers for Insulated Wood Frame Constructions," *Proceedings of the Symposium and Day of Building Physics*, August 24–27, 1987, Lund University, Swedish Council for Building Research.

[17] Popp, W., Mayer, E., and Kuenzel, H., "Untersuchungen über die Belüftung des Luftraumes Hinter Vorgesetzten Fassadenbekleidung aus Kleinformatigen Elementen," *Forschungsbericht B Ho* 22/80, Fraunhofer Institut für Bauphysik, April 1980.

[18] Straube, J. F. and Burnett, E. F. P., "Vents, Ventilation Drying, and Pressure Moderation," Building Engineering Group Report for Canada Mortgage and Housing Corporation, 1995.

[19] Kuenzel, H. M., *Simultaneous Heat and Moisture Transport in Building Components—One- and Two-Dimensional Calculation Using Simple Parameters*, IRB Verlag, 1995.

[20] Karagiozis, A., Kuenzel, H. M., and Holm, A., "WUFI ORNL/IBP—A North American Hygrothermal Model," *Performance of Exterior Envelopes of Whole Buildings VIII*, Clearwater Beach, FL, Dec. 2–7, 2001, ASHRAE Special Publication.

[21] Tichy, R. and Murray, C., "Developing Innovative Wall Systems That Improve Hygrothermal Performance of Residential Buildings Progress Report, Part A," *Report No.* NETL DE-FC26-02NT41498, Department of Energy, Washington, D.C., May 2007.

[22] ASHRAE SPC 160: ANSI/ASHRAE 160–2009: "Criteria for Moisture Control Design Analysis in Buildings," Amer Soc. of Heating , Refrigerating, and Air Conditioning Engineers, Inc,. Atlanta, GA.

Reprinted from JAI, Vol. 5, No. 7
doi:10.1520/JAI101275
Available online at www.astm.org/JAI

Loren D. Flick,[1] *Linda M. McGowan,*[2] *Ned S. Kirschbaum,*[3]
and Craig D. Carson[4]

Design Responsibility for Weathertight Perimeter Detailing for Non-Flanged Windows: Current Practices, Common Problems, and Possible Solutions

ABSTRACT: Architects typically design details for conditions around the perimeter of window openings prior to the final selection of the actual windows used in the building. This requires the architect to make reasonable, general details regarding the attachment of the window frames, the position of the windows in the wall cross-section, and the weathertight details around the perimeters of the windows. Often, once the final selection of the windows has been made, these general details no longer apply or are not sufficiently detailed to clearly reflect the design intent. In some instances, the details for the windows are intentionally shown in a general, approximate fashion, with the assumption that the actual details will be "designed" during the shop drawing phase. However, the shop drawings typically do not accurately reflect all of the conditions surrounding the windows, and the window installation subcontractor understandably does not want the liability of showing or designing all of these details which they will not build and for which they have

Manuscript received May 31, 2007; accepted for publication June 20, 2008; published online July 2008.

[1] P.E., President, Building Consultants & Engineers, Inc., 1520 West Canal Ct., Suite 240, Littleton, CO 80120.

[2] P.E., A.I.A., Consultant, Building Consultants & Engineers, Inc., 1520 West Canal Ct., Suite 240, Littleton, CO 80120.

[3] A.I.A., CCCA, LEED®AP, Principal and Director of Technical Design, Fentress Architects, Ltd., 421 Broadway, Denver, CO 80203.

[4] Vice President, A-1 Glass, Inc., 3070 South Wyandot St., Englewood, CO 80110.

Cite as: Flick, L. D., McGowan, L. M., Kirschbaum, N. S. and Carson, C. D., "Design Responsibility for Weathertight Perimeter Detailing for Non-Flanged Windows: Current Practices, Common Problems, and Possible Solutions," *J. ASTM Intl.*, Vol. 5, No. 7. doi:10.1520/JAI101275.

no responsibility. Further, while the window shop drawings are reviewed by the architect, the purpose of the architect's "approval" of the shop drawings is limited. Additionally, shop drawings are not part of the contract documents and, therefore, not part of the design. This results in a common situation where there is no clear basis of design for the weathertightness detailing around the windows. Unfortunately, at present, the authors believe this situation represents the state of the design practice in the building industry. This paper explores common, current practices for designing perimeter weathertightness details for non-flanged windows in commercial applications and how these practices influence the potential for performance problems and water leakage. Suggestions are provided for improvements and alternative methods in design practices. While the paper generally discusses window openings, similar conditions occur at doors.

KEYWORDS: non-flanged windows, window perimeter detailing, weathertightness, design responsibility, mock-up, testing, shop drawing, value engineering, construction documents

Introduction

The interface between the opaque exterior building envelope and the windows is complex. The building envelope is often composed of various building materials and typically constructed by a relatively large number of trades. In order for this interface to perform correctly, the proper installation of all materials and systems, including the cladding and drainage systems and air, vapor, and weather-resistive barriers, must be ensured for each to perform their intended function. In spite of the complexity, importance, and relatively high incidence of failure associated with this part of the building envelope, the attention and level of detail to address weathertightness around the window perimeter in the architectural drawings and specifications varies widely.

This paper explores the issue of design responsibility associated with the detailing around the perimeter of non-flanged windows in commercial buildings to ensure their weathertight performance. For this paper, the broad term "window" typically relates to aluminum-framed windows and/or curtain wall or storefront framing systems in "punched" openings in exterior walls or a "ribbon" of windows. The term also applies to curtain wall or storefront framing systems interfacing with exterior wall claddings and to non-flanged doors set in exterior walls.

In addition, this paper examines the current state of practice with regard to the window detailing design process during the development of construction documents; what represents a sufficient level of detailing for construction documents; why this typical detailing may provide insufficient information to allow a contractor to construct a weathertight perimeter around the window; how weathertight perimeter construction details are ultimately determined; and what additional and/or alternative practices should be considered.

The authors include engineers with expertise in investigating and designing repairs for building envelope problems, a design architect, and a window installation contractor. The four authors have a combined experience of over 75 years in the design and construction of building and window systems and the investigation and repair of leakage problems with windows. This paper represents a consensus view of the four authors and, as such, none of the authors fully agree with all of the contents of this paper. It is for this reason that we believe this paper presents an unusually balanced perspective on the uncertainties that exist with regard to whom is responsible for designing the weathertight details around the window perimeter, and how these uncertainties can and should be improved.

According to the American Institute of Architects, the term "construction documents" refers to the set of drawings and specifications which set forth in detail the requirements for the construction of the project and establish in detail the quality levels of materials and systems required for the project [1]. In this paper, the term "construction documents" will mean the drawings and specifications prepared by the architect for use by the contractor in performing the work, and will be considered to be the "design" for the project, that is, that which indicates the design intent.

Also, according to the American Institute of Architects, the "contract documents" include the construction agreement, conditions of the contract, drawings, specifications, and addenda, change orders, construction change directives, and other modifications and amendments [2]. The construction documents are usually incorporated into the "contract documents" by the general provisions of the contract. Neither the construction documents nor the contract documents include the shop drawings, manufacturers' literature, or installation instructions, or other documents that may be submitted by the contractor and reviewed by the architect during construction. Therefore, these are not part of the "design," but are still considered part of the "work" [3].

Current Practices

Design and Development of Construction Documents

In the authors' opinion, the level of information found on architectural window details and the scale of those details varies among architectural design offices and with the nature of the building. The details produced by many offices show only the major building wall and window components with small-scale, generic diagrams that rely primarily on specifications to describe the inclusion of flashings, air barriers, vapor retarders, and weather-resistive barriers. These often rely on the manufacturers' installation instructions, and typically do not address coordination between the various components. Some offices have improved details which depict all of the materials that come together at the window/wall interface including the cladding, air and weather-resistive barrier, weeps, metal and self-adhering flashings, exterior sheathing, insulation, sealants, vapor retarders, building wall structure, etc. However, the relationship, lapping, sealing, and termination of these materials are either not addressed or inadequately or incorrectly shown, resulting in details that, if constructed as drawn, would probably fail. A few offices produce details that clearly indicate all of these and show the appropriate relationship, lapping, sealing, and termination of these materials in head, jamb, and sill details for each condition. In some cases, large-scale, isometric, exploded views that attempt to depict both the configuration of all the enclosure components and their sequence of installation are included in the construction documents for at least the most typical conditions.

The level of detail with which the window frames themselves are currently shown seems to have increased in recent years due to readily available CADD details provided by window and curtain wall manufacturers. However, in the authors' opinion, this does little to enhance the quality of the details from the point of view of providing information for weathertight construction, or to address thermal and air leakage concerns at the window perimeter. It also gives the false perception that the quality of the rest of the information provided in the construction detail is drawn with the same level of detail and accuracy as the window frame itself.

In most cases, the architect selects a window system or a "generic" system around which to base the window design. Often, the architect will select one window product of a manufacturer as the "basis of design," although the details for the window product could vary significantly from the window that is actually installed on the project. Often, the windows are specified in a general manner by stating acceptable manufacturers and indicating performance requirements for the window for criteria such as design pressure, water penetration resistance, and air leakage resistance. Each of the performance requirements is quantified and can be approved for the window system selected for construction.

It is clear that the multitude of possible materials and systems which interface at the window perimeter makes proper detailing of these conditions challenging and complex. Each perimeter detail needs to address concerns regarding drainage, continuity of the air and weather-resistive barrier and vapor retarder, thermal insulation, anchorages, construction tolerances and sequences, and aesthetics, among other things.

Bidding and/or Guaranteed Maximum Pricing and Compressed Design Schedules

The typical bidding process includes the issue of "bid documents" or "pricing documents" by the architect for use by the general contractor in bidding the work. The general contractor selects possible subcontractors for each specific portion of the work (i.e., window and glazing systems, cladding systems, weather-resistive barriers, sealants, etc.). This selection process is typically a combination of previous working relationships developed between the general contractor and each subcontractor, and through competitive bidding by the subcontractors. Alternatively, general contractors can select subcontractors using a Guaranteed Maximum Price (GMP) process and still utilize competitive bidding in the process. In the authors' experience, the more complex and larger projects are presently trending toward the use of GMP pricing, with some competitive bidding on particular aspects of the construction.

During the bidding or pricing process, the window subcontractor reviews and bids or provides pricing on documents that often coincide with the 50 % Construction Documents or even the 100 % Design Development documents, but rarely are their prices based on the 100 % Construction Documents, particularly for large projects where multiple bidding stages occur. In the authors' experience, pricing is based on a number of assumed factors that are typically not finalized at the time pricing is provided. The primary factors on which bids are based are the performance requirements of the window system, and the design of the window framing sizes, glazed opening sizes, and other factors having to do with the overall design aesthetic. Other factors include installation methods and techniques, schedule and sequencing of work, staging, and storage of materials. During the bidding or pricing process, although the materials to be installed around the window perimeters are taken into account, the specifics of the installation of these materials are not often considered.

Further complicating this process has been the steady compression of the time allowed for design, bidding or pricing, and interaction between the architect and contractor prior to construction. This rush to price the project and begin construction before construction documents are fully completed began during the 1970s when interest rates were high, and owners and developers wanted to minimize interest charges associated with these high interest rates. This eventually became commonplace in the industry, with projects moving from design to construction even more rapidly than before the 1970s.

Value Engineering

Typically, after bids are received by the general contractor or by the architect, and if the cost of the project exceeds the owner's budget (as is almost always the case these days), a "value engineering" process is implemented. This often includes seeking alternative materials and construction methods that would lower the overall cost for the building. In the authors' opinion, this often means a reduction in the quality along with a reduction in the cost of the window systems. The proposed modifications may or may not have a significant effect on the weathertight performance of the windows. However, in the authors' experience, the modifications can sometimes have a significant effect.

Usually, the general contractor and window subcontractor are asked to review their bid in relation to the "design," and to reduce their pricing by submitting alternate (i.e., less expensive and lower performance) window systems or methods of installation. These submittals are then usually reviewed by the architect for general compliance with the construction documents (such as for structural adequacy and resistance to water penetration and air infiltration), but may not be fully evaluated (such as for the weathertightness details around the window perimeter). One reason for this is that architects generally believe they are not adequately compensated to perform such a thorough evaluation of each alternate product. The architect is then put in the position of needing to assume that most of the issues with the interfacing of the value-engineered window system and the materials around the window perimeter will be resolved in the field. In the authors' experience, the construction drawings are almost never redeveloped to incorporate the changes or modifications for a selected value engineered option. In some instances, new details are sometimes developed via architect's supplemental instructions (ASI's) and contractor requests for information (RFI's), but these are usually not comprehensive for the entire building.

Thus, at this time in the project, there is essentially no accurate "design" for the critical weathertightness details around the window perimeter, at least as it relates to the new "value-engineered" window product or system. Resolving and trying to design these details during construction is well-intended, but is typically not adequately performed due to the myriad of seemingly more pressing issues that confront both the architect and contractor. At the end of such a project, it is often impossible, or nearly so, to reconstruct the architect's "final" design details, as there are typically no "final" construction documents.

One example of this might be the change from a window system with a solid tubular jamb extrusion to one with an open-back channel extrusion. Modifications to the jamb flashing to create a proper seal at the weather-resistive barrier tie-in can easily be overlooked, and may not ever be properly addressed. It is important to note that it is not the responsibility of the window subcontractor to note each of these differences (since some may be quite minor) and it is also not the window subcontractor's responsibility to determine how the perimeter detailing of the alternate window system is to be designed (although, realistically, he may offer some suggestions for this option).

Because of the shortened design schedule and the sometimes numerous value engineering options and responses, these issues can be overlooked, and it may not be possible for the architect to respond adequately to the owner with his opinions and recommendations. In the authors' opinion, it is important for the architect to make the owner aware of the potential sacrifices in performance associated with such changes; even through the owner is focused on cost savings relative to his overall budget and not on changes in window perimeter details. Nevertheless, in the authors' experience, there is reluctance for the architect to make owners aware of such issues as it could jeopardize the owner–architect relationship. Of, perhaps, greater concern to many architects is whether or not they will be adequately compensated for evaluating each value engineered option (or at least the selected value engineered option) in as much detail as the original design, to ensure the quality of the detailing of the window perimeter, since the cost savings of value engineering alternatives rarely takes this into account.

Shop Drawing Process

Following the final selection of a window system, the window subcontractor begins the shop drawing process. As defined by the American Institute of Architects, the purpose of shop drawings is to demonstrate "the way by which the contractor proposes to conform to the information given and the design concept expressed in the construction documents [4]. Ideally, the shop drawings would be based on the "100 % Construction Documents" set of drawings. However, as noted above, due to the limitations of the design drawings and the value engineering process, this set often does not accurately show the perimeter details of the selected window system. In some cases, the 100 % Construction Documents set may never be issued, and to meet the owner's schedule, the window shop drawings are often based on the 50 % Construction Documents or, even in some cases, the 100 % Design Development documents. It is the experience of one of the authors that most window systems at the beginning stages of the shop drawing process are "under-engineered," that is, additional significant decisions (such as engineering attachments and perimeter weathertight details) are made after bidding and selection of the window system.

Typically, shop drawings include the following: building elevations and window elevations identifying each window system, size, and type; window head, jamb, and sill sections in cross-section for each condition; relative position of the window system in the wall; flashing and subsill flashing, perimeter sealants, and insulation to be installed by the window subcontractor as part of his work; manner of anchorage of the windows (but not the specific size and number of fasteners), and end-load reactions and intermediate anchor point locations of the window system on the base building. The window subcontractor is not responsible for the structural design of the base building or its ability to resist end-load reactions induced by exterior forces upon the window system. These end-load reactions are to be evaluated by the structural engineer relative to the structural design of the base building. The shop drawings by the window subcontractor should include all items and information for which he is responsible and are within his scope. While the window subcontractor is typically responsible for noting deviations from the construction documents to be directed to the architect's attention (in writing) and to be approved in writing before such deviations are effective, in the authors' experience, this step is frequently overlooked.

Window shop drawings do not typically include the following (except as may be included in a very general sense): the weather-resistive barrier system; flashings (except those installed by the window subcontractor); interior vapor retarder; interior finish materials such as jamb returns, stools, aprons, etc. (except those installed or provided by the window subcontractor); sealants and flashing by others (such as end dams on masonry flashing); cladding systems and anchorages of the claddings, etc. If shown, these are usually indicated as "NIC" (not in contract) or "by others." In other words, these adjacent materials and systems may be reflected in the shop drawings in a general sense to indicate the presence of other adjacent materials and systems, but the window shop drawings are not intended to show how all of these materials interface with one another or the sequence of installation.

The shop drawings are submitted to the architect for review. While the architect typically reviews and approves the shop drawings, the standard of care among many practicing architects is that the purpose of the review is limited to "checking for conformance with the information given and the design concept" [5]. According to the American Institute of Architects, and as commonly accepted practice, the review of the shop drawings "is not conducted for the purpose of determining the accuracy and completeness of other details" [5]. This would include the interfaces with other materials provided by other trades. By reviewing and approving the shop drawings, the architect does not take responsibility for the shop drawings, and this process does not relieve the window subcontractor of his obligations under the contract. As discussed above, neither the construction documents nor the contract documents include the shop drawings; therefore, the shop drawings are not part of the "design." In the authors' opinion, the architect still has design responsibility for the weathertight details around the perimeter of the window.

Following the shop drawing review by the architect, it is constructive to have a review meeting with the architect and window subcontractor to discuss the architect's comments on the shop drawings. In general, however, the window subcontractor (or any other subcontractors) does not communicate directly with the architect, since there is no contractual relationship between the architect and the subcontractors. Therefore, these meetings should be scheduled and directed by the general contractor. In the authors' opinion, many of the initial questions can be handled promptly, and others can be discussed to ensure proper communication. In some cases, the general contractor may organize a coordination meeting with all parties involved in the design and construction of the building envelope. It is important that a responsible party for the architect and a responsible party for the window subcontractor be present to represent the interests of each and to allow for prompt decision making. These responsible parties should maintain involvement throughout the construction to reduce the risk of miscommunication.

At this stage, if the shop drawings are satisfactory to the architect, they can be issued as "approved as noted" and the window subcontractor can begin ordering materials. Otherwise, "revise and resubmit" will require another round of development, review, and perhaps another meeting. On larger projects, it is useful to issue "product drawings" to allow the window subcontractor to order the material in advance of the shop drawings. The shop drawings would then be developed to confirm sizing so that fabrication can commence. At the time of authorship of this paper, one of the most pressing issues for a window subcontractor is the time factor associated with the manufacturer's schedule for engineering the window system. As getting in the manufacturing queue used to be an issue, getting in the "engineering" queue is today's problem. For this reason, it is important to make certain decisions regarding the design with as much advance time as possible.

Construction Mock-Ups and Testing

Construction mock-ups are informative to the architect, general contractor, and other subcontractors to see and understand how all of the pieces and parts of the window and wall system are to be installed. If mock-ups are required, the specific requirements (including testing) of the mock-ups should be included in the specifications. In the authors' experience, the mock-up needs to be performed early enough in the construction process to allow for design changes to be made without delaying the construction schedule. Mock-ups should start following the completion of the shop drawing process. In the authors' experience, mock-ups on the building are limiting in that they cannot usually allow for significant modifications to the actual construction, since the building construction is usually so far advanced so as to make changes much more difficult. The mock-up should generally be based on the most typical condition; in some cases, unusual conditions should also be mocked-up. More than one mock-up should also be constructed for different window systems or other major conditions or cladding systems.

The materials used to construct the mock-ups should be installed in the same sequence as the intended construction to allow sequencing and coordination issues to be understood and modified if necessary. Because design details are often changed during the construction of the mock-up, the architect should be involved during the construction of the mock-up. This allows the architect to determine the impact of even slight modifications to the design on the performance of the as-constructed assembly. Lessons learned from the mock-up can be incorporated into the construction documents by an ASI in accordance with the terms of the construction contract; however, other methods may also be employed. This information can often be provided in photographic format indicating the installation of the materials and the sequence of installation, as well as "as-built" sketches.

Water penetration testing and/or air leakage testing are helpful on the mock-ups, since water leakage (if any) on the mock-up usually does not create water-related damage to the building. It is not uncommon for mock-up windows to fail a water leakage test, and this failure often occurs in the weathertight details around the window perimeter. In the authors' opinion, the design architect should determine the testing procedures, and these should be stipulated in the construction documents. Generally, the testing should be performed by the window subcontractor or an independent third party who should determine whether the assembly passes or fails the test, and what the mode of failure (if any) is. However, observation by the architect or a consultant specializing in such areas is useful to diagnose potential causes of failure. Although it can be difficult to ascertain whether the failure around a window perimeter is due to the design or construction, it is important to establish the cause in order to remedy the condition.

While uncommon in the authors' experience, contractors can initiate the construction of mock-ups and testing of window systems as part of their own quality-assurance program. While these types of voluntary activities by the contractor enhance the overall performance of the window system by early detection of design and construction problems, ensuring mock-up construction and testing by inclusion in the construction documents is more proactive.

Common Problems with Current Practice

What Represents a Sufficient Level of Detail for Construction Documents?

Architects generally believe that they are not paid to detail each and every condition on the building, and that the contractor has some obligation to know how to construct the building in a weathertight manner. However, unless the construction documents show the perimeter details of each window at each condition, the contractor may lack adequate information to indicate how to properly execute the work to ensure its weathertight performance. It is a common problem to determine who is responsible for water leakage if a less-than-well detailed window perimeter leaks. Some architects believe that they should be able to specify "build it weathertight" and reasonably expect the contractor to do so. On the other hand, some contractors believe that the architect should provide sufficient detailing and specifications such that, if the perimeter is constructed in compliance with the construction documents, the perimeter will be weathertight.

The authors' believe that, for most conditions, the design can be adequately expressed in quarter-scale head, jamb, and sill details. While three-dimensional, isometric, exploded, installation-sequencing views may help to clarify the design intent (particularly for unusually complex details), the authors do not believe that these are paramount to the contractor in bidding or in achieving a successful installation.

In the authors' opinion, architectural details in the construction documents should at least show and identify each of the components of the window/wall interface, as well as the proper relationship, lapping, sealing, and termination of each of these materials, including (and particularly) at corners or other changes in plane. If the wall is designed as a rain screen (rather than a barrier), the details should clearly indicate the path whereby moisture that infiltrates to the drainage plane is directed back to the exterior. Similarly, management of the drainage from the window itself should be clearly indicated.

In the authors' opinion, relative to the window perimeter detailing, the construction documents should clearly convey the level of attention to detail and quality for a particular installation. Additionally, the authors believe that the details should clearly indicate the design of back-up or redundant systems, if any, and their interface with the other materials so that the redundant system functions properly. An example of this is clearly indicating watertight end and back dams on subsill flashing systems, how the construction of the watertight dams can realistically be achieved, and how water on the subsill flashing will be discharged to the building exterior.

In the authors' experience, not all designs require redundant systems, such as subsill or jamb flashing or double-rows of perimeter sealant, and not all owners are willing to pay for redundant systems. If redundant systems are not employed (which are usually at a cost savings to the owner), the system should not be expected to perform to as high a standard as one which employs redundant systems. In the authors' opinion, it is the responsibility of the architect to inform the owner of the probable performance of the construction quality to which the building will be designed, and to clearly convey to the general contractor the level of construction quality necessary to achieve this level of probable performance.

Conflicts in Responsibility of Window Perimeter Detailing

Given what has been said, it would be easy to fault the architectural profession for providing insufficient information on details in order to properly install windows. Yet, millions of windows a year are successfully installed; they do not appear to leak, they are not perceived as drafty, and condensation, if any, is not objectionable. This is because the building industry relies heavily on experienced installers and manufacturer's installation instructions and shop drawings to supplement the information contained in the construction documents. There is a long-standing tradition that requires the building contractor to provide complete and operational systems based on the design indicated in the construction documents. The construction documents are not intended to be complete installation instructions.

Nevertheless, when problems do arise related to the weathertightness of the window perimeters, many parties are looked at as being responsible or partially responsible. These include the architect, contractor, window subcontractor, cladding subcontractors, subcontractors who installed materials around the window perimeters, and the manufacturers of the many materials which interface at the window perimeter. Excluding the obvious possible causes of problems such as installation errors or material failures and focusing on problems related to the details of the design and the interfacing of the materials at the window perimeters, determining responsibility for these problems is not always easy.

The architect should be able to rely on the contractor's experience, expertise, and skill, as well as the wealth of information contained in manufacturer's installation instructions for windows, weather-resistive barriers, self-adhered window flashings, etc. However, there may be unclear or conflicting information for each of these, and the architect is responsible for determining which requirements apply to the specific conditions of the window perimeter. While it could be argued that coordination is the responsibility of the contractor, the authors do not believe this to be completely accurate in this application. The contractor is typically responsible for the coordinating of all portions of the work and for coordinating information contained within each submittal; however, the contractor is not responsible for determining how the materials around the window perimeters interface. This could similarly be said for the window subcontractor, cladding subcontractor, and other subcontractors whose work involves the window perimeter.

It could also be argued that the manufacturers of window systems, claddings, weather-resistive barriers, flashing systems, etc., should dictate how their products are to be installed relative to window perimeter detailing. While some manufacturers' offer recommendations for a variety of applications, these do not apply to all situations, and frequently conflict with one another. Further, the manufacturers do not have control over how their product will be used relative to other products and, therefore, cannot reasonably be responsible for the multitude of possible configurations.

As discussed above, this situation is often further complicated during the value engineering process, where the design details for the window perimeters shown in the construction documents are no longer necessarily accurate. Revisions to the construction documents by the architect to reflect changes required by selected value engineered options are uncommon. On most projects during the construction work, the architect is responsible to report deviations from the construction documents and has the authority to reject work that does not conform to the construction documents. However, if the construction documents do not accurately reflect the value engineered option, then the basis upon which the as-constructed condition is to be judged is not clear.

Lastly, the issue has been raised that the window shop drawings generated by the window subcontractor should show all adjacent materials and components, regardless of whether the window subcontractor will install these items or not. In order for these to be shown properly on the window shop drawings, the design of the window perimeters in the construction documents should show all of these items and the proper interface of these items. In the authors' experience, coordination drawings generated by the contractor for window perimeter details are rarely required by the specifications and are, therefore, rarely provided. While the contractor is obligated to coordinate the information in submittals, the contractor has no obligation to generate coordination drawings, unless otherwise specifically required in the construction documents.

Maintenance of Design Responsibility

Maintenance of design responsibility for the architect is important; the architect should not be responsible for the design errors of others. Problems caused by deficiencies in the design work of others could impact the architect's work and reputation. Therefore, the authors believe the architect's responsibilities for these window perimeter details should be clearly defined in the architect's scope of services in his contract with the owner. Attempting to deal with this uncertainty by leaving things out of the drawings or being deliberately vague does not relieve the architect of design responsibility and often increases the risk of problems.

Often, the contractor tries to obtain information regarding the proper interface of the materials around the window perimeter from the architect, who may or may not be responsive enough. In the authors' experience, the contractor usually tries to make the best choice he can out of a given situation. Often, it is the perimeter details that are not developed or are not clearly thought out that cause the request for information. Timing of the installation of the windows and the claddings is part of the means and methods controlled by the general contractor, unless the architect specifies the sequencing of a particular aspect of the work, such as the sequencing of the window installation relative to the wall cladding. Sometimes, the out-of-sequence but in-schedule installation prohibits the installation of a component or detail as shown on the construction drawings (for instance, flashing along a jamb of a window after the cladding is installed and before the window is installed). In other cases, installation methods not readily apparent to the architect may impact the design. For instance, the window subcontractor may select an inside-glazed window system for a particular area that does not allow for proper sealing of a flashing system. While it is typically the responsibility of the contractor to report to the architect design errors or omissions found, this is in the contractor's capacity as a contractor and not as a design professional, unless the contractor is specifically charged with this duty. This again affirms the architect's responsibility for the design of the window perimeter detailing.

If allowed by the construction contract, field changes approved by the architect are usually incorporated into the construction documents by ASI or RFI. These changes then become part of the "design." When these changes are authorized by the architect, the authors believe that the architect maintains responsibility for the design. If the general contractor, window subcontractor, or an independent third party makes recommendations for design changes, and these changes are approved by the architect, the authors believe the architect would similarly maintain design responsibility. However, if the architect does not approve these changes, the question of who is responsible for the design remains ambiguous. While it can be argued that if it is not approved then it should not be built, in the authors' experience, this is not an uncommon occurrence.

Possible Solutions to Address Problems with Current Practice

Improvements to the current practice are needed and are possible. We offer three possible solutions below:

Selection of Window Systems Early in the Design Process

The window systems could be selected during the design phase so that the systems can be accurately reflected in the construction documents. The architect (with the possible help of the general contractor or window subcontractor) can select the window system and design all of the details around that system. This would need to be performed relatively early in the design, possibly at 100 % Design Development or sooner. The details would be much more accurate than selecting a "generic" window and then adjusting the construction as necessary to suit the particular conditions. Since the general contractor and window subcontractor will provide additional services during the design phase, this will likely impact their costs (which will likely be reflected in the bid price). These services are now offered by some window subcontractors as "preconstruction fees." Historically, this information was provided to the architect with the input from window manufacturer representatives who are technically trained in such matters. However, the window manufacturer's representative does not know all of the factors that are associated with the window installation, so the design responsibility (and the responsibility for the final selection of the window system) remains with the architect.

This scenario eliminates the potential cost savings associated with alternate window systems that could be achieved by competitive bidding, and might not be suitable for public-sector projects that require competitive bidding. This option might not result in a cost increase, however, since the savings realized from moving to an alternate system could easily be offset by changes that are necessary to accommodate the alternate system. If a contractor also knows that he will get the project, he can also lock in pricing on the window system, which also reduces the cost.

Of additional importance would be the need to make final selections on the cladding systems, weather-resistive barriers, and other factors early in the design. Therefore, a relatively high-quality building envelope design would need to be developed early.

In this instance, the architect clearly maintains design responsibility. The installation instructions of the window system manufacturer are often very useful in this approach, as the architect can understand all the pieces, parts, and methods in the window installation, and can, therefore, successfully integrate them into his design. This level of detail is greater than the typical standard during the design, but will resolve significant potential problems in the field and during the life of the building. In this case, the general contractor and window installer can provide important information on method of installation and scheduling of various items to make sure the building can be constructed in a manner consistent with the architect's drawings.

The basis of the design is the 100 % Construction Documents. Changes to these documents can more easily be handled by ASI's and RFI's and other traditional methods. Also, since the design drawings should match the actual conditions, there is less confusion to address in the field. This method is common in design/build contracts. The disadvantage of this is that the architect needs to show what he wants and to address all conditions in order for this to be effective.

An owner would still have the opportunity to change the windows after they were selected and designed, but the Owner-Architect agreement would need to clearly state that any changes and redesigns would be an extra service and require extra compensation and time.

Additional Design Phase Following Shop Drawing Submission

A second option is to require an additional phase of design work by the architect following the submission of shop drawings. In this case, the typical design drawings are initially developed by the architect, including up to 100 % Construction Documents drawing and specifications. The project is sent out for bids, and value engineering occurs. Finally, a window system is selected. The window subcontractor develops the shop drawings for the window system and submits them to the general contractor and architect, as usual. The architect uses these drawings to generate another set of large-scale construction drawings to show how all of the materials of the exterior building wall integrate with each other. The window manufacturer's installation instructions are helpful in developing these large scale drawings, as the architect can understand all the pieces, parts, and methods in the window installation, and can, therefore, successfully integrate them. Large-scale drawings are necessary to show how all of the various pieces and parts adequately fit together.

This would be an additional service by the architect, which is not currently part of the typical scope of services, and would need to be clearly defined in the owner-architect agreement as such. Alternatively, this could be performed by a specialty consultant providing subconsultant services to the architect. In this way, the architect maintains design responsibility. These drawings ultimately become part of the construction documents. This method does not require advance coordination or pricing with the general contractor or window subcontractor, and accommodates changes for alternate window assemblies and value engineering.

The suggestion has been made for the architect to include in the construction documents the requirement for the general contractor to prepare coordinated shop drawings, based on the window shop drawings, showing the integration of the work by the various subtrades that interface at the window perimeter. One potential downside to this is the uncertainty regarding design responsibility. The architect did not prepare the coordinated shop drawings and, therefore, they are not part of the construction documents or contract documents, and none of the subtrades are necessarily required to follow these shop drawings.

Assign Design Responsibility to Window Subcontractor

The shop drawings are not intended to show all of the material interfaces between the window system and nearby cladding system and related parts because the window installer does not install the cladding system. The shop drawings are the property of the window subcontractor and are limited only to his work. These are not developed for the use of any other subcontractors and, therefore, do not show all of the other parts.

To overcome this restriction, a third option is to have the window subcontractor also install the cladding materials and related parts. In essence, the "window subcontractor" becomes the "window-wall" subcontractor. In this way, the window subcontractor would be responsible for the window, cladding, weather-resistive barrier, flashings, sealants, etc. In this way, it would be more of a design-build approach. Depending on the extent of this arrangement, the window subcontractor would take on much of the design responsibility and construction liability and reduce the architect's design responsibility. The window subcontractor would, of course, need to be capable of this type of project and systems, and would need to possess design liability insurance.

One significant advantage of this approach is that both the design and construction responsibility rests with one party, the window subcontractor. In the authors' experience, some window subcontractors seek this type of work for this very reason; that is, they have responsibility and control of the design and the installation. On the downside, the architect looses some design control, and this may decrease the architect's ability to make aesthetic decisions. There are other items that the architect is still responsible for, such as the interface at the parapet, firesafing, etc. Additionally, even with this approach, under the requirements of AIA documents, the window subcontractor would not be responsible for the adequacy of the performance or design criteria required by the construction documents, which remains the responsibility of the architect.

Summary and Conclusions

Based on the current design and construction process related to window perimeter detailing as described above, in the authors' opinion, the process is often flawed, is contributing to the relatively large number of problems with buildings, and needs improvement. As discussed previously, the construction documents frequently do not include accurate details for all of the window perimeter conditions or show how all of the materials come together at the wall/window interface. Compressed schedules for design and construction and design changes during value engineering efforts further complicate design responsibility. The current shop drawing submittal and review process, as well as construction mock-ups and testing, do not generally adequately address all of the issues related to the design of window perimeter detailing.

The questions of what are the "design details" for the weathertight window perimeter and who maintains the design responsibility for these are unclear and remain highly contentious. While further examination and debate regarding these issues will likely continue, the authors present three possible solutions. These include the following: (1) the selection of window systems early in the design process so that the systems can accurately be reflected in the construction documents, (2) an additional design phase following the shop drawing submission so that accurate details are developed for the as-selected window system, and (3) the assignment of the design responsibility for the window perimeter detailing to the window subcontractor. Each of these options has advantages and disadvantages, which are discussed.

References

[1]   AIA Document B141-1997 *Standard Form of Agreement Between Owner and Architect with Standard Form of Architect's Services*, Sec. 2.4.4.1, The American Institute of Architects, Washington, DC 20006.

[2]   AIA Document A201-1997 *General Conditions of the Contract for Construction*, Sec. 1.1.1, The American Institute of Architects, Washington, DC 20006.

[3]   AIA Document A201-1997 *General Conditions of the Contract for Construction*, Sec. 1.1.3, The American Institute of Architects, Washington, DC 20006.

[4]   AIA Document A201-1997 *General Conditions of the Contract for Construction*, Sec. 3.12.4, The American Institute of Architects, Washington, DC 20006.

[5]   AIA Document A201-1997 *General Conditions of the Contract for Construction*, Sec. 4.2.7, The American Institute of Architects, Washington, DC 20006.

Reprinted from JAI, Vol. 5, No. 9
doi:10.1520/JAI101211
Available online at www.astm.org/JAI

Raymond W. LaTona[1] *and Octavian Vlagea*[2]

How to Detect and Observe Hidden Window Leaks Using Infrared Thermography

ABSTRACT: Water intrusion through residential window assemblies is one of the leading causes of damage to the interior. The source is frequently the result of failed seals at window frame jamb/sill intersections or incorrectly installed window flashings. To find the source of and pinpoint the cause(s) of this type of leakage can be destructive, time consuming, and results in high investigation and repair costs. Several instruments can be used to detect and trace water intrusion nondestructively; the most popular are conductive or capacitance-type meters. These meters measure the electrical properties of building materials to indicate wet or dry materials. Often, the readings may be falsely interpreted as an indication of elevated moisture levels when metal is present in the region of the readings. Infrared thermography is successfully being used to detect and trace leakage in building envelopes. Its ability to detect and graphically display heat radiated from a target building area enables an operator to quickly detect leakage with very little interpretation. Although this technology is not new, its use for building envelope diagnostics is new; capabilities in this area are still being discovered. We recently conducted an infrared thermography survey to detect water intrusion at interior window sill regions from failed window frame corner assemblies. The investigative team also used a time-lapse survey to visually track the leakage path. We verified the leak with a capacitance-type meter and through visual observation of materials that became wet from the leak. An infrared thermography survey provides another useful method for quickly and efficiently detecting this type of window leakage.

KEYWORDS: nondestructive testing, infrared, thermography, moisture, window leaks

Manuscript received May 1, 2007; accepted for publication August 21, 2008; published online October 2008.

[1] Senior Principal, Simpson Gumpertz & Heger, Inc., Los Angeles, CA 90017.

[2] Formerly Senior Engineer, Simpson Gumpertz & Heger Inc., Los Angeles, CA 90017.

Cite as: LaTona, R. W. and Vlagea, O., "How to Detect and Observe Hidden Window Leaks Using Infrared Thermography," *J. ASTM Intl.*, Vol. 5, No. 9. doi:10.1520/JAI101211.

List of Notations

Abbreviations		Latin Symbols	
LCD	Liquid Crystal Display	K	Kelvin
CPU	Central Processing Unit	°F	Degrees Fahrenheit
PVC	Polyvinyl Chloride	k	thermal conductivity
μm	micrometer		

Introduction

We ask a lot of windows: to keep weather out; to hold conditioned air in; to provide sound control; to allow light to enter; to keep drafts out when closed, but allow fresh air in when we want it; to resist wind loads; to have aesthetic appeal; and to do all this for a long service life without the need for extensive maintenance or repairs. With such a long list of requirements, it is no wonder that windows have their share of problems [1]. Water leakage is a common problem with windows. Sometimes window installations have problems from the start; other times, age and weather take their toll. For all these reasons, water intrusion from failed window assemblies is a growing part of building envelope investigation.

There are several investigative methods to nondestructively detect water intrusion from failed window frame corners; the most common methods make use of commercial moisture meters because they are relatively inexpensive and easy to operate. Leaks can be located quickly while minimizing intrusive investigation and associated repairs. Conversely, moisture meters have several limitations which can affect the accuracy of the readings.

This paper reports on the use of infrared thermography, an emerging technology that can be used in conjunction with other methods to detect leakage originating from failed window frame corner assemblies. Although window leakage can be attributed to several factors, this paper will focus primarily on detecting leakage through window frame corner joints of installed aluminum residential windows.

Common Investigative Protocols

Typical windows that the authors have previously investigated are aluminum or PVC residential windows with a nail fin or flange that is used to attach the window into the framing opening. The interior window surround has painted gypsum wallboard with a painted wood sill trim piece (Fig. 1). In some cases, the painted gypsum wallboard surround continues across the sill instead of a wood sill. Water testing is needed as a part of any nondestructive method for leak detection. Most of the serious, recurring leaks in windows can be replicated. By performing a sill track test (AAMA 502), generally, we can determine if the frame corner leaks. By using a water spray test (ASTM E1105, "Standard Test Method for Field Determination of Water Penetration of Installed Exterior Windows, Skylights, Doors, and Curtain Walls, by Uniform or Cyclic Static Air

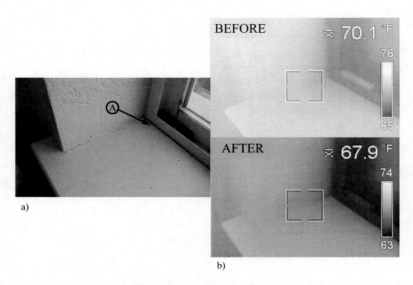

a)

b)

FIG. 1—(a) *Typical painted wood sill trim piece against the window sill; paper inserted between trim piece and sill track back leg at location "A" instantly became wet, (b) thermogram before and after the sill track testing indicating an anomaly due to the 2.2°F drop.*

Pressure Difference"), [2] we can observe differences in the leakage patterns from those that we observed in the sill track test and isolate other leak sources. Although there are numerous possible sources of leakage associated with windows, this paper will focus on leakage through the jamb/sill frame corners of aluminum residential windows.

Common Leakage Source [1]

Most manufacturers of aluminum windows seal frame corners with a narrow joint seam sealer. This procedure applies to expensive "architectural" grade window systems as well as to economical "residential" grades. A few manufacturers use a compressible gasket between the frame sections at the corner, but most manufacturers use seam sealers only.

When corner seals fail, water leakage occurs for one or more of the following reasons:

- *Design and Manufacturing Defects*–Window assembly is labor-sensitive, and there are inevitable variations in workmanship and quality control. The window frame design includes irregular mating surfaces of complex extrusion cross sections that are waterproofed with seam sealer. These corners are difficult to seal effectively, and manufacturers do not routinely water test all frame corners before they leave the factory.
- *Handling Damage*–After the window unit is fabricated, it is loaded on a truck, subjected to vibration and shifting during transportation to the construction site, unloaded to a storage location, and then moved into

position in the building. During the handling process from the time the frame is fabricated in the shop to the time it is installed on the building, the frame may get twisted and racked; during this process, the joint seals may be broken.

- *Environmental Degeneration*–Ponding water in contact with corner sealants can accelerate deterioration and loss of adhesion. The lower corner seals are especially prone to leakage because the sill track collects and may retain water for a period of time.

Instrumentation to Detect Leakage: Moisture Meters

Moisture meters are commonly used because they are a relatively inexpensive method to quickly detect moisture intrusion. The most widely used moisture meters are portable conductance and those known as capacitance-type moisture meters. These meters depend on the electrical properties of building materials. The moisture meter reading is affected when a material is in contact with other building materials with different electrical properties, particularly if metal is in the field of measurement. Different materials have a different effect on the final reading of the moisture meter which may contribute to inaccurate or inconclusive readings.

Conductance-Type Meters

A portable conductance-type moisture meter is battery-operated and calibrated in percent moisture content for three materials (usually wood, gypsum, and masonry); most have correction tables for other materials [3]. To measure the electrical conductance of a material requires electrical contact with the material at two points. The most common type of contact uses penetrating electrodes consisting of short pins attached to the top of the hand-held unit; the pins are driven into the material to be tested. Also, longer shielded pins are used to penetrate further into the material being tested. For shielded pins, the conductance is almost exclusively measured in the material at the pin depth and on a plane parallel to the surface of the material. For unshielded pins, the measured conductance is influenced by the electrode type and the moisture distribution in the subject material.

Capacitance-Type Meters

According to James [3], moisture meters that are commonly called capacitance-type moisture meters are more accurately termed dielectric-type meters. They usually contain nonpenetrating electrodes which the operator slides on the material surface. They operate on the principal of measuring capacitive reactance [4]. Coplanar electrodes are fitted on the base of the instrument, and low frequency signals are transmitted into the material being tested. The meter measures the change in radio-frequency impedance caused by the presence of moisture [4]. This reading is translated by the instrument into a moisture content reading [4].

Capacitance-type meters (as well as conductance-type meters) do not work well with electrically conductive construction materials in a wall system. Metal building materials such as steel studs, nails, electrical conduit or boxes, interior plaster lath, and gypsum corner beads in a wall system are likely to affect impedance and thus the meter reading. When metal objects are present in the measurement field, the meter is likely to provide a false indication of elevated moisture conditions.

Accuracy of Moisture Meters

Conductance and capacitance-type meters lose accuracy above the material fiber saturation point (moisture content between 26 % and 30 % for wood materials) [5]. Although these meters produce readings above 30 %, they are less accurate in this range; however, a high reading such as 60 % *does* indicate more moisture than a lower reading like 40 %.[3] Readings of 23 % and greater in wood generally indicate that excessive moisture is present. For the purpose of investigating leaks, the accuracy of these meters is usually adequate. The accuracy of both conductance and capacitance meters is roughly the same.

Instrumentation to Detect Leakage: Infrared Thermography

Any form of matter above absolute zero (0 K, −459.67 °F) contains internal energy. All matter emits a fraction of its internal energy in the form of thermal energy heat radiation. This heat radiation is emitted in the form electromagnetic waves in the infrared spectrum. Infrared cameras detect infrared waves in two different wavelength ranges: 3 to 5 μm for midwave and 8 to 12 μm for longwave range cameras. Visible light is in the range of 0.4 to 0.75 μm.

How It Works

Infrared cameras are designed to detect infrared heat radiation in the field of the lens. A small microchip called a "bolometer" rests behind a special camera lens coated with germanium. The germanium blocks visible light waves, but allows infrared waves to transmit through. Each individually emitted wave travels in a straight line from the target, through the lens, and hits a micro-detector on the bolometer. A micro-detector is basically an electrical bridge circuit, and there can be hundreds of thousands of micro-detectors on one bolometer, depending on the camera's resolution. When an infrared wave hits a micro-detector, the heat radiation (or lack thereof) causes the micro-dectector to expand or contract, changing the resistance in the detector. The amount of the resistance in the micro-detector is associated with a specific temperature, and a CPU monitors and converts these resistance changes for all the micro-detectors, and associates a specific color (assuming a color palette) for each

---

[3]Although moisture meters generally lose accuracy above the fiber saturation point when measuring moisture content by dry weight, information in Ref [6] found that the volumetric moisture content remains fairly accurate at moisture contents above the saturation point.

different temperature value. Each pixel on the LCD is colored based on the previously associated temperature for its corresponding micro-detector. Ultimately, the pixilated image is a rendering of target surface temperatures and is known as a thermogram.

Heat Transfer

Heat constantly flows within and across a wall system. Heat transfer across solid matter (such as across a building material or materials in contact with another) is known as conduction. The ability of a material to transfer heat by conduction is known as its thermal conductivity, k. Water has a much higher k than most dry building materials. When water diffuses into a building material, it increases the thermal conductivity and more heat can transfer through the wet building material than through the adjacent dryer areas. The result is an elevated rate of heat flow through and adjacent to the wet material, an increase in heat storage capacity at the wet location, and resultant latent heat effects. Any or all of these conditions can ultimately change the surface temperature of the material at the wet location.

Applications

Infrared technology has been used since the mid 1980s for detecting adequacy of insulation (ASTM C1060 "Standard Practice for Thermographic Inspection of Insulation Installation in Envelope Cavities of Frame Building") [7]. Recently it has become one of the tools available for use in investigations and building diagnostics. Generally, there needs to be more than one method of investigation. The methods should include visual observations to identify building materials and finishes and their condition at the time of the investigation, conditions of frame joints, estimation of the age of the building components, and other pertinent conditions. Moisture meters and the use of infrared thermography are tools for nondestructive investigation. Since none of the nondestructive methods actually measure water, some intrusive investigation or other physical confirmation is required to verify the results of the nondestructive method. Nevertheless, nondestructive testing reduces the amount of intrusive investigation required, thereby reducing the overall time and cost of a leak investigation.

Qualitative infrared surveys are used extensively in troubleshooting building subsystems. Infrared technology used for building envelope diagnostics and investigations is mostly used for qualitative air and water leak detection. A qualitative infrared thermography survey can be used in conjunction with other methods and can improve reliability of results because:

- It is not limited by the material properties of the construction components. It is capable of surveying locations not easily accessible with hand-held moisture meters.
- It is capable of surveying across a wide variety of different building materials simultaneously.
- It is capable of surveying large areas quickly, not just discrete locations.
- It permits continuous viewing of a leak during its development and the

path the water travels as it spreads through the assembly after the leak occurs.

There are also several disadvantages and limitations to infrared thermography. Most of them do not directly affect the objective of a qualitative infrared thermography survey. Some of the disadvantages are:

- IR cameras are more expensive than hand-held moisture meters.
- Apparent temperatures of most reflective materials do not represent actual surface temperatures and may lead to inaccuracies.
- Bulk moisture on a surface blocks the infrared heat emitted by that surface. IR waves do not pass through water.
- Anomalies created by air or moisture leakage may look similar at times.
- Some surveys, depending on location, may only be conducted at certain times of the day.
- Changing conditions of sun or shade during the test may lead to inaccuracies.

Even though the infrared camera provides advantages over moisture meters, it still has its limitations. It is always good practice to check the detected leaks with other methods such as moisture meters, and some physical determination to verify the leak.

A Brief Case Study

The authors used an infrared camera to determine if they could detect window frame corner leakage under the interior window wood sill trim piece. Due to the thickness of the wood sill trim and the paint coating on the surface, we did not expect to visually detect any moisture on the surface of the window trim during the short, 15 minute sill track test. We conducted a qualitative survey to verify the surface temperature before, during, and after the sill track testing. The camera is sensitive to small changes in temperature. We expected a temperature drop because the tap water used for the test was cool (62°F–65°F) relative to the temperature of the target materials at the window corner (67°F–72°F). The difference in temperature ultimately decreases the amount of heat at the surface and results in a drop of surface temperature. Additionally, the camera was set to display an average temperature (measured inside a boxed pointer) in lieu of the default spot pointer.

The authors conducted this survey at twelve interior window corners in two different homes in different cities; the houses were constructed by different contractors. The same manufacturer made all of the windows. Infrared thermography provided definitive, useful results for eleven of the twelve corners we investigated. One of the window corners became exposed to direct sunlight during the test period which led to an inconclusive result. The authors detected a temperature drop of 1.5°F to 4.8°F at five of the eleven corners and no temperature changes at the other corners. We tested all wood trim corners with a capacitance-type meter and confirmed the five corners with a temperature change also showed an increase in moisture content. Figure 1 shows a wood trim corner and a before-and-after test thermogram. The authors also inserted a piece of water sensitive paper between the wood trim piece and window sill

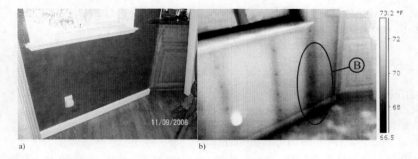

FIG. 2—(a) *Digital photo, and* (b) *corresponding thermogram showing a condition at the wall below the right window corner (location "B" as viewed from the interior). In the IR camera during the test, the authors observed the path of the leakage as the spread of water caused the temperature to change along the leak path. The window corner leakage continued down the double wall stud and accumulated at the wood flooring. The authors measured the moisture content with a capacitance-type moisture meter; it also indicated elevated moisture levels.*

frame, and it instantly became wet, thereby providing visual physical verification of the leak.

Figure 2 shows a condition at one of the five window corners caused by water traveling down the double wall stud at the jamb of the window and accumulating under the wood flooring. During the test, in the IR camera we could see the condition prior to the test, the spread of wet regions as water from the leak spread through the system and leak path as the temperature changed along the path of leakage from the window corner down the double stud and spread out in the flooring. Detecting the path of the water can be important information in some cases. The authors also tested a number of points along the leak path with a capacitance-type moisture meter; it indicated elevated moisture levels along the leak path and on the wood flooring.

Summary

The authors performed window sill track water testing of aluminum windows to determine if the jamb/sill frame corners leaked. We conducted time-lapse, qualitative infrared thermography surveys to nondestructively detect leakage at the window corners. We checked those leak areas with a moisture meter and by physical testing to corroborate the findings obtained using the infrared thermography. The authors found infrared thermography to be a useful diagnostic tool for nondestructive water intrusion detection at window corners. It can be used advantageously in conjunction with current moisture meter technology to detect leaks in a nondestructive manner. Time-lapse IR observations cannot only detect the occurrence of a leak, but also allow the investigator to observe the leak path and the extent of the spreading of moisture from the leak. To effectively use infrared thermography as a nondestructive investigative tool, one must have a clear understanding of the technology to interpret and achieve accurate results.

Current and Future Work

The authors continue to use infrared thermography to detect the type of leakage described in this paper, as well as other building envelope diagnostics. We constantly experiment with infrared thermography to find new uses and accurate methods for nondestructive testing.

The authors suggest that a collaborative effort be undertaken involving the development of a new ASTM standard for nondestructively detecting building envelope water intrusion using infrared thermography.

References

[1]   Louis, M. J. and Schwartz, T. A., "Technics: Designing Replacement Window Systems," *Progressive Architecture*, Oct., 1992, pp. 42–44.

[2]   ASTM, Standard E1105, "Standard Test Method for Field Determination of Water Penetration of Installed Exterior Windows, Skylights, Doors, and Curtain Walls, by Uniform or Cyclic Static Air Pressure Difference," *Annual Book of ASTM Standards*, Vol. 4.11, ASTM International, West Conshohocken, PA.

[3]   James, W. L., "Electric Moisture Meters for Wood," General Technical Report FPL-GTR-6, United States Department of Agriculture, Forest Service, Forest Products Laboratory, 1988, pp. 6, 9, 14, 15.

[4]   Tramex Ltd. *MEP 1004 Product Data Sheet*.

[5]   Quarles, S. L., "Physical Limitations of Moisture Meters," Paper, University of California, Forest Products Laboratory, Richmond, CA, pp. 37–38.

[6]   Moses, C. S. and Scheffer, T. C., "Using a Resistance-Type Wood Moisture Meter to Appraise Decay Hazard," FPL Report Number 2147, USDA Forest Service, Forest Products Laboratory, Madison, WI, 1959.

[7]   ASTM, Standard C1060, Standard Practice for Thermographic Inspection of Insulation Installation in Envelope Cavities of Frame Building," *Annual Book of ASTM Standards*, Vol. 4.06, ASTM International, West Conshohocken, PA.

Reprinted from JAI, Vol. 5, No. 10
doi:10.1520/JAI101236
Available online at www.astm.org/JAI

Collins Ofori-Amanfo[1] *and Matthew J. Spink*[2]

Condensation Damage Behind Self-Adhering Membrane Flashing and Interior Furnishings on Exterior Residential Walls

ABSTRACT: This paper will present case studies of condensation damage behind self-adhering membranes installed around windows and other penetrations in exterior walls, as well as case studies of condensation damage behind large interior furnishings installed on the interior surfaces of exterior walls, and in unventilated spaces in Minnesota. The self-adhering membranes that are often used to integrate water-resistive barriers with residential doors and windows can, under certain conditions, lead to condensation and subsequent damage. While wider membranes help prevent inward movement of liquid water to the sheathing and stud framing, they also inhibit outward movement of interior water vapor. By increasing the distance that outward moving vapor must travel, wide membrane flashings trap moisture that can condense in cold climates and cause deterioration of degradable materials. In cold climate regions, condensation damage can also occur in exterior walls behind furnishings such as large mirrors and large cabinets. These interior decorations act as thermal reflectors and prevent interior heat from migrating into the exterior walls. When moisture behind these thermal reflectors is cooled below the dew point, condensation and related deterioration of the wall framing can occur. This paper discusses suggestions for the width of applied self-adhered membranes in cold climate regions and recommends locations for thermally reflecting interior furnishings.

Manuscript received May 17, 2007; accepted for publication September 15, 2008; published online October 2008.

[1] P.E., Associate Principal of Wiss, Janney, Elstner Associates, Inc., Minneapolis, Minnesota.

[2] P.E., Former Associate Engineer III of Wiss, Janney, Elstner Associates, Inc., Minneapolis, Minnesota.

Cite as: Ofori-Amanfo, C. and Spink, M. J., "Condensation Damage Behind Self-Adhering Membrane Flashing and Interior Furnishings on Exterior Residential Walls," *J. ASTM Intl.*, Vol. 5, No. 10. doi:10.1520/JAI101236.

KEYWORDS: water intrusion, condensation damage, self-adhering membrane, pan flashing, water-resistive barrier, inward water movement, outward moisture movement

Introduction

Moisture-related damage to the exterior building envelope (i.e., walls, windows, and roofs) is a prevalent source of claims for the insurance industry. The authors of this paper performed investigations of moisture damage in over 1400 residential buildings in the upper Midwest region, most of which were located in Minnesota and western Wisconsin. In these investigations, two types of moisture damage were observed: (1) damage from water intrusion, and (2) damage from condensation. The damage can be confined within the wall cavity and remain concealed or can create unattractive conditions on interior and exterior finishes (Fig. 1). These damages have been found behind various cladding systems including stucco, lapboard siding, and brick and stone masonry.

Damage from Water Intrusion

Damage from water intrusion (i.e., the most obvious moisture damage) is typically caused by wetting of the exterior envelope by rain. Conventionally, rain water penetrates into the wall cavity through defective joints or improperly flashed openings. In residential construction, damage from water intrusion to the exterior envelope commonly occurs at the following locations:
- At window openings due to water leakage through deficient window unit or flashing. Until recently in the upper Midwest region, either no materials or a strip of felt paper have been installed behind the nailing flange

FIG. 1—*Stained window frame due to water penetration at the window head.*

FIG. 2—*Deteriorated sheathing and stud framing below a window caused by deficient window and improper flashing.*

at the sill during the window installation. After the window installation, the water-resistive barrier was lapped over the window nailing flange on all sides, creating a reverse lap at the sill. This method of installation was not weatherproof; it allowed water to migrate behind the water-resistive barrier and reach the sheathing. The absence of sealant at cladding joints around windows or doors allows for more water penetration behind the cladding and through these deficiencies. In addition, if a window sill pan flashing is not provided, water that leaks through the window frame or perimeter joints may migrate into the wall assembly (Fig. 2).

- Below roof edge terminations in walls as a result of the lack of diverter or kick-out flashing. The absence of kick-out flashing and sealant joints between the fascia board and cladding below the roof edge terminations directs water behind the cladding and into the wall cavity (Fig. 3).
- Below decks due to the lack of continuous metal flashing atop the deck ledger board or the lack of end dams on the metal flashing.
- Below utility through-wall penetrations (i.e., pipes, electrical outlets, light fixtures, and meter cabinets). At these penetrations, the water-resistive barrier is not integrated with the penetrating element.
- Along exterior grade lines. Inadequate clearance between finished grade and wood framing permits water seepage to the wood framing.

The condition of the sheathing or wood framing behind the exterior cladding is assessed by performing moisture content testing on the exterior wall materials. Moisture probes are inserted into small holes drilled into the exterior

FIG. 3—*Deteriorated sheathing due to the lack of kick-out flashing at the roof edge terminations on the chimney.*

wall cladding at the above-listed five areas where there is a likelihood of water penetration. Areas showing elevated moisture or areas where the sheathing is soft or unable to be detected during drilling are assumed to be moisture damaged. Areas that are not below openings or penetrations are generally not tested because water penetration and resulting damage is assumed to be unlikely.

Damage from Condensation

Problematic moisture accumulation from cold weather condensation has been recognized as a potential problem for decades [1–7], and has been observed in occupied residences in the Upper Midwest [8,9]. The case studies that are discussed in this manuscript indicate that problematic cold-weather condensation is still an issue. In each of the case studies, excessive moisture accumulation resulting from condensation was observed in recently constructed single-family residential buildings in the Upper Midwest.

The condensation damage observed by the authors commonly, but not always, occurred at expected locations. Penetrations made in vapor retarders for the installation of electrical outlets, phone jacks, and light fixtures, as well as discontinuities or unsealed joints in the vapor retarder, allow interior moisture to move into the wall cavity, carried by air movement. In addition, the absence of caps at the top ends of hollow masonry foundation walls, the lack of a moisture barrier below floor slabs-on-grade, and on the interior surface of below-grade foundation walls, or water in transit (under-floor heating) ducts, allows below-grade moisture to diffuse into the wall cavity. The ability of the wall cavity to retain moisture is reduced as the cavity temperature is decreased. Condensation occurs when moisture laden air is cooled below the dew point (i.e., the temperature at which air becomes saturated with water vapor and the vapor condenses out of the air). Damage from condensation observed by the authors can be categorized as: (1) condensation damage associated with self-adhering membrane flashing, or (2) condensation damage associated with interior furnishings and conditions. These two types of damage are explained below.

Condensation Damage Associated with Self-Adhering Membrane Flashing

This damage occurs behind wide, self-adhering membrane flashing with essentially no vapor permeance that is installed in attempts to stop inward water movement to the sheathing or stud framing at openings in the exterior walls. Due to the recent prevalence of moisture-related construction defect claims, designers and contractors are applying construction methods aimed at inhibiting water intrusion into walls. Designers and contractors appear to focus on preventing inward water movement, with attention being given to the installation of properly detailed sealant joints between the cladding and the windows or doors and other penetrations, as well as the installation of self-adhering membrane flashing at openings or penetrations in the cladding. Self-adhering membranes are used for pan flashing the window sills or door thresholds. Additional strips of self-adhering membranes are used to seal the window nailing flanges to the sheathing or water-resistive barrier to protect the wood framing from damage due to inward water movement. The self-adhering membranes provide waterproofing and an air or vapor seal around window penetrations. The advantages of their use include: (1) ease of application (no unique tools required, peel and stick), and (2) adequate adherence to a variety of building materials (wood, OSB, vinyl, metal) (Fig. 4).

When self-adhering membrane flashing is properly integrated with the surrounding water-resistive barrier, the sheathing is protected from incidental amounts of water that may move inward behind the building cladding. Because membranes offer a better resistance to inward water movement than many water-resistive barriers (e.g., felt paper), there is a tendency for designers and installers to provide wider membranes at openings where there is the greatest opportunity for inward water movement. It is worth noting that ASTM E2112 "Standard Practice for Installation of Exterior Windows, Doors and Skylights" [10] provides only minimum width requirements for self-adhering membrane usage at window and door penetrations. The space between the rough opening framing and the window/door unit is available for the outward movement of interior moisture (through air movement or vapor diffusion). When membranes with essentially no vapor permeance are installed, outward moving moisture generally cannot migrate through the membrane but would have to traverse around the membrane. As the width of the membrane is increased, both the distance and time for the outward moving moisture to traverse around the membrane increases and the moisture may accumulate behind the membrane (Fig. 5). The self-adhering membranes on the exterior plane of the wall are virtually exposed to the exterior temperatures. In the warmer climates of

FIG. 4—*Installation of self-adhering membrane flashing at the perimeter of a window before the installation of weather-resistive barrier on the sheathing.*

the southern United States, where freezing temperatures are seldom experienced and the wall cavity temperature remains warm, no adverse effects to the wood framing generally occurs. However, in cold climate regions, like Minnesota where below-freezing temperatures are common, the delay in outward movement can result in problematic accumulation during cold weather in the vicinity of the window nailing flanges. Repeated wetting of the sheathing (over successive heating seasons) can cause deterioration of degradable materials behind the self-adhering membrane (Fig. 6).

When self-adhering membrane flashing is installed at the window perimeter, what provisions must be provided to ensure that not only is inward water movement stopped but that outward moisture movement from the wall cavity is fostered? What is the industry standard for the installation of self-adhering membrane flashing around windows? How far should self-adhering membrane flashing extend beyond the boundary of the window frame? What should the permeance of the self-adhering membrane be? Unless these questions are addressed, condensation damage behind the self-adhering membrane in cold climates may not be averted.

Condensation Damage Associated with Interior Furnishing

This damage occurs behind large furnishings (e.g., mirrors, tiles, wood paneling, picture frames (mounted with glass), cabinet, head boards, unvented closets, and stairwells) that are installed on the interior surface of exterior walls (Fig. 7). Even with careful workmanship and material selection, moisture can

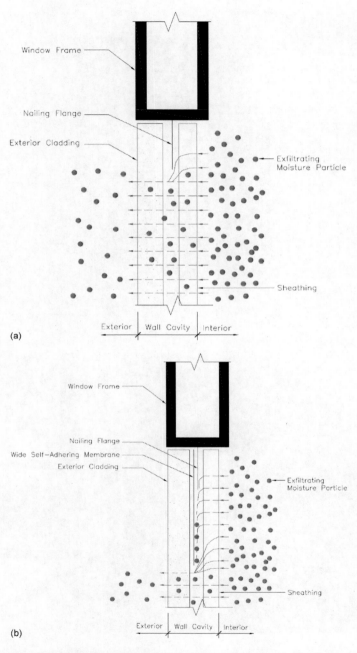

FIG. 5—*Outward movement patterns of moisture around a self-adhering membrane applied around a flanged window.*

(a)

(b)

FIG. 6—*Deteriorated sheathing behind self-adhering membranes at the window perimeter.*

FIG. 7—*A built-in cabinet that acts like a thermal reflector on an exterior wall.*

migrate into the wall cavity through imperfections in the air or vapor barrier or from the release of moisture contained in the construction materials. Large furnishings act as thermal reflectors to prevent interior radiant heat from migrating into the exterior walls. Again, in a cold climate region such as Minnesota, where below freezing temperatures are common, moisture inside the exterior wall cavities behind these large furnishings can be cooled below the dew point and condense. The authors have in a number of cases observed deterioration to wood sheathing and framing behind such large furnishings.

Assignment of Responsibility

As part of the investigation of moisture damage in exterior walls, the authors categorize defects as follows:
- Design defects caused by poor design through selection of defective, inferior, or incompatible materials.
- Workmanship defects that relate to improper installation during the construction or repair of the residence.
- Pre-existing defects which occurred before a specific construction or repair was performed.
- Other defects caused by lack of routine maintenance during occupancy.

The responsibility for defect is usually assigned to the general contractor, subcontractors, architects, and in some cases the homeowners. For damage from condensation, the authors specifically recommend the subcontractor who installed the wide self-adhering membrane, the subcontractor whose activities caused deficiencies in the air/vapor barrier system, the insulating subcontractor, and those involved in the location or installation of large furnishings that act as thermal reflectors on the exterior walls, to be included in the list of responsible parties.

Case Studies

In the remainder of this paper, ten case histories from field investigations conducted by the authors in Minnesota and western Wisconsin are presented. The cases focus on: (1) condensation damage associated with self-adhering membrane flashing, and (2) condensation damage associated with interior furnishings in residential buildings. During the field investigations, the cladding was removed from the perimeter of windows to observe the as-built flashing and water-resistive barrier details and the condition of the sheathing. The exterior wall construction consisted of oriented strand board, fiberboard, or plywood sheathing, 2 by 6 (50 mm by 150 mm) stud framing, fiberglass batt insulation in the wall cavity, and a polyethylene vapor retarder placed behind the interior gypsum wallboard. The space between the rough opening and the window framing was insulated. The polyethylene vapor retarder was sealed to the rough opening framing with sealant but the vapor retarder did not extended to the window frame. Typically, the authors performed window spray testing or window sill pond testing as part of their investigations of moisture damage. Except for Case 1 where window testing was performed, visual inspections were performed to judge the cause(s) of the moisture damage in the remaining cases where damage occurred below window openings. The decision not to perform water testing was based on the pattern and the location of the staining or damage at the inspection openings, which suggested to the authors that window units or joints between the windows and cladding were not contributing causes of the moisture damage.

Case 1: Condensation Damage Behind Self-Adhering Membrane Flashing (Behind Stucco Cladding)

The residence was constructed circa 2003, and is a single-story, wood-framed structure with a basement located in Rochester, Minnesota. The exterior walls were clad with stucco. The residence was equipped with a fresh air exchange system.

Water damaged sheathing was observed around the windows of the residence. The authors performed an investigation of moisture damage in the residence in spring 2006. Exterior inspection openings made through the stucco revealed self-adhering membrane flashing was installed on the rough openings at the sill. The membrane flashing and window nailing flanges were properly integrated with the felt paper behind the stucco in a manner that would channel water leakage to the exterior of the felt paper. Water spray testing was performed at two separate window openings using ASTM E1105-01 [11] and AAMA 502-02 [12]. The testing was performed in two phases. Phase 1 tested the window units, and Phase 2 tested the joints between the stucco and the windows. No leakage occurred through the window units or the joints between the stucco and windows at the test areas during both phases of testing. The damage was a result of condensation of interior moisture behind the membrane.

Case 2: Condensation Damage Behind Self-Adhering Membrane Flashing (Behind Stucco Cladding)

The residence was constructed circa 1994, and is a single-story, wood-framed structure with a basement located in a western suburb of the Twin Cities metropolitan area, Minnesota. The exterior walls were clad with stucco. The residence was not equipped with a fresh air exchange system.

The authors performed an investigation of moisture damage in the residence in winter 2002. Severe frost was observed at interior inspection openings made through the gypsum wallboard away from windows on the main and lower levels of the rear elevation. Exterior inspection openings made through the stucco, away from the windows, revealed that a self-adhering membrane with no vapor permeance was utilized as the water-resistive barrier behind the frosted sheathing. On other elevations where felt paper was applied as the water-resistive barrier, the interior of the sheathing was dry. The frost on the rear walls was a result of condensation of interior moisture behind the membrane.

Case 3: Condensation Damage Behind Self-Adhering Membrane Flashing (Behind Vinyl Siding)

The residence was constructed circa 2000, and is a two-story, wood-framed structure with a basement located in a northeastern suburb of the Twin Cities metropolitan area, Minnesota. The exterior walls were clad with vinyl siding. The residence was equipped with a fresh air exchange system and a humidifier was operated within the residence.

The authors performed an investigation of moisture damage in the residence in October 2006. No water-resistive barrier was applied over the fiberboard sheathing. A 6-in. (150-mm) wide self-adhering membrane that appeared to be impermeable to moisture was installed to seal the window nailing flanges to the fiberboard sheathing during the construction. The membrane was fully adhered to the substrates. The sheathing was dry and firm outside of the membrane perimeter; however, moisture stains were present and the sheathing was at the beginning stages of deterioration along the window perimeter. The staining and deterioration occurred behind the membrane only and were due to condensation (Fig. 8).

Case 4: Condensation Damage Behind Self-Adhering Membrane Flashing (Behind Stucco Cladding)

The residence was constructed circa 2000, and is a one-story, wood-framed duplex with a basement located in a western suburb of the Twin Cities metropolitan area, Minnesota. The exterior walls were clad with stucco. The residence was equipped with a fresh air exchange system.

Moisture content testing showed elevated moisture levels below a few windows. During an inspection of the residence in February 2007, stucco was re-

FIG. 8—*Condensation on fiberboard sheathing behind a self-adhering membrane (Case 3).*

moved to expose the as-built flashing details below a window where an elevated moisture content reading had been reported. Two layers of felt paper were installed behind the nailing flange at the sill. Two self-adhering membranes, approximately 6-in. (1500-mm) in width that appeared impermeable to moisture, were applied for pan flashing the rough opening and to seal the window nailing flange over the felt paper. The membrane was fully adhered to the window nailing flange. The sheathing was deteriorated behind the membrane. No evidence of water penetration to the sheathing through the window unit or

FIG. 9—*Stained and deteriorated sheathing behind self-adhering membrane applied at a windowsill (Case 4).*

joints between the window and cladding was observed. The source of the moisture was due to condensation behind the self-adhering membrane (Fig. 9).

Case 5: Condensation Damage Behind Self-Adhering Membrane Flashing (Behind Stucco Cladding)

The residence was constructed circa 1998, and is a one-story, wood-framed structure located in a western suburb of the Twin Cities metropolitan area, Minnesota. The exterior walls were clad with stucco. A 4-in. (100-mm) wide self-adhering membrane that appeared impermeable to moisture was applied to seal the window nailing flange over the felt paper around the window. During repairs in February 2007, the contractor found an unusual damage unrelated to inward water movement around the window (i.e., along the sill, jambs, and head). The authors observed that the sheathing was saturated with frost behind the self-adhering membrane around the window unit. The frost was due to condensation behind the self-adhering membrane.

Case 6: Condensation Damage Behind a Large Unvented Closet

The residence was constructed circa 1997, and is a two-story, wood-framed structure with stucco and brick masonry cladding located in western Wisconsin. The residence was equipped with a fresh air exchange system.

In April 2005, the authors observed water/brown stains on the curtains in a lower level door on the rear elevation. The door was below a large unvented

FIG. 10—*Deteriorated sheathing behind a large unvented closet (Case 6).*

closet on the main level (approximately 8 ft by 10 ft (2.438 m by 3.048 m)). The exterior wall sheathing was damp and deteriorated within the confines of the closet. The deterioration was most severe in the vicinity of unsealed lap joints in the vapor retarder and at an electrical outlet penetration. The staining of the blinds and door frame on the lower level was the result of condensation and deterioration behind the large unvented closet (Fig. 10).

Case 7: Condensation Damage Behind a Hutch

The residence was constructed circa 1997, and is a two-story, wood-framed structure with stucco cladding located in an eastern suburb of the Twin Cities metropolitan area, Minnesota. The residence was equipped with a fresh air exchange system in 2002.

In spring 2002, the authors observed deteriorated sheathing in a rectangular pattern away from windows and roof edge terminations in the wall. A hutch was installed on the interior side of the damaged sheathing. The perimeter of the damaged sheathing closely matched the dimensions of the large hutch. The deterioration was due to condensation behind the large hutch.

Case 8: Condensation Damage Behind a Built-In Cabinet

The residence was constructed circa 1991, and is a two-story, wood-framed structure with stucco and brick masonry cladding located in a northwestern suburb of the Twin Cities metropolitan area, Minnesota. The residence was not equipped with a fresh air exchange system.

FIG. 11—*Deteriorated sheathing on a side elevation wall. The damage occurred behind a built-in cabinet (Case 8).*

The authors performed an investigation of moisture damage at the residence between August and September 2003. Deteriorated sheathing was observed below a few windows as suggested by a moisture content testing report. In addition, damaged sheathing was found behind a large built-in cabinet on the main level of a side elevation (away from window or roof edge penetrations) where moisture testing was not performed. The perimeter of the damaged sheathing closely matched the dimensions of the large built-in cabinet. The deterioration was due to condensation behind the large built-in cabinet (Fig. 11).

Case 9: Condensation Damage Behind a Large Bathroom Mirror

The residence was constructed circa 1993 and is a two-story, wood-framed structure with stucco and manufactured stone masonry cladding located in an eastern suburb of the Twin Cities metropolitan area, Minnesota. The residence was not equipped with a fresh air exchange system.

The authors performed an investigation of moisture damage at the residence in April 2005. In addition to deteriorated sheathing below a few windows and roof edge terminations, damaged sheathing was found behind a large mirror in the bathroom (away from window penetrations). The deterioration was due to condensation behind the large mirror.

FIG. 12—*Deteriorated sheathing behind a bathroom. Clay tiles were installed on the interior of the wall (Case 10).*

Case 10: Condensation Damage Behind Bathroom Glazed Clay Tiles

The residence was constructed circa 1993, and is a two-story, wood-framed structure with vinyl siding on most of the exterior walls located in a northwestern suburb of the Twin Cities metropolitan area, Minnesota. The residence was equipped with a fresh air exchange system.

The authors investigated moisture damage at the residence in April 2007. Damaged sheathing was found in an exterior wall. The damage was restricted to the part of the wall that corresponded with the location of a full bathroom (Fig. 12). There is reason to suspect that humidity levels in the bathroom were, at least periodically, significantly higher than in the rest of the residence. Rousseau et al. [13], in a survey of humidity conditions in buildings in northern Canada, found that high humidity events occurred regularly in "wet rooms" (bathrooms and kitchens). A researcher located in Wisconsin[3] has also informed the authors that in an as yet unpublished survey, very significant humidity peaks were observed in bathrooms of residences, with no peaks of

---

[3]Personal communication with Charles Carll, Research Technologist at the U.S. Forest Products Laboratory, concerning a survey of homes in southern Wisconsin conducted in cooperation with Achilles Karagiozis and Florian Antretter, of Oak Ridge National Laboratory and Fraunhofer Institute of Building Physics, respectively.

equivalent magnitude being observed in other rooms. The interior of the bathroom walls were finished with glazed tiles. The deterioration was due to condensation of moisture behind the glazed clay tiles.

Recommendations

We observed problematic condensation-related moisture accumulation in a number of recently-constructed residential buildings in the Upper Midwestern United States. Damage from condensation in the cold northern climates can be prevented by incorporating some of the following recommendations in the construction process to manage the flow of moisture within the wall cavity:

- Install an adequately sized fresh air exchange system to regulate the indoor humidity levels. The presence of moisture on the window glass is an indication of elevated humidity levels in the residence and possibly in the wall cavities. The capacity of the fresh air exchange systems should be selected to match the moisture load and size of the residence. These exchange systems require frequent inspections and maintenance to operate properly.
- Use a vapor permeable self-adhering membrane flashing around window/door openings. We thus suggest that consideration be given to the development of membrane flashing with measurable vapor permeance. In the meantime, we suggest that self-adhesive flashing sheets be used with caution in cold climates.
- Limit the width of self-adhering membranes, particularly those with low vapor permeance around window penetrations to 4 in. (100 mm). This would reduce the time and distance traveled by outward moving moisture around the self-adhering membrane and may eliminate the potential for condensation.
- Provide adequate insulation and air barrier between the window/door units and the rough opening framing. All other joints in the air or vapor barrier should be properly sealed.
- Install large interior furnishings (e.g., mirrors, tiles, wood paneling, picture frames (mounted with glass), cabinet, head boards) that act as thermal reflectors on interior walls. Leaving these furnishings on exterior walls increases the risk for condensation damage.
- Provide adequate ventilation within enclosures such as closets that are installed on exterior walls to expose exterior walls to interior radiant heat. Louver doors or windows enhance better air exchange within the enclosure.
- Provide heat permeable backing behind cabinets installed against exterior walls to promote heat migration to the wall cavity.

By taking these relatively simple precautions, damage from condensation can be avoided or significantly reduced.

References

[1]   Teesdale, L. V., "Condensation Problems in Modern Buildings," Report # 1196

(originally published in 1939, reviewed and reaffirmed in 1959), U.S. Dept. of Agriculture, Forest Service, Forest Products Laboratory, Madison, WI, 1959.

[2]   Duff, J. E., "Moisture Content Distribution in Wood-Frame Walls in Winter," *For. Prod. J.*, 18, No. 1, 1969, pp. 60–64.

[3]   Marshall Macklin Monaghan Ltd., "Moisture-Induced Problems in NHA Housing, Part 1: Analysis of Field Survey Results and Projections of Future Problems," Prepared for Canada Mortgage and Housing Corp., Ottawa, 1983.

[4]   Sherwood, G. E., "Condensation Potential in High Performance Walls—Cold Winter Climate," Research Paper FPL-RP-433, Madison, WI: U.S. Dept. of Agriculture, Forest Service, Forest Products Laboratory. Madison, WI, 1983.

[5]   Tsongas, G. A., "Case Studies of Moisture Problems in Residences," *Moisture Control in Buildings, ASTM MNL 18*, H. R. Trechsel, Ed., ASTM International, West Conshohocken, PA, 1994, pp. 254–280.

[6]   TenWolde, A., Carll, C., and Malinauskas, V., "Airflows and Moisture Conditions in Walls of Manufactured Homes," *Airflow Performance of Building Envelopes, ASTM STP 1255*, M. Modera and A. Persily, Eds., ASTM International, West Conshohocken, PA, 1995, pp. 137–155.

[7]   Rose, W. B., and McCaa, D. J., "Temperature and Moisture Performance of Wall Assemblies With Fiberglass and Cellulose Insulation," *Proceedings, Thermal Performance of the Exterior Envelopes of Buildings VII*, American Society of Heating, Refrigeration, and Air-Conditioning Engineers, Atlanta, GA, 1998, pp. 133–144.

[8]   Angel, W. J., "Condensation-Related Problems in Cold-Climate Panelized Houses," *Condensation and Related Moisture Problems in the Home*, American Association of Housing Educators and Small Homes Council, Building Research Council, University of Illinois at Urbana Champaign, 1987.

[9]   Merill, J. L., and Ten Wolde, "Overview of Moisture-Related Damage in one Group of Wisconsin Manufactured Homes," *ASHRAE Trans.*, Vol. 95, No. 1, 1989, pp. 405–411.

[10] ASTM Standard E2112-01, 2001, "Standard Practice for Installation of Exterior Windows, Doors and Skylights," *Annual Book of ASTM Standards*, Vol. 04.12, ASTM International, West Conshohocken, PA.

[11] ASTM Standard E1105-00, 2000, "Standard Test Method for Field Determination of Water Penetration of Installed Windows, Skylights, Doors and Curtain Walls, by Uniform or Cyclic Static Air Pressure Difference," *Annual Book of ASTM Standards*, Vol. 04.11, ASTM International, West Conshohocken, PA.

[12] AAMA 502-02, "Voluntary Specifications for Field Testing of Windows and Sliding Glass Doors," 2002.

[13] Rousseau, M., Manning, M., Said, N. M., Cornick, S. M., and Swinton, M. C., "Characteristics of Indoor Hygrothermal Conditions in Houses of Different Northern Climates," *Proceedings Thermal Performance of the Exterior Envelopes of Whole Buildings X (Ten)*, American Society of Heating, Refrigeration and Air-Conditioning Engineers, Atlanta, GA, 2007.

Reprinted from *JAI*, Vol. 6, No. 9
doi:10.1520/JAI101446
Available online at www.astm.org/JAI

M. A. Lacasse,[1] *S. M. Cornick,*[2] *M. Rousseau,*[2] *M. Armstrong,*[2]
G. Ganapathy,[2] *M. Nicholls,*[2] *and S. Plescia*[3]

Towards Development of a Performance Standard for Assessing the Effectiveness of Wall-Window Interface Details to Manage Rainwater Intrusion

ABSTRACT: Laboratory water spray testing identifies the performance of a component or assembly under a specified set of simulated wind-driven rain conditions. Well-developed water spray test protocols can also help identify where an assembly is vulnerable to water entry, the test loads at which water entry occurs, and whether the water entry is managed by the installation details in such a way that it does not result in within-wall damage. This paper presents a proposed laboratory test protocol for assessing the effectiveness of wall-window interface details with regard to management of rainwater and provides a rationale for a performance-based approach to the evaluation method. An overview of the test approach is provided, and details of the test apparatus and test specimen are given, including information on implementation of the test method. Examples of testing performed according to the proposed protocol are provided. Finally additional tests for evaluating the performance of installation details are suggested. The additional tests are for field evaluation of installation details and for laboratory evaluation of installation details with regard to the risk of condensation along window frames.

Manuscript received September 19, 2007; accepted for publication July 28, 2009; published online September 2009.
[1] Senior Research Officer, Institute for Research in Construction, National Research Council Canada, 1200 Montreal Rd., Building M-20, Ottawa, ON K1A 0R6, Canada, e-mail: michael.lacasse@nrc-cnrc.gc.ca
[2] Institute for Research in Construction, National Research Council Canada, 1200 Montreal Rd., Building M-20, Ottawa, ON K1A 0R6, Canada.
[3] Canada Mortgage and Housing Corporation, Housing Technology, 700 Montreal Rd., Ottawa, ON K1A 0P7, Canada.

Cite as: Lacasse, M. A., Cornick, S. M., Rousseau, M., Armstrong, M., Ganapathy, G., Nicholls, M. and Plescia, S., "Towards Development of a Performance Standard for Assessing the Effectiveness of Wall-Window Interface Details to Manage Rainwater Intrusion," *J. ASTM Intl.*, Vol. 6, No. 9. doi:10.1520/JAI101446.

KEYWORDS: installation details, laboratory testing, performance test, rainwater intrusion, wall-window interface, watertightness

Introduction

The issue of water penetration associated with window installations has been a recognized concern for decades. In the United States prior to the establishment of the International Code Council (which superseded the three regional model code writing agencies), each of the regional model codes (the Uniform Building Code, the Basic Building Code, and the Standard Building Code) promulgated that exterior openings be flashed so as to "be weatherproof," "be leak proof," or "prevent entrance or water." The regional codes each promulgated essentially the same general requirement; none of them however provided guidance concerning what constituted an adequate level of leak resistance, nor did they address how an adequate level of leak resistance might be attained.

In Canada, the National Building Code (NBCC) has consistently required protection from precipitation at openings through wall assemblies and in particular the requirement for flashing at the window head. However these performance requirements are likewise provided in general terms similar to those given by the Codes bodies in the United States. The most recent NBCC 2005 edition nonetheless provides significantly more guidance information regarding protection from precipitation relative to past editions. Whereas the NBCC provides the basic guidance on protection from precipitation, such guidance does not constitute a substitute for accepted good practice. In Canada, the Canada Mortgage and Housing Corporation (CMHC) has often been a useful resource for guidance concerning construction practice. Documents regarding window installation were published by CMHC in the mid to late 1980s [1,2]. The information provided in these documents largely concerned windows of traditional design and thus did not address installation of windows with mounting flanges (often termed "nail-on" windows). Flanged windows were increasingly being installed in wood frame buildings in the late 1980s, and the (often inadequate) methods by which they were installed led to a number of construction defect investigations [3].

It was not until the 1990s that issues relating to water penetration at windows began to be addressed by practitioners in North America [4,5]. Concerns over water penetration led to the development of an ASTM window installation standard in 2001 [6]; revisions of the standard were issued in 2004 and 2007. The ASTM standard, in any of its versions, states that it "places greater emphasis on preventing or limiting rainwater leakage than on any other single performance characteristic." The ASTM standard, even in its most recent form [7], is however (by the admission of its developers) an imperfect document and in need of continued refinement. Unresolved issues concerning installation details for windows remain.

Ongoing concern relating to water penetration associated with window installation methods is reflected in the state of California's recent sponsorship of investigations concerning the level of risk associated with different window installation methods. The work undertaken by Leslie [8,9] concerned evaluation of installation details pertaining to flanged vinyl windows installed in wood

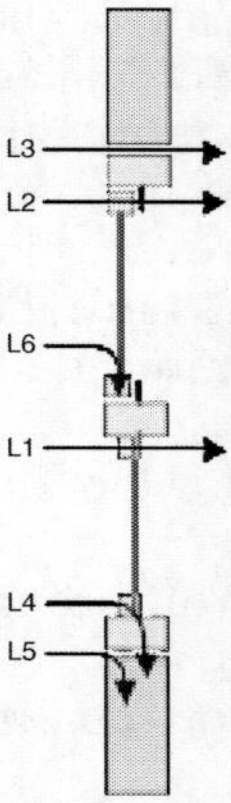

Leakage Paths	Risk of Consequential Damage Rating	Applicability of A440 Testing to Leakage Path
L1-Through fixed unit to interior	Moderate	Good
L2-Around operable unit to interior	Moderate	Good
L3-Through window to wall interface to interior	Moderate	Never
L4-Through window assembly to adjacent wall assembly	High	Sometimes
L5-Through window to wall assembly interface to adjacent wall assembly	High	Never
L6-Through window assembly to concealed compartments within window assembly	Minor	Good

* Depends on where window frame is attached to test frame

FIG. 1—*Schematic of water entry points following Ricketts [11].*

frame walls clad with stucco. Laboratory evaluations nominally permitted evaluating the ability of the different installation methods and use of different components to permit adequate drainage to the exterior of the assembly. The evaluations identified conditions under which observable liquid water leaked to the interior when the test assembly was subjected to simulated rain and leakage events. The work concluded that when windows leak, additional design elements are necessary to manage the water entry. Given the unpredictable amounts of and locations for water entry, pan sill drainage was considered essential. Additionally, it was found that an effective interior air barrier is required around window perimeters. Finally, with regard to testing, it was suggested that performance assessing the performance of window installations in different wall assemblies that are "realistic" and supported by field data and "validated models" [9].

In Canada, the utility of the Canadian Standards Association (CSA) standard specification for windows [10] has recently been brought into question. Ricketts [11,12] focused on assessing the watertightness of windows and the wall-window interface on behalf of CMHC. Results indicated that the two principal paths for problematic water leakage are associated with the wall-window interface. The principal paths (Fig. 1) were found to be through the window assembly to the adjacent wall assembly (path L4) and through the window to wall interface with the adjacent wall assembly (path L5). The risk associated with leakage via these two paths reflects that moisture within the stud space of the wall cannot readily be dissipated (by either drainage or evaporation) and therefore is likely to cause damage. Water that moves through the window assembly and is visible on the interior (paths L1–L3 in Fig. 1) may cause damage to interior finishes but is less likely to cause damage to components within the wall.

Ricketts [12] indicated that the criteria for water penetration addressed in the CAN/CSA A440 specification [10] are unlikely to address leakage via the L4 path and will not address leakage via the L5 path. An estimate of the applicability of the test procedure cited in CAN/CSA A440 to detect leakage via the different leakage paths is provided in Fig. 1; the figure indicates that the leakage paths posing the greatest risk of consequential damage are insufficiently addressed by the test methodology cited in the standard. Moreover, this standard concerns selection of the units themselves; it does not address installed performance, which is of ultimate importance. Some recommendations that followed from the reports [11,12] included the following:

- assessment of in-service and micro-exposure (at window proximity) conditions;
- provision for redundancy in water penetration control through the installation of sub-sill drainage;
- consideration of the durability of water penetration control performance; and
- development of a water penetration testing protocol for the window to wall interface.Given the level of interest in window performance and installation details, the Institute for Research in Construction (IRC) undertook work to assess the capacity of different wall-window interface installation details to manage rainwater intrusion. Several publications have been produced of selected results [13–16]. The work primarily focused on window installations typical of North American low-rise wood frame construction; this work at the IRC is continuing.

The investigations undertaken at the IRC provided a basis for proposing a standardized approach to the performance evaluation of window installations in a laboratory setting. This paper provides a rationale for the proposed approach, details on the implementation of the test method, and information regarding instrumentation of specimens. Brief examples of testing performed following the protocol are provided. These examples are for test specimens representative of typical low-rise wood frame construction. The test protocol can also be adapted to commercial installations. Additionally, proposals for standard tests directly related to the proposed air and watertightness test protocol are offered; such tests include assessing the risk of condensation along window frames for given installation details and a method for the evaluation of installation details in the field.

Approach to Evaluating Water Management of Window Interface Details

Performance Assessment through Testing

It is useful to draw linkages between performance and durability given that performance assessments are useful in helping ensure the durability or long-term performance of an assembly. Indeed, durability implies satisfactory performance of the basic functions of a wall and its components when subjected to environmental loads and other factors that may have a deteriorating or degrading effect [17]. However, the useful life of a material or component always relates to the particular combination of environmental factors to which it is subjected, so that durability must always be related to the particular conditions involved [18]. When consideration is given to assessing the performance of the assembly, it evidently is dependent on the performance of individual wall components. Hence, it is necessary to understand how wall components as well as wall assemblies respond to the range of climatic conditions to which they will be exposed. However, the manner in which the continuity of building envelope is implemented at junctions and penetrations, such as windows, ventilation ducts, electrical outlets, and pipes, is necessarily important. Unquestionably, the long-term performance of the assembly depends on providing functional details at these vulnerable points of the assembly [19,20]. Hence, to achieve functional performance of the assembly, the installation details themselves must meet a similar degree of acceptable performance as the components incorporated in the assembly.

Laboratory water spray testing establishes the degree to which a component or assembly performs under a given set (or given sets) of test conditions. Laboratory water spray testing also helps to determine the location of vulnerable points in a wall assembly. If testing is conducted at a number of different loads, the loads at which water entry either occurs or does not occur can be identified. Furthermore, a test protocol may be designed so as to discern water entry that can be managed from water entry that will result or is likely to result in damage. For purposes of this paper, laboratory spray testing performed according to a well-developed protocol is termed "performance testing." Performance testing may be used to relate the response of a test specimen to specific details under loads that simulate design conditions in a specified climate. Results derived from performance tests may provide useful insights for estimating the long-term performance of products when combined with knowledge of in-service conditions and information on the performance of similar products in the field.

Current Weathertightness Standards

In North America, the preeminent standard specification that addresses the weathertight performance of fenestration is the North American Fenestration Standard (NAFS) specification for windows, doors, and skylights [21]. This standard was developed jointly by the American Architectural Manufacturers Association (AAMA), Window and Door Manufacturers Association (WDMA), and the CSA. The NAFS defines watertightness testing requirements for windows according to four performance classes designated R, LC, CW, and AW. The class descriptions are given in Table 1. The test method referenced in NAFS is ASTM E331-00 [22]. The differential air pressures at which water penetration resistance tests are performed are based on the design pressure (DP) associated with the performance grade, where the minimum test pressure for R, LC, and CW windows is specified as being 15 % of the DP and for AW windows is specified as being 20 % of the DP. The standard further specifies the minimum water penetration resistance test pressure as 140 Pa (2.9 psf) and the maximum test pressure as either of 580 Pa (12.0 psf) (for U.S. applications) or 730 Pa (15.0 psf) (for Canadian applications).

The term "water penetration" is defined narrowly in ASTM E331-00 [22];

TABLE 1—*Summary of information relating to watertightness testing provided in NAFS [18].*

Product Specification	Test Method for Window Watertightness	Water Penetration Resistance Test Pressure Pa (psf)			
		R[a]	LC	CW	AW
AAMA/WDMA/CSA 101/I.S.2/A440-08	ASTM Designation E331-00 Standard Test Method for Water Penetration of Exterior Windows, Skylights, Doors, and Curtain Walls by Uniform Static Air Pressure Difference	140 (2.9)	180 (3.75)	220 (4.5)	390 (8.0)

[a]Window performance class. R: Commonly used in one- and two-family dwellings; DP: 720 Pa (15.0 psf). LC: Commonly used in low-rise and mid-rise multi-family dwellings and other buildings where larger sizes and higher loading requirements are expected; DP: 1200 Pa (25.0 psf). CW: Commonly used in low-rise and mid-rise buildings where larger sizes, higher loading requirements, limits on deflection, and heavy use are expected; DP: 1440 Pa (30.0 psf); commonly used in high-rise and mid-rise buildings to meet increased loading requirements and limits. AW: On deflection and in buildings where frequent and extreme use of the fenestration products is expected; DP: 1920 Pa (40.0 psf).

water that passes inward beyond a plane defined by the innermost edges of the fenestration unit's frame is classified by the standard as water penetration. Given this narrow definition of water penetration, water that leaks through a unit's frame and enters the wall below the unit would not be deemed water penetration unless the water happened to also spill to the interior of the wall (past the vertical plane defined by the innermost edges of the unit's frame).

Existing standard test methods for evaluating the weathertightness of installed fenestration include AAMA 501-05 [23], AAMA 504-05 [24], and ASTM E1105-00 [25]. AAMA 501-05 [20] relates primarily to testing of curtain walls, storefronts, and sloped glazing. Given that this paper primarily concerns qualifying the installation of fenestration in low-rise wood frame construction, AAMA 501-05 [24] largely concerns installations outside this paper's scope. AAMA 504-05 [24], which is the "Voluntary Laboratory Test Method to Qualify Fenestration Installation Procedures," references ASTM E331-00 together with other test methods. This method, in contrast to ASTM E331-00, calls for identification of water penetration between the window perimeter and the rough opening (or, more specifically, lack thereof). The performance criterion for this method regarding watertightness requires that no water penetration be evident through the installation system or into the wall cavity around the fenestration product perimeter at the specified test pressure. The utility of ASTM E1105-00 [25] is primarily to determine the resistance of fenestration units to water penetration. The scope section of the standard indicates that the test method "can also used to determine the resistance to penetration though joints between the assemblies and the adjacent construction," but the means by which this might be accomplished are not outlined in the standard. Moreover, the definition of water penetration in ASTM E1105-00 [25] is identical to that in ASTM E331-00 [22] and thus is narrow. The proposed test protocol outlined in this manuscript more closely approximates AAMA 504-05 [24] than any other standard test method.

Although AAMA 504-05 [24] specifies a minimum test load and suggests that more severe loads can be applied to the test specimen, it does not outline means for adjusting test conditions to simulate climate loads. Additionally, it does not outline means for measuring water penetration via various paths through the assembly. The test method specifies that test specimens be subjected to "durability cycling," the assumption being that assemblies will or should essentially retain watertightness after the durability cycling. In contrast, it can be argued that the watertightness of all components and assemblies will eventually deteriorate and thus that robust installation procedures will by definition accommodate some degradation of watertightness of the components or assemblies. The test protocol being proposed in this paper follows this line of reasoning, specifically that deficiencies in watertightness of components and assemblies will eventually occur.

Estimating the long-term performance for new or innovative products is challenging, given the need to obtain results in a time frame considerably smaller than the expected life of the product. Key elements to consider when developing performance test protocols include the following:

- understanding the behavior of component parts of an assembly in relation to the performance of the system. The essential elements of the protocol are:

- consideration of performance of products when installed according to in-service conditions; and
- knowledge of environmental loads and the manner in which these affect the assembly or components, specifically having information on the intensity, duration, and frequency of occurrence of key climate parameters affecting the assembly.In this manner, interfaces of adjacent products are delineated, details defined, and in-service conditions estimated. On the basis of test results, key elements that help ensure the long-term performance of the component or assembly can be recognized.

Overview of Approach

The proposed test protocol is intended to provide information on whether different window installation details can adequately manage rainwater intrusion. It provides quantitative information on the degree to which the various approaches manage rainwater in relation to simulated climate loads. Under the protocol, the range of loads may be selected as being representative of "design" loads for the region or locale of interest. Hence, information on the primary test parameters is provided in which the basis for the selection of values for test conditions is given.

Thereafter, information is given on the test apparatus and generic configuration of the specimen. The proposed protocol is adaptable to different types of assemblies. It can be carried out by many test facilities that currently perform watertightness tests.

With regard to the configuration, mention is made of the overall size, the location of the window specimen, and details regarding the test set-up. As indicated previously, an inherent part of the protocol is the assumption that over time windows will leak and given that there is leakage, the wall-window installations details should be designed and implemented such that inadvertent water entry is contained and drained to the exterior of the assembly. To verify that this is achieved and the capacity of the installation design to manage water entry at different test loads, deficiencies are purposely introduced in the window assembly, thus permitting water entry to the sill area; this is further described in the generic description of the test specimen.

Two important aspects of the approach are that water entry be observed and be quantified. To meet these goals the test specimens incorporate transparent sheathing components (to permit observation of water presence behind the sheathing membrane) and means for collection and measurement of water that penetrates between the window and the rough opening and of water that leaks into the stud cavity.

Primary Test Parameters—The key climatic factor that affects the severity of a wall assembly's exposure to water that may penetrate the assembly is the wall's exposure to wind-driven rain. Although drying potential after rain events also has an effect on the long-term performance of the wall, wind-driven rain is the factor that influences water penetration. Knowing the intensity, duration,

TABLE 2—*Notional set of test combinations for assessing the water management performance of the window-wall interface.*

Pressure Differential (Pa)	Spray Rate (L/min m²)			
	0.4	0.8	1.6	3.4
0				
75				
150				
200				
300				
500				
700				
1000				

and frequency of rainfall along with coincident wind conditions at a locale provides a means of characterizing wind-driven rain exposure at the locale. As regards simulation of wind-driven rain in laboratory testing, the two primary test parameters are air pressure difference and water spray rate. Combinations of pressure differential and water spray would ideally be based on known climate parameters. Pressure differentials during spay testing correspond to wind speeds coincident with rain, whereas water spray rates correspond to rainfall rates.

If the likelihood of occurrence of values of both wind speed coincident with rain fall and rainfall rates are known for specific climate regions, then one can assess the extent to which window-wall systems attaining specific performance levels might perform in a given region. The selection of a specific set of differential pressure and water spray rate combinations would permit establishing the level of performance at which assemblies can function. The proposed protocol involves subjecting specimens to different levels of simulated wind-driven rain of increasing severity, such that the limit below which systems can adequately perform can readily be determined. From the test protocol then, a specified window-wall assembly is subjected to specific combinations of simulated wind-driven rain by application of pressure differentials across the wall assembly and water spray onto the cladding. The set of combinations is chosen such that these encompass the range of values of simulated wind-driven rain that might be expected to occur at the geographic location within a specified return period. A notional set of test combinations is provided in Table 2; these were derived from a review of wind-driven rain events in North America as reported by Cornick and Lacasse [26]. Spray rates may vary between 0.4 and 3.4 L/min m² and pressure differentials between 75 and 1000 Pa. Rates of water penetration at no pressure differential (0) are also determined to help understand the effects of water entry when the force of gravity alone is acting. Such effects would be evident when water cascades onto window-wall interfaces from adjacent building elements in the absence of a significant pressure differential (i.e., <5 Pa).

Proposed Laboratory Test Protocol

The proposed protocol involves full-scale testing of installed fenestration units in wall sections that incorporate a cladding system. What is meant by "full scale" is that the wall test sections are of single-storey height and have a length equal to their height. The wall sections are representative of complete constructed walls in buildings, except for incorporation of transparent interior and exterior sheathing materials (in lieu of opaque gypsum wallboard or opaque wood-based or gypsum sheathing, respectively) and for incorporation of collection devices to quantify water penetration at various locations within the wall. In the protocol, the air leakage characteristics of the wall sections are determined before spray testing is commenced. The protocol also allows for determination of air pressure profiles (pressure levels at the various layers within the wall sections) at various levels of pressure differential across the wall. The air leakage and pressure distribution characteristics are likely to influence the potential for water entry via various paths during spray testing. Knowledge of the air leakage and pressure distribution characteristics of the wall section can thus be helpful in interpretation of spray test results. In cases where there is a significant "plane" of air leakage restriction on the interior side of the wall, the air leakage characteristics of the test wall section may (as described later in this manuscript) be modified (adjusted). Modification to the airtightness of the wall may have an appreciable influence on the watertightness of the installation. Details relating to the apparatus and the instrumentation needed to conduct the protocol are addressed in the following sections.

Description of Test Apparatus—The proposed protocol requires an apparatus capable of subjecting a full-scale test specimen (e.g., 2.4×2.4 m^2; 8×8 ft^2) to simulated wind-driven rain conditions. The required capabilities of the test facility with regard to exertion of air pressure differentials and spray rates depend on the local climatic conditions being simulated. Table 2 indicates a range of capabilities that would allow simulation of essentially the full range of conditions that may be anticipated across North America. As implied previously, the apparatus would incorporate instrumentation that allows the air leakage characteristics of the specimens to be identified. The water spray system should be pressure regulated and should deposit water evenly across the front of the specimen through an array of spray nozzles. As will be discussed later in this paper, there are cases in which water application in a "cascade" mode (as opposed to application through an array of nozzles) can be instructive.

Generic Description of Test Specimen—An example of the generic step-up for a test specimen is shown in Fig. 2, in which both a vertical sectional view and an elevation view of the specimen are provided. The figure shows a test configuration for a single window and related interface details. The application of simulated wind-driven rain conditions, characterized by water spray and pressure difference across the test assembly (ΔP), is depicted on the sectional view as is the notional location for water entry points representing possible deficiencies in the cladding or window. A notional path for water leakage and accumulation to the sill is shown in the elevation view. The generic configuration also provides the location of a water collection trough as a means of quantifying water entry to or drainage from the sill.

As indicated previously, the introduction of deficiencies (at the interface

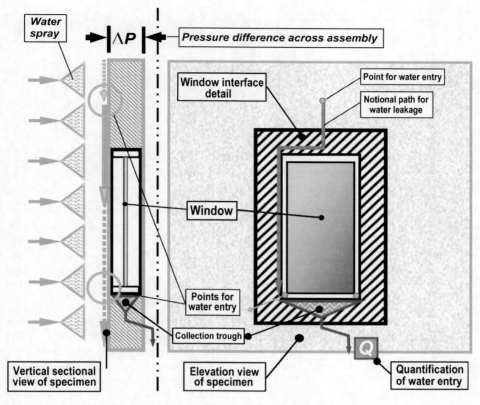

FIG. 2—*Schematic of test assembly showing vertical and elevation views and actions of simulated wind-driven rain on specimen. Also provided are locations of window, collection trough, and notional points for water entry and leakage in assembly.*

between the window and cladding or in the window proper) is a key element of the protocol. For example, the introduction of deficiencies at window corners, depicted as points of water entry in Fig. 2, can be achieved by boring small openings (e.g., <1 mm diam) in the window frame, providing direct access to the sill area. Such deficiencies mimic failed or improperly sealed window frame joints. In this manner, tests can first be conducted with no deficiencies and thereafter with deficiencies introduced in the interface or at the window. A specimen having no deficiencies would be representative of a recently installed window assembly, whereas a specimen with deficiencies incorporated in it would represent either a prematurely failed system or one that over time developed entry paths for rainwater. In either case, the introduction of deficiencies permits discerning the vulnerability of the assembly to water entry or, conversely, the extent to which specific installation details may provide robustness to the installation.

Inclusion of a single large window opening in a test specimen would be

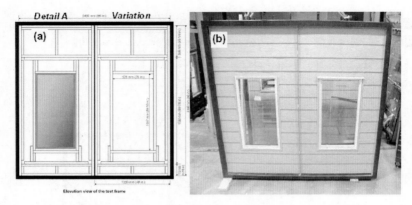

FIG. 3—(a) *Schematic of front elevation of* 2.44×2.44 m² (8×8 ft²) *specimen show-ing location of* 600×1200 mm² (2×4 ft²) *windows and adjacent wood framing studs. Detail "A" might be representative of installation details used in current practice, whereas detail "V" is a variation of that practice.* (b) *Photo of a completed specimen clad with hardboard siding.*

useful when investigating installation details for mulled windows. In mulled installations two or more window units are joined to form a single assembly; these assemblies are vulnerable to water entry at the joints between units.

If comparison between details of individual windows is of interest, the width of the window can be reduced, and side-by-side comparisons are then possible. An example of a specific configuration for two side-by-side window installation details is provided in Fig. 3. These types of configurations were used in previous studies to compare the comportment of alternate design de-tails to simulated conditions of wind-driven rain [13–16].

Summary of Test Protocol—The protocol provides values for spray rate (wa-ter deposition rate) on the cladding and pressure difference across the assembly [26]. The essential elements of the protocol are the following:

(1)   Characterization of air leakage and pressure equalization potential of the wall assembly.

(2)   Water spray testing without deficiencies in the test specimen over a series spray rates and over a series of static differential pressures at each spray rate. The most extreme combination of spray rate and dif-ferential pressure may be chosen to simulate the expected design load (rainstorm) over a specified return period (usually ten years or more) for the geographic locale.

(3)   Water spray testing with a deficiency or deficiencies in the test speci-men over the same series of conditions as in the second step (listed directly above).Specimens are thus subjected to simulated wind-driven rain conditions for specified periods of time. The conditions are intended to replicate the main features of rain events. During spray testing, the rate of water entry behind the cladding and the rate of drainage from the sill area of

the rough opening, are to be determined by measuring water collected from troughs.

Criteria for Performance Assessment—The test protocol is designed to identify the potential for water entrapment within the wall assembly. More specifically, the protocol addresses the management of water that may enter the space between the window frame and the rough opening. Water that enters this space typically finds its way to the sill area of the space. The expectation is that a robust installation will allow drainage of water from this area to a place where it is evacuated from the wall assembly. Hence in conducting tests, observations are made as to whether water is present at the sill area of the rough opening and whether water accumulates in the sill area or drains from it. Collection of water in specialty troughs permits determining whether the rates of entry to the sill are less than, equal to, or greater than rates of drainage from the sill; evidently if rates of entry exceed those of drainage, accumulation at the sill occurs and spillage into the stud cavity may occur. Such threshold conditions for which entry exceeds the drainage capacity of the design are critical points that set the limits as to the expected performance of the installation method. This condition may occur at a particular set of test conditions or over a series of conditions, but in every instance this would be noted over the course of the test. From a series of such tests, acceptable levels of performance of the installation method may be determined.

Instrumentation of Specimens

The test protocol requires that both the pressure differential across the assembly and water spray rates on the cladding be maintained at prescribed conditions over selected periods of time. Hence, the minimum required instrumentation to assess performance would include the following:

- pressure sensor to monitor the pressure differential imposed on the specimen;
- water flow meter in line with the spray rack capable of measuring rates of flow to the nearest 0.5 L/min; and
- water collection troughs for quantifying water entry to the sill space and drainage from it.Each of these items will be briefly discussed in turn.

Pressure Sensors

Conducting tests up to 1000 Pa covers a substantial pressure range. Selection of sensors over this threshold would reduce the level of accuracy at the pressure differentials most commonly associated with wind-driven rain events in North America, although it would provide for measurement of pressures associated with hurricane-force winds (i.e., 104–131 km/h; 65–82 mph). Inasmuch as the vast majority of rainstorms in North America are not accompanied by hurricane-force winds,[4] choice of a pressure sensor having a maximum range of at least 1 kPa with ±10 Pa accuracy (1 % full scale) will for most cases be adequate.

Water Flow Meter

With respect to the spray rack and water deposition on the cladding surface, the most commonly referenced test method (ASTM E331-00 [22]) specifies a default water deposition rate of 3.4 L/min m^2. For a specimen of ca. 6 m^2 (approximately 8 ft^2) this would amount to a nominal flow rate of 20 L/min. If the rain conditions to be simulated are as high as the default condition specified in ASTM E331-00 [22], a flow meter capable of measuring beyond 20 L/min (say, 30–50 L/min) is needed. We recommend a flow meter accuracy of 0.5 L/min or better. Typically, the spray is applied with specialty nozzles. The operational features of such nozzles are such that they are performance rated at specific water pressures. Hence, the provision of pressure gauges along spray rack water delivery lines is useful for monitoring the line pressure over the course of testing to ensure that the spray is being evenly applied.

Water Collection Troughs

As indicated previously, a defining characteristic of the test protocol is its ability to assess the rate of drainage from the sill area of the space between the window and the adjacent wall. This is accomplished with specially constructed collection troughs.

Examples of different collection troughs are provided in Fig. 4. Figure 4(*a*) shows a photo of a trough used for collection of water draining from the sill area and the related vertical sectional view. The photo of the trough is taken prior to installation of the cladding overtop the trough. Water collected in this trough is channeled through a tube (shown in photo) to a collection vessel located beneath the specimen, where rates of collection can be measured. Figure 4(*b*) shows an alternative configuration for a trough to collect water draining from the sill area. It contains a front elevation photo of the collection trough and the related vertical sectional view. The sectional view indicates that drainage from the sill area is collected in a trough beneath the sill area. Water from this trough is evacuated to a vessel located beneath the specimen (in this case through a tube on the interior face of the specimen). The accompanying photo shows a yellow diamond meshed component used to funnel water to the collection trough. Figure 4(*c*) shows a photo of a trough used to collect water that penetrates past the window and moves fully to the interior. This trough is shown in the related vertical sectional view (along with two other troughs). In the sectional view, the trough located at the bottom of the assembly collects water that may accumulate at the base of the wall behind the cladding.

The collection troughs are evacuated to collection vessels located beneath

---

[4]Severe thunderstorms may produce rain accompanied by hurricane-force winds, but the duration of these rain events at any given location at or near the ground is typically quite short.

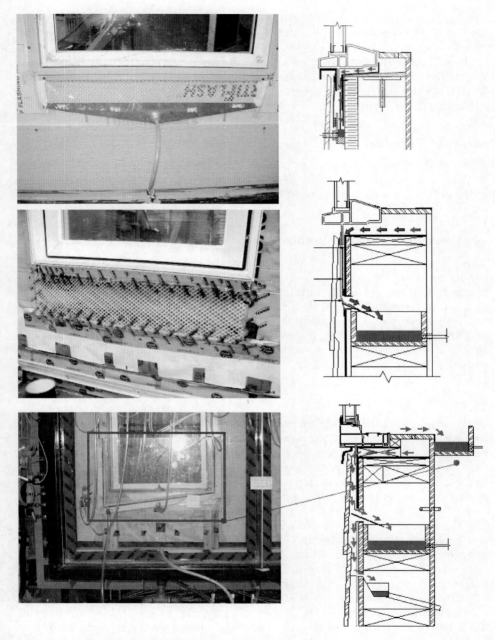

FIG. 4—*Examples of water collection troughs. (a) Collection trough for water draining from sill. (b) Alternative trough configuration—water draining from sill. (c) Collection trough for water that penetrates window (photo) and collection troughs for water penetration past the window, for drainage from the sill space, and for water drainage to the base of the wall (sectional sketch).*

the specimen. Each of the collection vessels is equipped with a capacitive level sensor. These sensors monitor the height of water in their respective vessels. Monitoring water levels in the vessels over time allows calculation of volumetric rate of collection and its fluctuation over the course of a test. Our experience is that the capacitive sensors have appreciable accuracy. Provided that the collection vessels are not too large, rate flow readings with an accuracy of ± 2 mL/min can be attained.

Useful Additional Sensors

Additional pressure sensors can permit measurement of pressure differentials at points within the assembly. This can identify driving potentials for water entry at locations in proximity to the pressure tap.

Implementation of Test Protocol

The proposed test protocol, as previously described, follows a series of test sequences that include (i) air leakage determination, (ii) pressure response characterization (optional), and (iii) watertightness evaluations. The test is carried out in sequential steps, the first of which is determining the air leakage of the test specimen. This ideally is followed by a step in which the pressure response of the specimen is identified. The final step of the protocol is the conduct of watertightness (spray) testing. Details for each of these steps are provided below.

Air Leakage

Determining the air leakage characteristics of the assembly and of the window (by use of masking techniques) permits assessment of the window's contribution to the overall air leakage across the assembly. This can indicate whether the primary water entry paths for wind-driven rain are expected to be through the window or through other paths in the assembly Although masking techniques can be instructive, we do not propose that they necessarily be included as part of the protocol.

The degree of tightness of an air barrier system (ABS) located at the interior finish to window frame interface is likely to affect the degree of driving pressure at the exterior interface. Hence, characterizing the degree of air leakage of wall assemblies having an interior ABS can provide significant insight with regard to interpretation of spray test results.

In walls with an interior ABS, we have been able to regulate the air leakage characteristics of the system by introducing a series of pluggable[5] openings in the plane of airtightness of the ABS (with the pluggable openings located near

---

[5]Pluggable holes allow the specimen to be tested in a relatively airtight mode (with holes plugged) or tested in a relatively non-airtight mode (with holes unplugged). The ability to re-test at different air leakage conditions permits determination of watertightness at different air leakage conditions over a series of different spray rates.

the perimeter of the window). The airtightness plane in the test specimens with which we have the most experience was the interior finish, which was a clear acrylic sheathing panel. Nominal leakage rates of 0.3 and 0.8 L/s m² through test specimens could be achieved by boring an array of small openings through the acrylic sheathing near where it interfaced with the interior surfaces of the window frame. The nominal values for air leakage (0.3 and 0.8 L/s m²) are those achieved at 75 Pa; they were derived from air leakage tests over which pressure differences across the specimens ranged from 50 to 700 Pa. The value of 0.3 L/s m².are considered representative of a "tight" assembly, whereas that of 0.8 L/s m² would be representative of an assembly with substantially lesser airtightness (but likely more closely representative of the degree of airtightness obtained in typical construction practice).

Pressure Response

With regard to pressure response, should there be a series of pressure sensors monitoring pressure in the different layers of the assembly, e.g., behind the cladding, in the stud cavity or in the interstitial space between the window frame and window opening, then obtaining pressure differences at these different locations in the dry condition provides some idea of the range of expected pressure differences at given driving pressures during spray testing. This in turn offers some measure of the anticipated driving pressures across the respective layers and thus provides some idea of the expected comportment of the assembly prior to testing under wet conditions. An example of such a pressure response diagram is provided in Fig. 5 in which the pressure response at a differential pressure of ca. 300 Pa is shown for two window installations each contained in a single test specimen. The configuration of the test specimen was as shown in Fig. 3. On the B-side (a) of the specimen, the head and jamb flanges of the window had been bedded in sealant ("caulking"), whereas on the V-side (b) of the specimen, there was no sealant behind the window flanges. The different locations at which pressure differentials were measured are shown in the elevation views (left) and also in the corresponding sectional views. The upper sectional views depict the horizontal cross-sections, showing the pressure in the space between the window and window opening; the lower sectional views depict vertical cross-sections. The sectional views indicate pressure levels (relative to the interior) at the respective taps. Comparison of results between different installation details can readily be made, e.g., differences in pressure differential at the window mounting flange are evident as greater differences ($\Delta P = 302 - 17 = 285$ Pa) are obtained for the detail with caulking applied as compared to when no caulking is applied ($\Delta P = 72$ Pa) to the back of the flange. Such type of information provides insights into vulnerability of different details and the magnitude of water leakage rates to and drainage from the sill.

Watertightness Evaluations

   Proposed Test Parameters—To be consistent with the most commonly used test procedure for assessing watertightness (ASTM E331-00 [22]), the evalua-

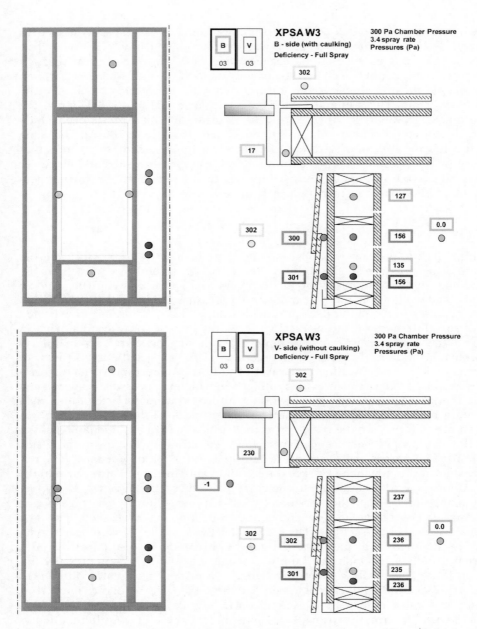

FIG. 5—*Pressure response on each of two sides of a wall assembly with each side having a window installed in an opening. The pressure responses are at ca. 300 Pa driving pressure, showing pressures (Pa) at specified locations in elevation view (left) and corresponding sectional views (top: horizontal x-section; bottom: vertical x-section). (a) Sample pressures on B-side having caulking behind window flange at head and jamb. (b) Sample pressures on V-side without caulking behind window flange.*

tions would be carried out at a water spray rate of 3.4 L/min m^2 (5 U.S. gal/ft^2 h). Considerable insights into the range of expected performance of an assembly may however be gained by conducting tests at different spray rates.

For example, by initiating tests at lower spray rates, threshold values for water entry can potentially be determined. This permits assessing the lowest level at which adequate performance can be achieved. For a comparison of the relative performance of different installation details, identification of the level for each at which adequate performance can be achieved is likely to be more instructive than testing each at a single fixed level of water spray (particularly when the test level is as high at the default rate specified in ASTM E331-00 [22]). Adjusting the spray rate to a value that simulates an expected climate load may also be more instructive than testing at the default spray rate.

An example of a set of test conditions is given in Table 3. In this example, test trials are first conducted without and thereafter with deficiencies incorporated in the assembly. The example is for a specimen with an interior ABS whose air leakage rate can be adjusted. The tests are carried out with the ABS adjusted to leak at a low leakage rate (0.3 ABS) and then at a greater leakage rate (0.8 ABS).

For each test trial and at each water spray rate, starting with the lowest rate of deposition (0.8 L/min m^2), tests are initiated with no pressure differential applied across the specimen, following which the test sequence follows in increasing pressure levels of up to 700 Pa or 1 kPa. Test intervals, as noted, are nominally 15 min in duration. The use of cascade spray as compared to full-spray conditions provides a means to better understand the features of the assembly that might affect the water load on the window corners. More information on the difference between cascade and full-spray conditions is provided in the subsequent subsection (i.e., *Choice of Water Deposition on Cladding*).

Choice of Water Deposition on Cladding—Water deposition in a test sequence is idealized as being representative of rainfall deposition on a façade; water is evenly sprayed across the entire specimen surface typically with a series of water spray nozzles arranged in a regular array that permits a reasonably even distribution of water, as illustrated in Fig. 6. The "full-spray" configuration, depicted on the left side of Fig. 6, results in water being deposited evenly across the height of the specimen; however, the resulting water load due to migration downward along the face of the cladding increases in proportion to the wall height, the maximum effective load being located at the base of the wall. The load on the wall at any given height can be estimated from knowledge of the average spray rate over the wall and the wall height.[6] Certain types of cladding have non-absorptive surfaces and water quickly accumulates on the surface and runs down its face. For claddings having a porous surface, water first needs to saturate the surface of the cladding sufficiently for a film of water to form; thereafter, water naturally cascades down the cladding.

Provision can be made for testing assemblies with water applied in a cas-

---

[6]Water deposition load $S_r(x)$ at height, x, from top of wall, $S_r(x) = (x/\boldsymbol{h}) \cdot 2S_r$, where $\boldsymbol{h}$ is height of wall and S_r is average spray rate (L/min m^2) over wall height.

TABLE 3—Proposed test parameters for evaluating wall-window interface details to manage water intrusion.

Test Trial	Deficiency	ABS[a] (L/s m²)	Spray Rates/Condition (L/min m²)	Differential Pressure (Pa)							Test Interval (min)
				0	75	150	300	500	700	1K	
1	No	0.3	0.8 full-spray	●	●	●	●	●	●		15
2			1.6 full-spray	●	●		●		●		15
3			3.4 full-spray	●	●	●	●	●	●		15
4			3.4 cascade spray	●	●			●	●	●	15
5	No	0.8	0.8 full-spray	●	●	●	●	●	●		15
6			1.6 full-spray	●	●		●		●		15
7			3.4 full-spray	●	●	●	●	●	●		15
8			3.4 cascade spray	●	●			●	●	●	15
9	Yes	0.3	0.8 full-spray	●	●	●	●	●	●		15
10			1.6 full-spray	●	●		●		●		15
11			3.4 full-spray	●	●	●	●	●	●		15
12			3.4 cascade spray	●	●			●	●	●	15
13	Yes	0.8	0.8 full-spray	●	●	●	●	●	●		15
14			1.6 full-spray	●	●		●		●		15
15			3.4 full-spray	●	●	●	●	●	●		15
16			3.4 cascade spray		●			●	●	●	15

[a]Nominal ABS leakage of 0.3 and 0.8 L/s m² at a pressure differential of 75 Pa.

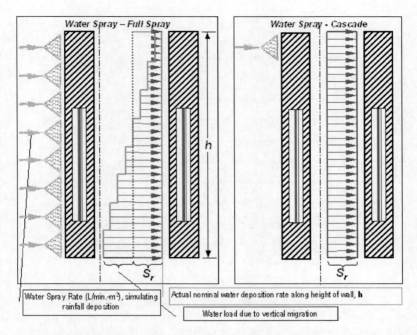

FIG. 6—*Difference in relative water load along height of specimen when applying full-spray as compared to cascade water deposition loads on cladding.*

cade mode; this is accomplished by providing for a supply of water at the head of the specimen (illustrated in Fig. 6 on the right side). In cascade mode, specimens with non-absorptive cladding are not exposed to cumulative water loads at lower locations on the specimen (as would be the case in full-spray mode). In cascade mode, the water load on specimens with non-absorptive claddings is, in principle, independent of vertical location on the specimen.

Expected Range of Values from Watertightness Tests—Examples of some results for water tightness tests that provide the expected range of water collection rates are provided in Figs. 7 and 8. In Fig. 7, rates of water collection at the window are given in relation to the pressure differential across the specimen (0–700 Pa); variations in collection rates (maximum values ranging from ca. 10 to >80 mL/min) relative to the water spray load on the specimen (0.8–3.4 L/min m^2) are clearly evident. It can also be seen that collection rates increase with increasing pressure difference and that rates of entry of different assemblies (i.e., A and W) can also be differentiated.

Figure 8 provides an example of test results, showing how the rate of water collection for drainage from the sill area below each of two installed windows (each in the same test specimen) related to spray rate and to pressure differential across the specimen. Collection rates in this example ranged from as low as

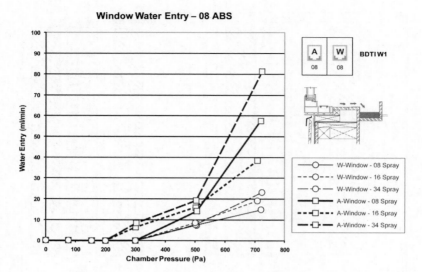

FIG. 7—*Rate of water collection at window in relation to pressure differential across specimen. Variations in collection rates in relation to the rate of water spray load on the specimen are clearly evident. Collection rates increase with increasing pressure difference. Rates of entry between different assemblies, A and W, are also evident.*

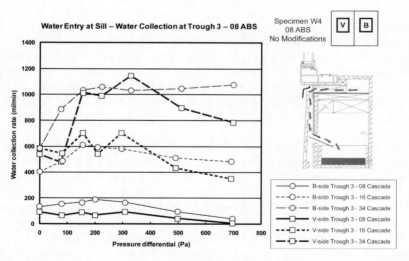

FIG. 8—*Rate of water collection for drainage from sill in relation to pressure differential across specimen. Variations in collection rates in relation to the rate of water spray on the specimen are evident. Collection rates are not dependent on pressure difference but on water spray loads. Similarities between rates of entry of different assemblies, V and B, are also evident.*

ca. 10 mL/min to rates substantially in excess of 1000 mL/min. Collections rates in this instance were largely insensitive to applied pressure differential but were highly dependent on water deposition (spray) rate.

Proposed Related Tests

Additional tests that relate to evaluation of window installation methodology are worthy of consideration, specifically a field test for evaluation of installation methods and a test to determine the risk of condensation associated with a given set of installation details. Notional aspects related to the completing each of these tests are provided below.

Field Test

Parameters for field testing can be derived from the laboratory test protocol and could be applied in situ once a window installation method has been tested in the laboratory. Requirements for such a test would be similar to that for other field tests, such as that provided in ASTM E1105-00 [25] (Field Determination of Water Penetration of Installed Exterior Windows by Uniform or Cyclic Static Air Pressure Difference) or ASTM C1601-06 [27] (Field Determination of Water Penetration of Masonry Wall Surfaces). Control of the water flow rate to the spray rack would require a flow meter, and control of the pressure difference across the window would require the room to be depressurized to a specified level (e.g., 75 Pa). The test would need to be carried out prior to completion of the interior finish, as otherwise the observation of inadvertent water entry is not likely to be possible. Field testing without interior finish in place however poses a risk for skewed results. This is because continuity of the ABS at the interface between the interior finish and the window is generally needed to ensure adequate watertightness of the installation, and with interior finish absent, continuity of the ABS is doubtful. Means can however be devised to provide a notational ABS for the purposes of testing. Providing a false interior finish, such as a clear acrylic sheet (as in the proposed laboratory test protocol), is an option. The acrylic sheet would be installed temporarily (for purposes of testing); it would have a width of at least a stud space on either side of the window opening.

Risk to Window Condensation at the Window Frame

Depending on the types of windows used and the wall construction into which windows are installed, there evidently are various possible methods for providing drainage; drainage methods are likely to vary primarily with regard to cladding type. The various drainage details may affect air leakage through the assembly. The provision of adequate thermal protection at the window-wall interface, as is currently recommended in building practice, may contradict recommended (or required) details for moisture management. Some approaches to window installation chosen with regard to their ability to manage water penetration may thus raise the risk of formation of condensation on the windows. Hence, there is a need to determine if, under cold weather conditions, the approaches do in fact pose a potential for problematic condensation.

There exist a number of standard laboratory test methods for determining the potential for the formation of condensation on windows, e.g., ASTM C1199-00, Standard Test Method for Measuring the Steady-State Thermal Transmittance of Fenestration Systems Using Hot Box Methods [28], and AAMA 1503-98, Voluntary Test Method for Thermal Transmittance and Condensation Resistance of Windows, Doors, and Glazed Wall Sections [29]. The essential elements of the methods, briefly described, consist of testing a window assembly in a hot (i.e., interior) and cold (i.e., exterior) box environmental chamber across which there is a specified temperature differential (e.g., 70°F; ca. 38°C), measuring the window and frame surface temperatures at specified locations on the window, and calculating a weighted average of the interior surface temperature on the window. If from testing the window, the estimated room-side surface temperature on the window is less than a specified dew point temperature (selected to be representative of "normal" indoor conditions), then condensation on the window is expected.

Existing test methods for evaluation of condensation potential of windows could be adapted for evaluating the relative risk of condensation associated with various window installation methods. The test results are likely to be most meaningful when performed on wall assemblies that include cladding systems. As well, one may be able to adapt the test methods to determine the effects of air infiltration on the potential for window condensation for specific installation details.

The extent to which windows actually perform when installed is not well understood, irrespective of the fact that the same windows may have been subjected to rigorous testing and evaluation following commonly used standard practice to evaluate thermal performance. Tests that help evaluate the risk to condensation at the window frame given specified installation details may prove useful in offering a more complete solution to the window installation conundrum.

Conclusion

A protocol for a laboratory test method on assessing the watertightness performance of window installation details is proposed. Information is provided on the specimen configuration, tests parameters, instrumentation, and performance criteria. Examples have been provided for the implementation of this test protocol, and the interpretation of test results from the examples has been discussed. Finally, information is a provided regarding additional proposed test methods for evaluation of window installation details, specifically a notional field test and a test for assessing the risk of condensation at the window frame.

Acknowledgments

The writers are indebted to Mr. Charles Carll for his thorough review of, many useful suggestions for, and keen effort in the preparation of this paper. The work carried out in the Wall-Window Interface consortium project was partially funded by the Canada Housing and Mortgage Corporation, Public Works and Government Services Canada, Building Diagnostic Technologies, DuPont Weatherization Systems, and the National Research Council Canada. The Extruded Polystyrene Association (XPSA) has also provided support for this work outside the consortium project. The writers would also like to extend their appreciation to others who contributed to this effort, in particular, Mr. Stacey Nunes, Mr. Alex Jacob, and Mr. Christopher Short.

References

[1] CMHC, Door and Window Installation: Problems, Causes and Solutions, Publication NHA 5890 08/87, Canada Mortgage and Housing Corporation, Ottawa, 1986, p. 16.

[2] CMHC, "Door and Window Installation," *Report No.* NHA 5890 09/88, Canada Mortgage and Housing Corporation, Ottawa, 1988, p. 28.

[3] Blackall, T. N. and Baker, M. C., "Rain Leakage of Residential Windows in the Lower Mainland of British Columbia," *Building Practice Note No.* 42, Institute for Research in Construction, National Research Council Canada, Ottawa, November 1984, p. 8 (BPN-42).

[4] Bateman, R., *Nail-On Windows: Installation and Flashing Procedures for Windows and Sliding Glass Doors*, DTA, Inc., Mill Valley, CA, 1995.

[5] Lies, K. M. and B. A. Faith, "Window Detailing Considerations for Leakage Prevention," *ASTM STP 1314*, ASTM International, West Conshohocken, PA, 1998.

[6] ASTM E2112-01, 2001, "Standard Practice for Installation of Exterior Windows, Doors, and Skylights," *Annual Book of ASTM Standards*, Vol. 4.12, ASTM International, West Conshohocken, PA.

[7] ASTM E2112-07, 2007, "Standard Practice for Installation of Exterior Windows, Doors, and Skylights," *Annual Book of ASTM Standards*, Vol. 4.12, ASTM International, West Conshohocken, PA.

[8] Leslie, N. P., "Window Installation Methods Test Results," *Task 3.3 Report, GTI Project No.* 15485, Gas Technology Institute, Des Plaines, IL, 2006, p. 38 (California Energy Commission/Contract No. 500-03-013).

[9] Leslie, N. P., "Laboratory Evaluation of Residential Window Installation Methods in Stucco Wall Assemblies," *ASHRAE Trans.*, Vol. 113, 2007, pp. 296–305.

[10] CAN/CSA A440, 2000, "Windows," Canadian Standards Association, Mississauga, ON.

[11] Ricketts, D. R., "Water Penetration Resistance of Windows: Study of Manufacturing, Building Design, Installation and Maintenance Factors," *Study* 1, Canada Mortgage and Housing Corporation, Ottawa, December 2002, p. 86.

[12] Ricketts, D. R., "Water Penetration Resistance of Windows: Study of Codes, Standards, Testing and Certification," *Study* 2, Canada Mortgage and Housing Corporation, Ottawa, December 2002, p. 91.

[13] Lacasse, M. A., Rousseau, M., Cornick, S. M., and Plescia, S., "Assessing the Effectiveness of Wall-Window Interface Details to Manage Rainwater," *Tenth Canadian Conference on Building Science and Technology*, Ottawa, May 12–13, 2005, Building Envelope Council Ottawa Region (BECOR), Ottawa, ON, pp. 127–138 (NRCC-47685).

[14] Lacasse, M. A., Manning, M. M., Rousseau, M. Z., Cornick, S. M., Plescia, S.,

Nicholls, M., and Nunes, S. C., "Results on Assessing the Effectiveness of Wall-Window Interface Details to Manage Rainwater," *11th Canadian Conference on Building Science and Technology*, Banff, Alberta, March 22, 2007, Alberta Building Envelope Council (South), Alberta, Canada, 2007, pp. 1–14 (NRCC-49201).

[15]   Lacasse, M. A., Rousseau, M. Z., Cornick, S. M., Manning, M. M., Nicholls, M., and Nunes, S. C., Performance Evaluation of Wall-Window Interface Details: Phase 1—Watertightness, Air Leakage and Rainwater Management of CMHC Specified Assemblies," *Client Report No.* B1229.1, Institute for Research in Construction, National Research Council Canada, 2007.

[16]   Lacasse, M. A., Rousseau, M., Cornick, S. M., Manning, M. M., Ganapathy, G., Nicholls, M., and Williams, M. F., "Laboratory Tests of Water Penetration Through Wall-Window Interfaces Based on U.S. Residential Window Installation Practice," *J. ASTM Int.*, Vol. 6, 2009, paper ID JAI10148.

[17]   Legget, R. F. and Hutcheon, N. B., "The Durability of Buildings," *ASTM STP 236, Symposium on Some Approaches to Durability in Structures*, Sixty-first Annual Meeting, American Testing Materials, Boston, MA, June 23, 1958, ASTM International, Philadelphia, PA, April 1959, pp. 35–44 (NRCC 4915).

[18]   Sereda, P. J., "Performance of Building Materials," Canadian Building Digest, CBD 115, National Research Council Canada, Division of Building Research, Ottawa, July 1969.

[19]   Legget, R. F. and Hutcheon, N. B., "Performance Concept in Building," *Symposium on Relation of Testing and Service Performance*, Atlantic City, NJ, June 26, 1966, American Society for Testing Materials, Philadelphia, PA, May 1, 1967, pp. 84–95 (NRCC-9593).

[20]   Legget, R. F. and Hutcheon, N. B., "Performance Testing Standards for Building," Canadian Building Digest, CBD 210, National Research Council Canada, Division of Building Research, Ottawa, December 1979.

[21]   AAMA/WDMA/CSA 101/I.S.2/A440-08, January 2008, "NAFS—North American Fenestration Standard/Specification for Windows, Doors, and Skylights, Canadian Standards Association, Mississauga, Canada, p. 121.

[22]   ASTM E331-00, 2000, "Standard Test Method for Water Penetration of Exterior Windows, Skylights, Doors, and Curtain Walls by Uniform Static Air Pressure Difference," *Annual Book of ASTM Standards*, Vol. 04.11, ASTM International, West Conshohocken, PA.

[23]   AAMA 501-05, 2005, "Methods of Test for Exterior Walls," American Architectural Manufacturers Association, Schaumburg, IL, p. 10.

[24]   AAMA 504-05, 2005, "Voluntary Laboratory Test Method to Qualify Fenestration Installation Procedures," American Architectural Manufacturers Association, Schaumburg, IL, p. 7.

[25]   ASTM E1105-00, 2000, "Standard Test Method for Field Determination of Water Penetration of Installed Exterior Windows, Skylights, Doors, and Curtain Walls by Uniform or Cyclic Static Air Pressure Difference," *Annual Book of ASTM Standards*, Vol. 04.11, ASTM International, West Conshohocken, PA.

[26]   Cornick, S. M. and Lacasse, M. A., "A Review of Climate Loads Relevant to Assessing the Watertightness Performance of Walls, Windows, and Wall-Window Interfaces," *J. ASTM Int.*, Vol. 2, No. 10, 2005, paper ID JAI12505 (NRCC-47645).

[27]   ASTM C1601-06, 2006, "Standard Test Method for Field Determination of Water Penetration of Masonry Wall Surfaces," *Annual Book of ASTM Standards*, Vol. 04.05, ASTM International, West Conshohocken, PA.

[28]   ASTM C1199-00, 2000, "Standard Test Method for Measuring the Steady-State Thermal Transmittance of Fenestration Systems Using Hot Box Methods," *Annual*

Book of ASTM Standards, Vol. 04.06, ASTM International, West Conshohocken, PA.

[29] AAMA 1503-98, 1998, "Voluntary Test Method for Thermal Transmittance and Condensation Resistance of Windows, Doors and Glazed Wall Sections," American Architectural Manufacturers Association, Schaumburg, IL, p. 4.

Erratum for JAI101446, Journal of ASTM International

Towards Development of a Performance Standard for Assessing the Effectiveness of Wall-Window Interface Details to Manage Rainwater Intrusion, Dr. Michael Lacasse, Mr. Steven Cornick, Ms. Madeleine Rousseau, Ms. Marianne Armstrong, Mr. Gnanamurugan Ganapathy, Mr. Michael Nicholls, Mr. Silvio Plescia, published JAI Volume 6, Issue 9, (October, 2009) and STP1509, Up Against the Wall: An Examination of Building Envelope Interface.

Page 4, should read: TABLE 1-*Summary of information relating to watertightness testing provided in NAFS [21].*

Reprinted from *JAI*, Vol. 5, No. 7
doi:10.1520/JAI101426
Available online at www.astm.org/JAI

Mark F. Williams, FAIA[1]

Evaluating Drainage Characteristics of Water Resistive Barriers as Part of an Overall Durable Wall Approach for the Building Enclosure

ABSTRACT: The most recent model residential building code has been modified to require increased use of water/weather resistive barrier (WRB) materials in construction, and to require some means of draining water from the building enclosure. However, "drainage" performance is not defined, and the Code is unclear about which currently available WRB products and design approaches help provide a durable water-resistant exterior wall enclosure. The present work is a qualitative, "order of magnitude" study of the drainage characteristics of various types of WRB materials (felts, housewraps, drainage wraps, drainage boards, and furring strips), and is a "first step" toward developing an overall durable wall approach for the building enclosure. The ASTM E2273 drainage efficiency test was used in 40 wall assembly mockups to evaluate 11 WRB materials in 8 design configurations. Traditional WRBs and housewraps provided little or no drainage capability to the exterior wall designs tested. Drainage-enhanced housewraps provided an improved level of drainage, but they still retained water. The retained water can migrate through fastener holes to the underlying construction. Best drainage performance was obtained by using WRBs with furring, drainage mats, and profiled sheets (drainage boards). These overall results are in general agreement with similar research by others. These results can guide designers and builders in the proper selection and use of such materials, which should be used as part of an overall durable wall approach to protecting the building enclosure.

Manuscript received August 29, 2007; accepted for publication June 20, 2008; published online July 2008.

[1] President, Williams Building Diagnostics Inc., Maple Glen, PA.

Cite as: Williams, M. F., "Evaluating Drainage Characteristics of Water Resistive Barriers as Part of an Overall Durable Wall Approach for the Building Enclosure," *J. ASTM Intl.*, Vol. 5, No. 7. doi:10.1520/JAI101426.

KEYWORDS: building enclosure, building codes, water resistive barrier, fasteners, water penetration, housewrap, building felt, furring strips, drainage efficiency

Introduction

The author's recent field experience indicates that many residential construction projects that utilize absorptive/reservoir type claddings (such as stucco, manufactured stone veneer, and masonry) have experienced water intrusion and entrapment with consequent deterioration of wood-based sheathing and wood framing members. These problems have occurred despite the widespread use of water/weather resistive barrier (WRB) membrane materials, as required by building codes for secondary moisture protection behind exterior claddings. Some dwellings are experiencing moisture related deterioration shortly after they are built. Unacceptable levels of moisture related building enclosure failures are occurring in areas of the country where this had not been a notable concern.

To help address these problems, an overall approach to promoting durable exterior wall performance is needed. This approach should begin with an understanding of the drainage and drying characteristics of water/weather resistive barriers (WRBs). The building enclosure includes the horizontal, vertical, and inclined assemblies that work together to provide separation between the interior and exterior environments. Proper selection and use of WRBs, which are intended to protect the underlying enclosure assemblies, and integration of these with other enclosure components, are key first steps to implementing an overall approach. Designers and builders have access to many types of WRB materials, including building felts, building papers, polymer-based housewraps, and "drainage enhanced" housewrap materials. However, there is minimal comparative information about the performance characteristics of WRBs, or about which products are most appropriate for specific project applications.

Concerns relating to WRB selection and performance have intensified in light of recent national building code developments. Prescriptive and performance-based Code requirements for WRBs have been modified in the most recent (2006) edition of the International Residential Code (IRC). The minimum IRC performance requirement is that "Exterior walls shall provide the building with a weather-resistant exterior wall envelope" [1]. Additionally, the 2006 IRC requires WRBs to be installed behind nearly every type of exterior siding (cladding) material, as set forth in Table R703.4. The previous (2003) edition of this Table allowed numerous exceptions, such as behind vinyl siding, aluminum siding, or beveled wood lap siding. Finally, IRC Section 703.1 was modified to require "...a means of draining water that enters the assembly to the exterior." While this is an important new performance criterion, which could help to address moisture related problems behind many types of claddings, the Code does not define what constitutes "drainage." A variety of new WRB products are purportedly designed to provide "drainage" in exterior walls. However, this attribute is not clearly defined, either by manufacturers or the Code.

The 2006 edition of Section R703.1 also includes several new exceptions.

(See the Code Comparison Table, Appendix A.) One of these drops the require-ment for a "means of drainage" if the exterior wall enclosure has been tested (per ASTM E331) and demonstrated to resist wind-driven rain. This new testing requirement does not appear to be commonly published by manufacturers of many types of claddings.

Section R703.2 was also modified to delete the prescriptive requirement for asphalt-saturated felt to weigh "not less than 14 pounds per 100 square feet" (0.68 kg/m^2). This removes one element of confusion. There are several ASTM standards for asphalt saturated felt. ASTM D226 lists two grades of the product. Type I (a.k.a. No. 15) is specified to weigh 0.56 kg/m^2 (11.5 lb/100 sf), and Type II (a.k.a No. 30) is specified to weigh 1.27 kg/m^2 (26 lb/100 sf) [2]. Based on this standard, only Type II (No. 30) felt would have been Code compliant. ASTM D4869 currently lists four grades of the product (Types I through IV). It specifies Type I felt (No. 8 Underlayment) as weighing not less than 0.39 kg/m^2 (8 lb/100 sf), which is less restrictive than the Type I felt specification in D-226 [3]. Specified weights for the other three grades in D4869 are as follows: Type II (No. 13 Underlayment) = 0.63 kg/m^2 (13 lb/100 sf); Type III (No. 20 Underlayment) = 0.98 kg/m^2 (20 lb/100 sf); and Type IV (No. 26 Underlayment) = 1.27 kg/m^2 (26 lb/100 sf).

It should also be noted that the weight of building felts apparently may never have actually been as much as 0.73 kg/m^2 (15 lb/100 sf), but has varied over the years from 0.68 kg/m^2 (14 lb/100 sf), in the mid 1960s, to the 0.56 kg/m^2 (11.5 lb/100 sf) set forth in ASTM D226 [4]. A quick check of some available felts by the author found that most weighed less than 0.56 kg/m^2 (11.5 lb/100 sf). Thus one cannot assume that today's "No. 15" felt provides as much water penetration resistance as in the past.

Section R706.3, "Water Resistive Barriers," now stipulates that, when using "exterior plaster" (e.g., stucco) over wood based sheathing (e.g., OSB or ply-wood), a water-resistive vapor permeable barrier with a water penetration re-sistance at least equal to two layers of Grade D paper must be installed. How-ever, if the WRB has a water penetration resistance equal to or greater than 60-min Grade D paper and is separated from the stucco by a "substantially" non-water-absorbing layer or "designed drainage space," then only one layer of WRB is necessary. This Code section introduces further options that allow the specifier and contractor some additional freedom to develop a customized en-closure drainage approach, but again, "drainage" remains undefined.

Finally, it should also be noted that, while the Code now addresses "drain-age," it does not mention "drying," although the "drying rate" is probably more significant than "drainage efficiency" for long-term performance and durability of the building enclosure.

In summary, the Code now requires increased use of WRB materials in construction, and requires them to have some means of draining water from the building enclosure. However, we are still left wondering if current WRB products will satisfy the "overall" performance requirement that exterior walls provide the building with a "weather-resistant exterior wall envelope."

Based on these considerations, the current study was undertaken to learn more about the drainage characteristics of various types of WRB materials commonly used in the Mid-Atlantic States (felts, housewraps, drainage wraps, drainage boards, and furring strips). Specifically, this study evaluated a material's "drainage efficiency." Drainage efficiency, expressed as a percentage, is calculated as 1) the amount of water that passes through a vertically oriented wall mockup and is collected, divided by 2) the amount of water that is initially applied to the mockup. This procedure is included in ASTM E2273 [5] and was used in the first series of laboratory tests reported herein. An additional test series further explored water related concerns that are not directly addressed by E2273, but were deemed to be significant. These results are also presented and discussed below.

The author has previously investigated specific wall durability issues, focusing on the performance of various WRB and pan flashing materials. A 2004 study [6] compared the water penetration resistance behavior of two commonly available housewrap products (which had different permeance values) and No. 15 building felt, when subjected to surfactant contamination from other sources; water intrusion through fastener penetrations; and water vapor diffusion through WRB materials. Among other things, it was found that fastener (staple) penetrations significantly reduced the moisture resistance of WRBs, thereby potentially degrading exterior wall "weather resistance" performance. In another study [7], the author conducted field evaluations of pan flashing/sill protection components installed in conjunction with fenestration units in a single-family dwelling and in a low-rise health care facility. Moisture levels were monitored in building walls in the vicinity of these fenestration units. All of the pan flashing/sill pan protection components performed satisfactorily. To date, no water retention has been detected beneath any of the sill pans.

Before initiating the study described in this paper, the author reviewed various methods used by manufacturers for evaluating the drainage characteristics of exterior wall claddings, water resistive barriers, and the like. ASTM E2273-03 was selected as the basis for the laboratory testing methodology. Overall, the procedure is simpler to use and requires less complex apparatus than other tests. It is worth noting that E2273-03 was originally developed in the late 1990s by the EIFS industry as they were developing alternatives to the face-sealed barrier claddings (e.g., concealed barrier/drainage type systems), in an effort to respond to water intrusion and entrapment concerns inherent in the face-sealed barrier approach. While this test remains useful, some concerns have emerged, which are discussed further below.

Another test employed by some manufacturers is ASTM D4716, "Test Method for Determining the (In Plane) Flow Rate per Unit Width and Hydraulic Transmissivity of a Geosynthetic Using a Constant Head." This procedure involves mounting the drainage material between two horizontal plates, compressing the "sandwich" from above, and then forcing a hydrostatic head of water through the material from one end to the other. A similar test, ASTM D4491, "Standard Test Methods for Water Permeability of Geotextiles by Permittivity," includes hydrostatic head tests meant to evaluate geosynthetic filter fabrics. In sum, we have an EIFS industry-based test on one hand, and some geosynthetic industry-based tests on the other, all of which are intended to analyze "drainage."

Methodology

Two laboratory test series were performed. In Series A, 40 wood framed wall mockups, 122 cm × 244 cm (4 ft × 8 ft) in size, were constructed to evaluate different combinations of water resistive barriers, drainage products, and mediums, utilizing the ASTM E2273 test method. These mockups were tested by an independent third-party laboratory (Architectural Testing, Inc., York, PA), which has performed similar testing for building component manufacturers.

In Series B, four smaller-scale mockups were constructed to further investigate some additional WRB performance characteristics, and also to demonstrate that a less cumbersome mockup size (i.e., one-fourth the size used in E2273) could be used. These mockups used the overall E2273 methodology, but included provisions for observing how bulk water interacts with the WRB and drainage surfaces within the wall assembly.

Series A: Modified ASTM E2273 Mockup Tests

In the ASTM E2273 test, water is introduced at a stated flow rate from a pair of standard nozzles into a "fault slot" near the top of the mockup; water that drains downward past the WRB material in the mockup assembly is collected at the bottom and weighed, and drainage efficiency is calculated.

The WRB specimens included traditional No. 15 and No. 30 building felts; three brands of traditional polymer based housewraps; five brands of surface-modified (drainage-enhanced) housewraps; one brand of "profiled sheet" (drainage board) material; and drainage mediums that incorporated a drainage mat or furring strips. These were tested in a variety of configurations, as follows:

- *Design A:* 1 layer WRB (No. 30 felt, housewrap, or drainage board).
- *Design B:* 2 layers of WRB (2 layers of No. 15 felt, or 1 layer of another WRB with 1 layer of No. 15 felt on "exterior" [front side, exposed to water entry] of the other WRB).
- *Design C:* 1 layer WRB, with 6.35 mm ($\frac{1}{4}$ inch) plywood furring strips on "exterior" (front side, exposed to water entry) of the WRB.
- *Design D:* 1 layer WRB, with 6.35 mm ($\frac{1}{4}$ inch) foam plastic furring strips on "exterior" (front side, exposed to water entry) of the WRB.
- *Design E:* 1 layer WRB, with 19 mm ($\frac{3}{4}$ inch) plywood furring strips on "exterior" (front side exposed, to water entry) of the WRB.
- *Design F:* 1 layer WRB, with 6.35 mm ($\frac{1}{4}$ inch) foam plastic furring strips on "interior" (back side, protected from water entry) of the WRB.
- *Design G:* 1 layer WRB, with 6.35 mm ($\frac{1}{4}$ inch) foam plastic furring strips aligned with each other, on both ("exterior" and "interior") sides of the WRB.
- *Design H:* 1 layer WRB, with drainage mat on "exterior" (front side, exposed to water entry) of the WRB.

Series "A" Procedure—Test mockups were constructed as follows. Each unit included a 122 cm × 244 cm (4 ft × 8 ft) sheet of 11 mm (7/16 in.) oriented strand board (OSB) sheathing. The back of the sheathing was fastened to a frame of 51 mm × 102 mm (2 in. × 4 in.) wood studs of the same overall dimensions. WRB specimens were installed on the face of the sheathing horizontally, shingle-fashion, and attached with T-50 staples spaced 203 mm (8 in.) on center. Some mockups included the WRB alone, while others included the WRB together with other materials such as a drainage mat or plywood/plastic furring strips spaced 203 mm (8 in.) apart. In mockups using furred material, the WRB was fastened to the sheathing only through the furring strips. The WRB specimens were then covered with a 122 cm × 244 cm (4 ft × 8 ft) sheet of 25 mm (1 in.) thick extruded polystyrene (XPS) board, which was intended to function as an exterior "faux cladding." The mockup edges were then caulked with sealant and self-adhering flashing. The field area of the XPS board was further secured through the WRB specimen to the sheathing with 51 mm (2 in.) cap nails. These cap nails were applied 203 mm (8 in.) on center with a compressed-air-driven coil nailer. The head of each cap nail was further caulked with sealant. The completed mockup was then affixed to the ATI testing frame to hold the mockup plumb and vertical for the test.

The upper portion of the XPS faux cladding included a 61 mm × 51 mm (24 in. × 2 in.) "fault slot," to receive bulk water from a dispensing device. This device consisted of a clear acrylic plastic box fitted with two spray nozzles that were mounted 127 mm (5 in.) to either side of the center of the box. The nozzles were connected to the water supply by plastic tubing. A pressure regulator, flow meter, and in-line water filter controlled water flow to the nozzles. The dispensing device was mounted at an angle to ensure that all water was directed into the slot. The water spray was delivered at the rate of 3.4 L/m^2/min (5.0 U.S. gal/ft^2 h), or 2.12 gal/75 min, with a tolerance of ±10 %.

Although not required by the E2273 procedure, a record was also made of the time that elapsed from the initial introduction of water to its first appearance at the bottom of the mockup. These data are noted in the matrix in Appendix B as "Time To First Water (TFW)." During the test proper, the weight of drained water was recorded every 15 min until the test was terminated at 75 min. Any remaining water was allowed to drain from the mockup for an additional 60 min, and this water was also weighed.

Results and Discussion—Data for the 40 test mockups is summarized in the matrix in Appendix B. Eleven WRB materials were evaluated in eight design configurations. Based on the results of these tests, some qualitative, "order of magnitude" comparisons can be made as follows. Test results are considered informative but not authoritative. The percentage figures provided are averages derived from the data on "drainage efficiency" and "Time to First Water" (TFW), and are intended to highlight what appear to be noteworthy patterns in the data.

1. Traditional WRBs, installed alone, provided little drainage.
    - The drainage efficiency of *building felts* was 0 %, while that of *traditional housewraps* was 9 %.
    - TFW for *building felts* was N/A (no water appeared), while that of *traditional housewraps* averaged 27 min 27 s.
2. Drainage-Enhanced WRBs performed better than traditional WRBs.

- The drainage efficiency of *drainage-enhanced* housewraps averaged 71 %; that of *traditional* housewraps averaged 9 %.
- TFW for *drainage-enhanced* housewraps averaged 3 min 5 s, while that of *traditional* housewraps averaged 27 min 27 s.

3. Drainage Board product performance was better than Drainage-Enhanced WRBs, and was on a par with those WRBs used with furring or a drainage mat.
   - The drainage efficiency of one *drainage board product* was 97 %, compared to an average of 71 % for *drainage-enhanced housewraps*.
   - TFW for the *drainage board product* was 16 s, compared to an average of 3 min 5 s for *drainage-enhanced housewraps*.

4. Building Felt, when used in conjunction with Drainage-Enhanced WRBs, negated the drainage benefits of the latter.
   - The drainage efficiency for *drainage-enhanced housewraps used with felt* was only 1.7 %, compared to an average of 71 % for *drainage-enhanced housewraps used alone*.
   - TFW for *drainage-enhanced housewraps used alone* was an average of 3 min 5 s, compared to None (no water appearance) for *drainage-enhanced housewraps used with felt*.

5. Furring installed behind the WRB (i.e., the side away from the fault slot) enhanced drainage.
   - The drainage efficiency of *building felt with furring* installed behind it was 38 %, compared to None for *felt used alone*.
   - TFW of *building felt with furring* installed behind it was 22 min, compared to None (no water appearance) for *felt used alone*.
   - The drainage efficiency of a *drainage-enhanced housewrap with furring* installed behind it was 77 %, compared to an average of 71 % for *drainage-enhanced housewraps used alone*.
   - TFW of a *drainage-enhanced housewrap with furring* installed behind it was 16 s, compared to an average of 3 min 5 s for *drainage-enhanced housewraps used alone*.

6. Furring or a Drainage Mat placed in front of the WRB (i.e., exposed to the fault slot) dramatically enhanced drainage.
   - The drainage efficiency of *building felt with furring* installed in front averaged 88 %, compared with 0 % for *felts used alone*.
   - TFW of *building felt with furring* installed in front averaged 15 s, compared to None (no water appearance) for *felts used alone*.
   - The drainage efficiency of *traditional housewraps with a drainage mat or furring strips* installed in front averaged 88 %, compared to an average of 9 % for *traditional housewraps used alone*.
   - TFW of *traditional housewraps with a drainage mat or furring strips* installed in front averaged 15 s, compared to an average of 27 min 27 s for *traditional housewraps used alone*.
   - The drainage efficiency of *drainage-enhanced housewraps with furring* installed in front averaged 89 %, compared to an average of 71 % for *drainage-enhanced housewraps used alone*.
   - TFW of *drainage-enhanced housewraps with furring* installed in front

averaged 10.5 s, compared to an average of 3 min 5 s for *drainage-enhanced housewraps used alone*.

7. Furring placed on both sides of the WRB generally performed better than when it was placed in front of the WRB. (Foam plastic furring strips tested.)

- The drainage efficiency of traditional housewraps with foam plastic furring *installed on both sides* averaged 87 %, compared to an average of 78 % for traditional housewraps with foam plastic furring *installed in front*.
- TFW of *traditional housewraps* with foam plastic furring *installed on both sides* averaged 18 s, compared to an average of 12 s for traditional housewraps with foam plastic furring *installed in front*.
- The drainage efficiency of a *drainage-enhanced housewrap* with foam plastic furring installed *on both sides* was nearly 100 %, compared to an average of 89 % for *drainage-enhanced housewraps* with foam plastic furring *installed in front*.
- TFW of a *drainage-enhanced housewrap* with foam plastic furring installed *on both sides* was 3 s, compared to an average of 11 s for *drainage-enhanced housewraps* with foam plastic furring *installed in front*. From these preliminary results, it appears that the highest level

of drainage performance (90 % and above) can be obtained by using WRBs with furring, drainage mats, or profiled sheets (drainage boards).

About "Time to First Water."—The "Time to First Water" (TFW) data obtained in these modified E2273 tests appeared to offer significant additional insights about how quickly bulk water will pass through a given wall assembly. The TFW period was generally shorter with furring strip/drainage mat or profiled sheet (drainage board) materials, than with "drainage-enhanced" WRB products. However, in several instances the author found significant differences in TFW between the same type of product, from the introduction of water to its first appearance at the bottom of the mockup. Thus, some "drainage-enhanced" WRB materials retained water in the drainage space for a considerably longer time than others with lower drainage efficiencies. (Compare, e.g., data for Mockups 7A and 8A in the matrix in Appendix B.) This finding further illustrates the need to better understand the behavior of WRB materials in service, as well as related drainage/drying mechanisms in exterior walls. Finally, in the author's experience, bulk water can easily flow through a WRB fastener/staple penetration and migrate to the underlying sheathing. It appears that products having a longer TFW may allow larger amounts of water to persist for a longer time in proximity to fasteners, with a potential effect on the long-term performance of the underlying sheathing/framing.

Further Thoughts on ASTM E2273—The author's mockup testing has revealed some problematic aspects of the ASTM E2273 procedure. The test is intended to provide information regarding the "drainage efficiency" of a wall cladding. Water is applied to the specimen via two spray nozzles. A pressure regulator, flow meter, and inline water filter control the flow rate of water supplied to the nozzles. The flow rate is stipulated as 106 g (0.234 lb) per minute,

±10 %. When calibrating this test, the flow rate must be adjusted to obtain a weight of water of 1590 g (3.5 lb) to 1745 g (3.8 lb) during a 15-min period. Theoretically, the required pressure regulator would hold the flow rate within this variable range of 155 g (0.3 lb) during the test. The author found that changes in water line pressure may affect the calibrated spray nozzles' output. If the line pressure changes, the nozzles may deliver more or less water to the specimen. Although this variability would be maintained within the ±10 % tolerance specified by the ASTM test, a ±10 % tolerance will affect the overall drainage efficiency. This makes it difficult to gauge water management performance within samples of the same wall assembly design, let alone trying to compare different designs.

For example, if one specimen tested at 92 % efficiency and another tested at 88 %, it is unclear what significance, if any, should be attributed to the 4 % difference between these two results. Such a difference would amount to a few ounces of water over the required 135 min of the test. Beyond this, it is impossible to know how quickly one wall assembly will dry out compared to the other wall assembly, based on this test. By design, the E2273 test is limited to assessing how quickly a wall assembly may drain bulk water. It is not intended to assess the fate of any water that is retained within that assembly. Based on this testing, it is not known if an assembly with a 98 % drainage efficiency will dry out more or less quickly than an assembly rated at 88 %. The "time to first water" data shed some light on this aspect of the problem. The author is aware of research by others, which also indicates that the ASTM E2273 test can give misleading results in its current form. Recent work by Canadian investigators [8] shows that wall designs using furring strips may dry more quickly than designs utilizing other drainage mediums. The actual amounts of water retained are also dependent upon the cladding type and by the manner in which water entry occurs.

A recent study by the Building Research Association of New Zealand (BRANZ) [9] measured drying rates of wall mockups over a three-year period. The study found that it is critical to isolate the back of a cladding from the framing, because framing lumber gives up moisture very slowly; water dried 100 times faster from the back of a given cladding than from the underlying framing. The study also found that drained/ventilated and "open rainscreen" walls dried approximately three times faster than walls without an airspace. However, drained/ventilated designs did not improve drying of wet framing, because the drying rate was still limited by moisture transport rates in the timber.

Series B. Additional WRB Mockup Tests

Some of the preceding ATI tests showed that asphalt felt and traditional housewraps, when used alone, had very low drainage efficiencies, on the order of 0 % to 9 %. Although these materials may comply with certain performance requirements, it would appear that they fail to meet the Code's performance requirement for drainage. Indeed, approximately 90 % to 100 % of the introduced moisture was retained in these particular mockups. While other tests showed that WRB products used with drainage mediums or furring materials had much higher drainage efficiencies, some portion of the introduced moisture remained within the mockup assemblies after the tests were completed. The E2273 test procedure was not intended to address the mechanisms by which water that does not drain is held in the test specimen. Specifically, the test procedure cannot identify the relative amount retained outboard of the WRB versus the amount which may penetrate or otherwise breach the WRB.

To further explore this concern, several smaller-scale mockup tests were conducted. The overall E2273 approach was utilized, but with some important differences. "Drainage efficiency" was not calculated. Rather, the intent was to qualitatively evaluate and compare the water resistance behavior of: (1) a "traditional" housewrap, (2) a "drainage-enhanced" housewrap; (3) a "traditional" housewrap used with furring strips; and (4) a "drainage enhanced" housewrap used with furring strips. All housewraps products were from the same manufacturer.

Series "B" Procedure—The mockups were one-fourth the size of the E2273 mockups (61 cm × 122 cm [2 ft × 4 ft]); a known quantity of water was delivered to the mockups using a reservoir/"trickle" dispensing method; and the substrate sheathing was coated with a fluorescent dye powder that would change color upon contact with moisture.

Test mockups were constructed as follows. Each unit included a 61 cm × 122 cm (2 ft × 4 ft) sheet of 11 mm (7/16 in.) oriented strand board (OSB) sheathing. The back of the sheathing was supported by 51 mm × 102 mm (2 in. × 4 in.) studs attached in an "I" pattern (horizontal members at each end, connected by a central midrib) which left the sides open to accommodate brackets for mounting the finished mockup on a testing frame. The face of the sheathing was coated with a water-miscible fluorescent dye to provide an indication of moisture intrusion.

WRB specimens were attached to this coated sheathing with staples and then covered with a 61 cm × 122 cm (2 ft × 4 ft) sheet of 25 mm (1 in.) thick extruded polystyrene (XPS) board, which was intended to function as an exterior "faux cladding." Some mockups included the WRB alone, while others included the WRB together with plastic furring strips spaced 203 mm (8 in.) apart, in which case the WRB was fastened to the sheathing only through the furring strips. The top portion of the "faux cladding" included a projecting "hopper" (similar to the "fault slot" of the Series "A" tests) to receive the water-dispensing device described further below. The faux cladding panel /hopper was secured to the OSB using paired 51 mm (2 in.) aluminum shelf angles at each side. The remaining mockup edges were then caulked with sealant and self-adhering membrane flashing. The field area of the faux cladding was further secured through the WRB specimen to the sheathing with 51 mm (2 in.) cap nails. These cap nails were applied 203 mm (8 in.) on center with a compressed-air-driven coil nailer. The head of each cap nail was further caulked with sealant. The completed mockup was then affixed to the testing frame using the brackets. The purpose of this frame was to hold the mockup plumb and vertical and to hold the water dispensing apparatus in place at the top of the mockup during the test.

Water was applied to the top of the mockup from the "trickle" dispensing device as follows. The bottom of a 3.8 L (1 gal) plastic bucket was fitted with a brass needle valve attached to a length of plastic tubing. The lower end of this tubing was connected to a manifold made from two segments of PVC tubing joined at the middle by a "T" connector. Both PVC segments were approximately 127 mm (5 in.) long, and were drilled with 1.6 mm (1/16 in.) diameter holes set 13 mm ($\frac{1}{2}$ in.) on center. This manifold was placed at the bottom of the "hopper" in the XPS faux cladding so that the holes faced toward the exposed exterior face of the WRB specimen. This manifold was intended to ensure that water was distributed evenly across the face of the specimen, over a constant period of time.

Water was released from the "trickle" dispensing device into the mockup for 19 min. As before, the bottom of the mockup was observed for appearance of the first water droplets. After each drainage test, the WRB specimen was removed from the substrate and examined using ultraviolet light, to examine the dye-coated sheathing surface for evidence of leakage.

Results and Discussion—When used alone, both the plain and drainage-enhanced housewrap products allowed water to migrate via fastener holes to the substrate sheathing, as indicated by visible areas of fluorescent dye activation on the sheathing surface. When both types of housewraps were tested in conjunction with furring strips, no dye activation occurred on the sheathing and no dye was observed in the drainage water. Therefore, water intrusion to the sheathing plane was prevented by installing the WRBs with furring. Test results are summarized in Table 1.

Summary and Conclusions

The 2006 *International Residential Building Code* requires increased use of WRB materials in construction and requires them to have some means of draining water from the building enclosure. However, this "drainage" performance requirement is not defined, and it is also not clear that current WRB products used in common design configurations will provide "a weather-resistant exterior wall envelope." Manufacturers, specifiers, and contractors are challenged to find ways to promote and use appropriate WRB materials to respond adequately to a public need. Given these factors, the author performed these studies to learn more about the "drainage efficiency" characteristics of various types of WRB materials and mechanisms (felts, housewraps, drainage wraps, drainage boards, and furring strips) as a "first step" towards developing an overall approach for the Building Enclosure.

Overall, based on tests using a working definition of "drainage efficiency" as set forth in ASTM E2273-03, it appears that traditional WRBs and housewraps do not provide a drainage capability (0 % to 9 %) to exterior walls. Drainable housewraps provide a much-improved level of such drainage (approximately 70 %), but they still retain water that can migrate through fastener holes to the underlying construction. The highest level of drainage performance

TABLE 1—*Series B/small-scale E2273 mockup results.*

Mockup Number	Test Modality (Note Sequence of Materials)	Time To First Water	Additional Observations
B.1	OBS/traditional housewrap/faux cladding	120 s	Dye observed on OSB and in catch basin
B.2	OBS/drainage enhanced housewrap/faux cladding	5 s	Dye observed on OSB and in catch basin
B.3	OBS/traditional housewrap/furring/faux cladding	Immediate	No dye observed on OSB or in catch basin
B.4	OBS/drainage enhanced housewrap/furring/faux cladding	Immediate	No dye observed on OSB or in catch basin

(90 % and above) is obtained by using WRBs with furring, drainage mats, and profiled sheets (drainage boards).

Some exterior claddings may include an integral drainage space (e.g., vinyl siding) and, therefore, may not require an enhanced drainage approach, under certain project conditions. Others, particularly absorptive / reservoir type claddings such as stucco and manufacture stone, may require it, depending upon the project. However, "drainage" appears to be only part of the equation for success. "Drying" of exterior walls must also be considered further; recent work by others [8,9] provides useful insights on this important issue.

Acknowledgments

The author gratefully acknowledges the support and advice of staff of the National Association of Home Builders Research Center (NAHBRC), who encouraged this research in partnership with the U.S. Department of Housing and Urban Development's PATH (Partnership for Advancing Technology in Housing) program. The author also acknowledges the assistance of the staff at Architectural Testing, Inc. (ATI), York, PA, for performing the 40-mockup portion of this study. Finally, the author acknowledges the assistance of WBD Inc. employees Peter H. Johnson for his editorial help, and Michael Knox and Denny Smith for constructing other test mockups.

Appendix A. International Residential Codes Comparison Chart

SECTION R703 – EXTERIOR COVERING (Excerpted)	
IRC 2006 PROVISIONS	**IRC 2003 PROVISIONS**

R703.1 General. Exterior walls shall provide the building with a weather-resistant exterior wall envelope. The exterior wall envelope shall include flashing as described in Section R703.8. The exterior wall envelope shall be designed and constructed in a manner that prevents the accumulation of water within the wall assembly by providing a water-resistant barrier behind the exterior veneer as required by Section R703.2. and a means of draining water that enters the assembly to the exterior. Protection against condensation in the exterior wall assembly shall be provided in accordance with Chapter 11 of this code.
 	
Exceptions:
1. A weather-resistant exterior wall envelope   shall not be required over concrete or masonry walls designed in accordance with   Chapter 6 and flashed according to   Section R703.7 or R703.8.
2. Compliance with requirements for a means of
    drainage, and requirements of Sec. R703.2 and Sec. R703.8, shall not be required for an exterior wall envelope that has been demonstrated to resist wind-driven rain through testing of the exterior wall envelope, including joints, penetrations and intersections with dissimilar materials, in accordance with ASTM E331 under the following conditions:
 	
    2.1.   Exterior wall envelope test assemblies shall include at least one opening, one control joint, one wall/eave interface and one wall sill. All tested openings and penetrations shall be representative of the intended end-use configuration.
    2.2.   Exterior wall envelope test assemblies shall be at least 4 feet (1219 mm) by 8 feet (1219 mm) in size.
    2.3.   Exterior wall assemblies shall be tested at a minimum differential
	R703.1 General. Exterior walls shall provide the building with a weather-resistant exterior wall envelope. The exterior wall envelope shall include flashing as described in Section R703.8. The exterior wall envelope shall be designed and constructed in such a manner as to prevent the accumulation of water within the wall assembly by providing a water-resistive barrier behind the exterior veneer as required by Section R703.2

SECTION R703 – EXTERIOR COVERING (Excerpted)	
IRC 2006 PROVISIONS	**IRC 2003 PROVISIONS**
pressure of 6.24 pounds per square foot (299.Pa).. 2.4. Exterior wall envelope assemblies shall be subjected to a minimum test exposure duration of 2 hours. The exterior wall envelope design shall be considered to resist wind-driven rain where the results of testing indicate that water did not penetrate: control joints in the exterior wall envelope; joints at the perimeter of openings penetration; or intersections of terminations with dissimilar materials.	
R703.2 Water-Resistive Barrier. One layer of No. 15 asphalt felt, free from holes and breaks, complying with ASTM D226 for Type I felt or other approved water-resistive barrier shall be applied over studs or sheathing of all exterior walls. Such felt or material shall be applied horizontally, with the upper layer lapped over the lower layer not less than 2 inches (51 mm). Where joints occur, felt shall be lapped not less than 6 inches (152 mm). The felt or other approved material shall be continuous to the top of walls and terminated at penetrations and building appendages in a manner to meet the requirements of the exterior wall envelope as described in Section R703.1.	**R703.2 Water-resistant sheathing paper.** Asphalt-saturated felt free from holes and breaks, weighing not less than 14 pounds per 100 square feet (0.683 kg/m^2) and complying with ASTM D 226 or other approved weather-resistant material shall be applied over studs or sheathing of all exterior walls as required by Table R703-4. Such felt or material shall be applied horizontally, with the upper layer lapped over the lower layer not less than 2 inches (51 mm). Where joints occur, felt shall be lapped not less than 6 inches (152 mm).
Exception: Omission of the water-resistive barrier is permitted in the following situations: 1. In detached accessory buildings. 2. Under exterior wall finish materials as permitted in Table R703.4.	1. In detached accessory buildings. 2. Under panel siding with shiplap joints or battens. 3. Under exterior wall finish materials as permitted in Table R703.4. 4. Under paperbacked stucco lath.

Appendix B: Drainage Efficiency (Percent), Per ASTM E-2273 And Number of Seconds to "First Water"

This matrix provides results of "drainage efficiency" and "Time to First Water" (TFW) testing of E2273 mockups, together with information on mockup construction. To locate data on Mockup #2-C, e.g., follow Row 2 (left-hand column) to where it intersects Column "C." The upper figure gives the "drainage efficiency," and the lower figure gives the TFW. Refer to the text for further explanations.

Design Approach:	A	B	C	D	E	F	G	H
	1 layer WRB	2 layers WRB	1 layer WRB with ¼" (6.35 mm) plywood furring on "exterior" (front) side	1 layer WRB with ¼" (6.35. mm) foam plastic furring on "exterior" (front) side	1 layer WRB with ¾" (19 mm) plywood furring on "exterior" (front) side	1 layer WRB with ¼" (6.35 mm) foam plastic furring on "interior" (back) side	1 layer WRB with ¼" (6.35 mm) foam plastic furring aligned with each other on both sides	1 layer WRB with Drainage Mat on "exterior" (front) side
Traditional WRBs (Building Felts)								
1 #30 asphalt saturated felt	0 %							
	N/A							
2 #15 asphalt saturated felt		0 %	97.0 %	75.4 %	90.9 %	37.9 %		
		N/A	23 sec.	10 sec.	13 sec.	1,320 sec.		
Traditional WRBs (Polymer-Based Housewraps)								
3 Hwp. # 1	5.6 %		97.6 %	72.1 %	82.9 %		85.3 %	97.1 %
	1,980 sec.		15 sec.	8 sec.	9 sec.		14 sec.	25 sec.
4 Hwp. #2	9.9 %		90.5 %	82.9%	92.8 %		88.5 %	92.8 %
	1,680 sec.		9 sec.	15 sec.	12 sec.		22 sec.	23 sec.
5 Hwp. #3	11.6 %		95.4 %	77.5 %	83.3 %			92.4 %
	1,280 sec.		17 sec.	12 sec.	13 sec.			18 sec.
Drainage-Enhanced Housewraps								
6 Drainage Wrap #1	76.3 %	0 %	99.5 %	87.7 %				
	50 sec.	N/A	9 sec.	7 sec.				

Design Approach:		A	B	C	D	E	F	G	H
7	Drainage Wrap #2	69.8 %	5.1 %	97.4 %	93.4 %		77 %	99.7 %	
		94 sec.	1,200 sec.	8 sec.	15 sec.		16 sec.	3 sec.	
8	Drainage Wrap #3	90.6 %	0 %	70.9 %	83.9 %				
		360 sec.	N/A	13 sec.	11 sec.				
9	Drainage Wrap #4	62.7 %							
		180 sec.							
10	Drainage Wrap #5	55.5 %							
		240 sec.							
Profiled Sheet (Drainage Board)									
11	Drainage Board #1	97.3 %							
		16 sec.							

References

[1]   International Code Council, Inc., *International Residential Code for One-and Two-Family Dwellings*. Editions of 2003 and 2006, at Section R703.1. Published by ICC, Country Club Hills, IL.

[2]   ASTM D226–97a, "Standard Specification for Asphalt-Saturated Organic Felt Used in Roofing and Waterproofing," *Annual Book of ASTM Standards*, Vol. 4.04, ASTM International, West Conshohocken, PA, pp. 35–37.

[3]   ASTM D4869–05, "Standard Specification for Asphalt-Saturated Organic Felt Underlayment Used in Steep Slope Roofing," *Annual Book of ASTM Standards*, Vol. 4.04, ASTM International, West Conshohocken, PA, pp. 232–235.

[4]   Butt, T. K., "Water Resistance and Vapor Permeance of Weather Resistive Barriers," *J. ASTM Int.* Vol. 2, No. 10, 2005, Paper ID JAI12495.

[5]   ASTM E2273–03, "Standard Test Method for Determining the Drainage Efficiency of Exterior Insulation and Finish Systems (EIFS) Clad Wall Assemblies," *Annual Book of ASTM Standards*, Vol. 4.12, ASTM International, West Conshohocken, PA, pp. 1043–1045.

[6]   Williams, M. F., "Evaluation of Water Resistive Barrier Performance Using Simple Ponding and Vapor Diffusion Tests," *Proceedings, Performance of Exterior Envelopes of Whole Buildings IX, International Conference.*, (*Materials/Barrier/Practices, Section II-B*) Dec. 5–10, 2004, Clearwater, FL. Special Pub. SP-5. American Society of Heating, Refrigerating, and Air-Conditioning Engineers, Atlanta, 2004.

[7]   Williams Building Diagnostics, Inc. *Laboratory and Field Evaluations of Pan Flashing and Methods of Integration With Water Resistive Barriers*—PATH 7. NAHB Res. Ctr./US DHUD, Office of Policy Development & Research. April, 2006. Available online at www.toolbase.org/Field-Evaluations/williams-building-diagnostics.pdf.

[8]   Onysko, D. M. et al., 2007. *Summary Report: Drainage and Retention of Water By*

Cladding Systems. One of a series of eight reports prepared on behalf of Forintek Canada Corp. for Canada Mortgage and Housing Corp. Ottawa: CMHC, Policy & Research Division.

[9]   Bassett, M., "Examining Drying Rates In Walls," *Build* #100, June/July 2007 (Building Research Association of New Zealand), pp. 66, 67. Available from www.branz.co.nz.

Reprinted from JAI, Vol. 6, No. 5
doi:10.1520/JAI101271
Available online at www.astm.org/JAI

James D. Katsaros[1] *and Charles G. Carll*[2]

Extreme Exposure Fenestration Installations—The Florida Challenge

ABSTRACT: Current standards for installation of fenestration units, such as ASTM E2112-07, "Standard Practice for Installation of Exterior Windows, Doors and Skylights" do not address regional considerations, or how the level of wind and rain exposure could influence installation methodology. In the coastal southeastern United States, where extreme wind-driven rain events occur with some regularity, more robust methods than those prescribed in ASTM E2112-07 are necessary. In Florida, single family houses are commonly constructed with surface barrier concrete masonry walls on the first story, and membrane-drainage, wood-frame walls on the second story. This "hybrid" construction is unique, or virtually so, to Florida. Finned windows of a particular design are made expressly for installation in cement masonry unit (CMU) walls as commonly found in Florida homes. The special considerations that relate to residential construction in Florida were of concern to an industrial consortium. The consortium thus formed an Installation Committee to develop methods for fenestration installation that would be applicable to the wall systems commonly found in the coastal Southeast, with consideration of the high wind-driven rain loads that accompany tropical storms. This paper addresses two general installation methods proposed by the Installation Committee, and presents test data for wall assemblies incorporating fenestration units installed using the methods.

KEYWORDS: construction, water management, flashing, sealants, extreme exposure, windows, buildings, durability, CMU, adhesives, Florida

Manuscript received June 15, 2007; accepted for publication March 17, 2009; published online April 2009.

[1] Ph.D., DuPont Flashing Systems Development Leader, DuPont Building Innovations, 5401 Jefferson Davis Highway, Richmond, VA 23261/Chairman of FMA Installation Committee.

[2] Research Technologist, U.S. Forest Products Laboratory, One Gifford Pinchot Dr., Madison, WI 53726-2398.

Cite as: Katsaros, J. D. and Carll, C. G., "Extreme Exposure Fenestration Installations—The Florida Challenge," *J. ASTM Intl.*, Vol. 6, No. 5. doi:10.1520/JAI101271.

Introduction

Moisture problems in buildings can originate from several sources, but in many buildings, water intrusion (often into walls) poses the greatest risk. The window-wall (w/w) interface is furthermore one of the most critical locations for water intrusion. In a recent study by RDH Building Engineering Limited [2], a wide variety of window types and assemblies were tested for leakage, with leakage via six potential leakage paths being monitored. Water leakage was found to occur to some extent via all six paths. However, leakage via the "through window to wall interface to adjacent wall assembly" path was prevalent for all the window types tested. Leakage via this path poses a high risk of consequential damage to the building. The causes for leakage via the "interface to adjacent assembly" path are many, but improper flashing installation and over-reliance on building sealants were noted in the study report [2] as consistently contributing to leakage via the path. The Durability by Design guideline [3] published by the Partnership of Advancing Technology in Housing (PATH) concurs with the RDH report [2]; the PATH Design guideline states: "most leakage problems are related to improper or insufficient flashing details or the absence of flashing."

Moisture management challenges occur with all types of wall systems and fenestration systems (windows and doors), and in all climates, but the potential for problematic leakage is greatest in regions that experience extreme wind-driven rain events, such as hurricanes and severe thunderstorms. In the coastal regions of the southeastern United States, problematic wall leakage from wind-driven rain is a common problem. The problem is not only due to the occurrence in the region of extreme wind-driven rain, but also because buildings in the region are designed to first maintain structural integrity during hurricanes. In designing with an emphasis on structural integrity (while remaining mindful of construction cost), water management principles have often been overlooked. For example, wide roof overhangs are effective for sheltering walls from wind-driven rain, but unless robustly constructed, are prone to removal from the building by hurricane winds at which point they become airborne projectiles. As a consequence, wide roof overhangs are uncommon in the region. In addition, the first-story walls of residences in Florida are commonly constructed of Concrete Masonry Units (CMUs) with direct-applied stucco rendering. These walls resist termite attack, which can be an issue in the Florida climate. If the CMU cores are grouted and reinforced, the walls are furthermore appreciably resistant to projectile penetration during hurricanes. CMU walls with direct-applied stucco are, however, prone to problematic water intrusion. After the hurricane season of 2004, water intrusion in the affected areas of Florida was widely observed, particularly near fenestration (window and door) wall openings [4]. While a portion of this water intrusion was associated with rain driven at pressures well exceeding the design leakage pressure of the windows, which is generally 15 % of the structural design pressure, much of the water intrusion was identified as being due to faulty or poorly-designed installation methods. The report [4], prepared for the Home Builders Association of Metro Orlando and the Florida Building Commission, states: "Water-managed

FIG. 1—*Typical residential home construction in Florida.*

window and door installation methods (should) be developed and the Florida Building Code altered to require them."

The need for fenestration installation methods that resist leakage has been recognized by Florida building officials. As a result, an installation committee was formed by the Fenestration Manufacturers Association (FMA). The objective of the committee was to develop installation methods applicable to the types of walls commonly constructed in Florida, with particular emphasis on resisting leakage, or managing it, or both. This paper reports spray test results for prototype assemblies fabricated in accord with proposed installation methods that were developed by the installation committee. The prototype assemblies were of w/w interfaces. Two different types of wall systems were investigated.

Residential Wall Systems in Florida

A typical two-story residential building in Florida incorporates two different types of wall systems (Fig. 1). Second-story walls are usually of wood-frame construction, with wood-based sheathing covered with a water-resistive barrier (WRB). The second-story walls are thus membrane-drainage walls, as classified by ASTM E2112 [1]; they would be termed "drainage walls" by the terminology of ASTM E2266 [5]. In contrast, first story walls are typically of CMU construction with stucco applied directly to the block. The stucco is coated with water-proofing paint; the paint serves as the water barrier. There is no provision for drainage of water that breaches the outermost surface of the wall. This would include water intrusion associated with fenestration units.

Second-story wood-frame walls in Florida are not conceptually different than membrane-drainage wood-frame walls elsewhere in North America. Finned windows installed in these walls are of similar design as elsewhere in North America; they may have higher design pressure ratings, but are otherwise similar. The conceptual difference between these walls and membrane-drainage wood-frame walls elsewhere in North America is the anticipated level of wind-blown rain to which they may be exposed.

First-story CMU walls in Florida pose unique challenges with regard to installation of fenestration units. Units made for installation in these walls are designed for installation in CMU walls; the design is not commonly found outside of the region. The fenestration units are flanged, but the flanges are not used for anchoring the unit. The units are commonly termed "frontal flange" units, indicating that the flanges are exposed in service, rather than being covered by trim or cladding.

Frontal flange units are anchored with screws through jamb and head members driven into pressure-treated 2 by 4 (38 by 89 mm) wood members. The wood members are in turn anchored into the CMUs with masonry anchors. The wood members form what is termed a buck. Inward/outward positioning of the window is determined by location of the outboard faces of the buck members; the top and side window flanges seat against the outboard faces of the buck members. The interfaces between the buck members and the CMU wall are potential leakage paths. The interfaces are essentially cracks, which are surface-filled with sealant. A pre-cast or site-poured concrete sill pan is found at the base of the window opening. The sill serves a structural purpose, tying together the CMUs at the bottom of the opening. The sill is also intended to serve a water management function, although this function is often not adequately achieved. The concrete sill incorporates a lip or ledge (back dam) against which the lower (bottom) flange of the window is intended to seat, a representative pre-cast concrete sill is shown in Fig. 2. Alignment and inward/outward positioning of the sill's ledge is important, as is subsequent alignment of members of the wood buck with the ledge in the sill. In residential construction practice, alignment is sometimes poor. To serve its water management function, the sill should shed water. In practice the concrete sill is often porous and permeable, allowing through-passage of water. Cracked sills, which are fairly common, will also allow water passage. Flaws at sill ends (casting flaws or faulty mortar joints) can also result in leakage. Examples of areas prone to water leakage with the concrete sill system are shown in Fig. 3. For the purpose of water management, it is desirable for the sill to protrude beyond the face of the CMU wall. More commonly, the concrete sill is flush with the outer surface of the CMU wall.

The Installation Committee, formed under the direction of the FMA, had the objective of developing effective installation methods for fenestration units in Florida. The committee has developed five installation practice documents, based on different window/door and wall configurations found in the southeastern United States. These are listed in Table 1. This paper reports on evaluation of wall assemblies constructed to be consistent with the first two documents listed in Table 1: (1) FMA/AAMA 100 for wood framed construction [6],

FIG. 2—*Pre-cast concrete sill. The sill shown protrudes past the outer face of the block wall.*

TABLE 1—*FMA (AAMA/WDMA) Installation Committee documents as of 5/31/07.*

Document	Window System	Wall System	Status
FMA/AAMA 100	Flanged or Mounting Fins (Wood, Al, or Vinyl)	Wood Frame	Draft/AAMA Ballot complete, third ballot pending wall test results
FMA/AAMA 200	Frontal Flanged (Aluminum and Vinyl)	Surface Barrier CMU	Draft/AAMA Ballot complete, third ballot pending wall test results
FMA/WDMA 250	Nonfrontal flanged (Wood)	Surface Barrier CMU	Draft under development/awaiting WDMA ballot
FMA/AAMA 300	Sliding Glass Doors	Wood Frame	Draft under development
FMA/AAMA 400	Sliding Glass Doors	Surface Barrier CMU	Draft under development

(a)

(b)

FIG. 3—*Common installation flaws. Cracks in joint between sill and rough opening, forced fitting of wood buck (a), and raised leg in sill back dam is cut out to fit anchoring hardware (b).*

and (2) FMA/AAMA 200 for frontal flanged windows in surface barrier CMU construction [7].

Testing and Results

Installations Conforming with FMA/AAMA 100

The forward of FMA/AAMA 100 [6] states: *"This standard is specifically designed for installations subject to extreme wind/water climate exposure, particularly in the coastal southeast United States, and addresses buildings that will be at high risk for water intrusion. Thus, preventative measures shall be taken that are above normal installation practice."*

FMA/AAMA 100 requires that the window rough opening be drainable through the use of sill pan flashing under the fenestration unit. In contrast, ASTM E2112-07 does not require the use of sill pans for installation of flanged windows in membrane-drainage walls, although it recognizes (recommends) use of sill pans. FMA/AAMA 100 also specifies that a perimeter air seal between the window frame and the rough opening be installed at or near the interior edge of the window frame. FMA/AAMA 100 includes details on specific installation steps for self-adhering flashing (100 mm/4 in. width) and mechanically attached flashing (230 mm/9 in. width), as well as pictorial illustration of the installation steps. The procedural steps of FMA/AAMA 100 are generally consistent with the A1 method of ASTM E2112-07, for installation of flanged windows in membrane drainage walls; the procedural steps are not consistent with the A, or B, or B1 methods of ASTM E2112-07. This reflects common construction sequencing in the southeast region. Although other sequencing methods are not explicitly recognized, they are not prohibited by FMA/AAMA 100. It is also important to note that manufacturer's instructions take precedence over the explicit procedural instructions outlined in FMA/AAMA 100.

Section 1.2 of FMA/AAMA 100 states: *"Representative installation methods described in this document have been water tested up to a design pressure of 575 Pascal (12 psf) water test pressure, using the ASTM E331 water test, to simulate extreme exposure conditions."*

Two wall assemblies, each containing a flanged window installed in accord with FMA/AAMA 100, were fabricated in a laboratory and spray tested. A summary of the installation features is listed in Table 2. The window in each wall assembly was installed according to the detailed steps of Section 7 of FMA/AAMA 100 [6]. Illustration of the installation are included in Figs. 4–7, which show the cut in the water-resistive barrier, the sill pan flashing, the jamb and head flashings, and the interior air seal method, respectively. After windows were installed, the wall assemblies were left in the laboratory for 24 hours before spray testing.

There was no interior finish on the wall framing and no cavity insulation between studs; the wall framing and the back (interior) side of the wall sheathing was visible during testing. Spray testing was according to ASTM E331 [8], with the pressurized chamber sealed against the exterior side of the test assemblies. Spray testing was performed before and after thermal cycling consisting

TABLE 2—*FMA/AAMA 100 wall test installation details.*

	FMA/AAMA 100 Wall #1	FMA/AAMA 100 Wall #2
Water Resistive Barrier	Installed before window (A1 method) with full "I-cut"	Installed before window (A1 method) with modified "I-cut"
Sill Pan Flashing	150 mm (6 in.) wide extendable self-adhered flashing	150 mm (6 in.) wide extendable self-adhered flashing
Sealant under flange	Polyurethane hybrid sealant: continuous application under jambs and head of flange, discontinuous bead at sill (two 50 mm gaps near either end)	Polyurethane hybrid sealant: continuous application under jambs and head of flange, discontinuous bead at sill (two 50 mm gaps near either end)
Jamb and Head Flashing	100 mm (4 in.) wide self-adhered flashing (butyl adhesive based)	230 mm (9 in.) wide mechanically attached flashing
Interior Air/Water Seal	Backer rod with polyurethane hybrid sealant—later changed to pure polyurethane sealant at sill area after initial test	Polyurethane low expansion aerosol foam

of fourteen 12-hour hot-cold cycles conducted in accord with ASTM E2264, Method A, Level 1 [9]. The test walls did not incorporate cladding systems; spray application was directly to the water resistive barrier, the flashing sheets, and the window unit. In most tests, water was applied at air pressure differentials of 145 Pascal (3.13 psf), 290 Pascal (6.2 psf), 440 Pascal (9.2 psf),

(a)   (b)

FIG. 4—*Cuts in water resistive barrier for FMA/AAMA 100 installations. Full I-cut used in Wall #1 (a) and modified-I cut used in Wall #2 (b).*

FIG. 5—*Extendable sill flashing used in both Wall #1 and Wall #2 for FMA/AAMA 100 installations, with discontinuous bead of sealant at sill (can also be applied to back of the flange).*

(a)   (b)

FIG. 6—*FMA/AAMA 100 completed installations, Wall #1 with 4 in. self-adhering flashing used at jambs and heads (a); Wall #2 with 9 in. mechanically attached flashing used at jambs and head (b).*

FIG. 7—*FMA/AAMA100 interior air/water seals: Wall #1 with backer rod and polyure-thane hybrid sealant in (a); Wall #2 with low expansion polyurethane aerosol foam sealant in (b).*

FIG. 8—*Water leak formed at 11.29 psf on FMA/AAMA 100 Wall #1 at interface between sealant and flashing, after 24 hour cure time.*

540 Pascal (11.29 psf), and 575 Pascal (12 psf). These pressures correspond with structural window pressure design ratings of approximately DP 20, 40, 60, 75, and 80 respectively, (per the 15 % of design pressure load rule of thumb for water test pressure). Water spray, at the rate of 3.4 L/m² min (5.0 U.S. gal./ft² min) at each differential air pressure was applied for 15 minutes, in accord with ASTM E331.

Results of FMA AAMA 100 Wall #1 Test—In the first round of testing of this wall assembly, water leakage was not observed until air pressure differential, reached 540 Pascal (11.29 psf), as shown in Fig. 8. At that 540 Pascal, leakage was observed between the sill pan and the sealant that served (along with backer rod) as the air seal (and the pan back dam) below the window unit's sill. It was noticed that the sealant had not fully cured; it was still wet/sticky to the touch. A spot or "patch" repair was made with additional sealant. The assembly was retested after seven days to allow the sealant to fully cure. During retesting the wall was taken directly to 440 Pascal (9.2 psf) pressure differential (the 145 and 290 Pa differential set-points were skipped). Within eleven minutes at 440 Pa, a leak was observed at the same area as before, and the leak was again between the pan flashing and the sealant. Upon inspection, two conclusions were drawn:

1. There was poor interfacial adhesion between the polyurethane hybrid sealant and the flashing topsheet—the sealant could be easily pulled away from the topsheet. This resulted in an insufficient bond to hold

water back against the pressure differential (the back dam would leak at the higher differential pressures).

2. Since the leak occurred at the same location as the first test, it was also concluded that the repair "patch" was ineffective.

Given the conclusions drawn above, the polyurethane hybrid sealant was removed at the sill area of the installation and a short distance up the jambs and replaced with pure polyurethane sealant. It was known from previous experience that the topsheet of this flashing adhered effectively to pure polyurethane sealants.

Wall #1 was retested with the polyurethane sealant. No leakage was observed at 575 Pascal (12.0 psf) differential. The wall thus met the criterion specified in FMA/AAMA 100. The pressure differential was then increased to 720 Pascal (15 psf) to explore the limits of the installation; this pressure is beyond the FMA/AAMA criterion and above normal exposure for typical window and door installations. A small amount of leakage occurred at 720 Pa at the lower corner of the sill.

After thermal cycling (as described previously), the wall was retested with water application at 145, 290, 440, and 575 Pa differential. Dye tracer was applied at the final test pressure. Water containing the dye was applied with a hand-held sprayer around the entire perimeter of the w/w interface while pressure was still applied, but with the spray racks turned off. After several minutes of pressure application, the spray racks were reactivated to wash residual dye tracer from the exterior surface. The wall was then dismantled for forensic inspection. No water intrusion was noted behind the flashing or in the wall cavities, although some water penetration was evident under the sealant at the sill. It was found that the backer rod had been displaced during the sealant "repair" from the first phase, resulting in potential leakage paths from this action.

FMA/AAMA 100 Wall #2 Test Results—Test Wall #2 was tested in a similar manner as Wall #1. This wall differed from Wall #1 in that a polyurethane low expansion aerosol foam was used for the interior air seal (it also served as the sill pan back dam), and mechanically attached flashing was used for the jambs and head (the cut in the WRB was also different, as previously described in Table 1).

During its first round of testing, Test Wall #2 was subjected to pressure differentials of 290, 440, 540, and 720 Pascal (6.06, 9.20, 11.29, and 15 psf, respectively). No leakage was observed at 540 Pascal differential. A very small leak was observed at the lower right corner at 720 Pascal (15 psf). The installation was repaired at the location of the observed leak and then retested at 575 Pascal (12 psf); a leak was observed in the same location as before. As had been the case with Test Wall #1, it was concluded that a spot repair would not seal the leakage path. The foam at the sill area was thus completely removed and replaced with new material. The wall was again retested at 575 Pascal (12 psf) differential. No leakage was observed; the installation then met the FMA/AAMA 100 criterion.

The wall was then exposed to thermal cycling (according to ASTM E2264, Method A, Level 1), and the wall was retested with water application at 290,

440, 540, and 575 Pa differential. No leakage was observed at 575 Pascal (12 psf). Dye tracer was applied as described previously and the wall was dismantled for forensic inspection. The tracer dye indicated that no water intrusion had occurred behind the flashing or into wall cavities.

FMA/AAMA 100 Wall Test: Discussion of Results—As summarized in Table 3, both of the FMA/AAMA 100 Test Wall #1 and Test Wall #2 showed no leakage at 575 Pascal (12 psf) differential when tested according to ASTM E331 (the criterion set forth in FMA/AAMA 100). The 100 mm (4 in.) self-adhered flashing system and the 230 mm (9 in.) mechanically attached flashing system can each qualify under this criterion, as can each of the methods evaluated for forming the interior air seal and sill pan back dam.

Key observations are summarized below:
1. The adhesive seal between the sill flashing topsheet and the sealant used for the interior air/water seal is important in meeting the FMA/AAMA 100 criterion.
2. Sealant/topsheet combinations that have a lesser seal (such as the initial test with Wall #1) are evidently capable of performing at lower differential pressures. In initial testing (before thermal cycling) the system with less-than-ideal seal did not leak at 440 Pascal (9.20 psf). This corresponds with wind impinging on the wall at approximately 55 mph ($\sim$90 km/h).
3. Once leaks formed in the backer rod and caulk method, the leaks could not be remedied by adding more of the same sealant. The sealant had to be fully removed and replaced (with a more effective sealant) in order for the installation to meet the criterion.
4. These installations did not utilize an upturned leg back dam, demonstrating that a continuous perimeter air/water seal at the interior interface between the window and wall cavity is able to serve as the "back dam" under high pressure loads up to 575 Pascal (12 psf). However, the small leakage observed at 720 Pa in test assemblies that were consistent with either of the methods could have been managed with an upturned leg back dam.

It is important to note that performance of the jamb and head flashings cannot be fully concluded until the wall is disassembled and inspection made behind the flashings. It is worth noting that in these investigations disassembly and subsequent inspection was performed after the walls were thermally cycled and retested.

FMA/AAMA 200 Wall Test

The FMA/AAMA 200 standard practice addresses the unique window and wall configuration utilized in the southeast United States/Florida residential market, with a surface barrier concrete block construction. The FMA/AAMA 200 standard practice is specific to frontal flanged windows, which are typically made from aluminum.

As with the FMA/AAMA 100 standard practice noted in the previous sec-

TABLE 3—*Results of initial FMA/AAMA 100 water testing.*

FMA/AAMA 100 Wall Number	Initial ASTM E331 Water Test Results	ASTM E331 Results After Thermal Cycling (per ASTM E2264 Method A, L1)	Comments/Observations
1	Pass (no leakage) at 575 Pascal (12 psf)	No water penetration behind flashing. Some leakage at interior sealant—pan flashing interface	Adhesion between interior air/water seal and pan flashing is critical. Performance appears sensitive to mis-alignment of backer rod
2	Pass (no leakage) at 575 Pascal (12 psf)	No water penetration behind flashing. No leakage at interior seal up to 575 Pascal (12 psf)	Low expansion aerosol foam was effective as interior air/water seal provided it was not exposed to excessive pressure differential (in excess of 575 Pa)

tion, the FMA/AAMA 200 standard practice specifies the same performance criterion—specifically an absence of leakage when tested according to ASTM E331 at 575 Pascal (12 psf) air pressure differential.

It is also important to note the following statement in the forward of the FMA/AAMA 200 standard practice: *The techniques demonstrated in this standard practice have been developed specifically to restrict liquid water from entering through the masonry opening and/or around the perimeter of the window frame. The major emphasis is focused on sealing the surrounding area of the window's masonry opening in such a manner as to restrict liquid water from penetrating the wall at the window opening* [7]. What this means is that the standard practice is only concerned with the surrounding area around the rough opening and not the entire wall system. Aligned with the test criterion set forth in Section 1.2, the following is noted: *Water resistance is demonstrated around the sealed portion of the rough opening and wall face only. This standard practice presumes that all other construction elements function to provide expected water resistance* [7]. Thus in FMA/AAMA 200, the focus is on the sealed area around the rough opening of the test assembly, rather than the entire block wall (although in the test assembly some area of block will be present).

Two assemblies, each incorporating an aluminum frontal flange window installed in a section of concrete block wall were fabricated. In each assembly, the window was installed in a manner consistent with FMA/AAMA 200 [7] and spray tested in accord with ASTM E331 [8]. In each assembly, the window was anchored to a pressure treated wood buck at the jambs and head of the rough opening, and polyurethane sealant was used to bed the frontal flange to the treated wood members that composed the buck. A discontinuous bead of sealant (also polyurethane) was applied at the sill of the window to allow for drainage. A fillet bead of sealant (also polyurethane) was installed between the wood buck members and the surrounding block wall. The interior perimeter of the window opening was sealed with backer rod and polyurethane sealant. It should be noted that the wall assemblies did not incorporate stucco rendering; this was conceptually similar to the wall assemblies constructed to be consistent with FMA/AAMA 100, (discussed previously), which did not incorporate cladding.

FMA/AAMA 200 Tests Results—All the blocks in the first of the two assemblies were sealed with a block sealer that is commonly used in the region. This included the rough opening return and the pre-cast concrete sill. The concrete sill in the assembly protruded beyond the face of the block wall. Figure 9 shows this assembly prior to spray testing.

The first testing of the assembly was performed during the fall of 2006. In that testing, leakage was observed between the concrete sill and the CMU wall below the sill without application of an air pressure differential (the only driving force being the momentum of the water droplets, imparted by the spray nozzles). A second application of sealer was made in January 2007. The assembly was then exposed to spray testing in February and March 2007.

In the first tests performed in early 2007, the window was masked with film. The masking covered the window flanges, including the sill flange. The only interface actually exposed to water spray was the joint between the wood

FIG. 9—*FMA/AAMA 200 setup for first test wall prior to wall testing in March 2007.*

buck and the concrete block wall. Pressure differentials of 145 Pascal (3.13 psf), 290 Pascal (6.2 psf), 440 Pascal (9.2 psf), and 540 Pascal (11.29 psf) were applied. At roughly 290 Pa differential, water seepage was noted at the interior lower corner of the concrete block, as shown in Fig. 10. Water leakage at the lower extremity of the wood buck was also noted (circled in Fig. 10). The test was continued to 1437 Pascal (30 psf) pressure before stopping. Additional leakage locations were not noted at the higher pressure differentials.

The masking film was removed from the sill flange; this exposed the sill flange and the joint between the sill flange and the concrete sill. The wall was

FIG. 10—*Water seepage through concrete block in first FMA/AAMA 200 wall test near lower corner at interior, as well as the lower buck area, as highlighted by the circle.*

then retested. At 440 Pascal (9.2 psf), a pool of water was noted at the lower corner of the interior on the same side as the leak observed in earlier testing (Fig. 11). Spray testing was suspended and dye tracer was applied to the exterior surface of the assembly around the window perimeter. Dye application was by the same method, described previously, for assemblies conforming with FMA/AAMA 100.

The window was subsequently removed from the assembly. After window

Water Puddle formed here

FIG. 11—*FMA/AAMA 200 water test—water puddle formed in lower corner with lower flange open.*

FIG. 12—*FMA/AAMA 200 wall after first test showing leakage at lower wood buck.*

removal, it was noted that the lower portion of the wood buck on the left side facing the wall was very wet. It was evident that leakage had occurred at a mortar joint in the vicinity of the wood buck; the water that entered at this location traveled between the buck and the sealed concrete blocks and then penetrated the fillet sealant joint between the wood buck and the block wall. Figure 12 shows the area where the buck was soaked. Figure 13 shows the water path between the buck and the concrete wall, made evident by the blue dye tracer. The sill area of the window was dry, indicating that no water penetrated the open sill region under the flange.

The interface between the wood buck and the sealed concrete block wall had (as described previously) been subjected to a 1437 Pascal (30 psf) pressure differential. Leakage, as described previously, had been observed at pressure differentials below and substantially above the criterion level. The dye tracer had only been applied, however, after the assembly had been exposed to a test pressure well beyond the criterion level, and a leakage path had been established.

A second assembly conforming with FMA/AAMA 200 was constructed. This assembly was tested in May 2007. In the second assembly, only 230 mm (9 in.) of the exterior perimeter face of the block was sealed (as directed in the AAMA/FMA 200 draft specification). Figure 14 shows the 230 mm (9 in.) coverage of the sealer, as well as the rough opening return and pre-cast sill. In this case, the pre-cast sill was flush sill with the block wall below the window. A flush sill is more common in actual field installations in Florida. The installation followed the detailed steps of FMA/AAMA 200.

Testing of this second assembly was conducted in two phases. First, water

FIG. 13—*FMA/AAMA 200 wall test indicating path of leakage with blue die entering at mortar joint between sealed concrete block and wood buck, penetrating the sealant.*

was applied only to the sealed area of the block, which is 230 mm around the exterior perimeter of the rough opening, in order to test the robustness of the sealed area and interface. Figure 15 shows the method used to mask the un-sealed portion of the wall; the method used an acrylic sheet and sealant. In the second phase of testing, the test was repeated, with the mask removed (with the entire wall exposed, as shown in Fig. 16). The test results are summarized in Table 4.

As noted in Table 4, the masked assembly did not show leakage at 575 Pa (12 psf) pressure differential. This means that leakage through neither the window-wall (w/w) interface nor the perimeter area of sealed block occurred when air pressure differential was at the criterion level. Leakage was further-more not observed through the interface via these pathways when the test pres-sure was increased to 720 Pascal (15 psf).

Some leakage was noted through the window glazing at the criterion pres-sure differential (575 Pa). This leakage collected at the interior of the pre-cast sill. The installation is not designed to manage this type of water intrusion. The system is designed to manage water that intrudes through or around the w/w interface or through window frame joinery, not water that intrudes through sash, between sash, or between the window sash and frame.

When the masking was removed and the entire CMU wall was exposed to water spray, water seepage to the interior occurred at the lowest pressure dif-ferential included in the test protocol (Table 4). Figure 17 shows the water penetration through the interior side of the unsealed area, but not the sealed area of the block. Unsealed portions of the CMU wall system were thus notably

FIG. 14—*Wall treatment for second FMA/AAMA 200 wall test, showing* 230 mm (9 in.) *sealant application around exterior perimeter and return of rough opening.*

incapable of meeting the FMA/AAMA 200 criterion. Additional testing has shown that water seepage through block walls occurs readily in the absence of any air pressure differential. A "whole wall" approach to water management is thus justified. This, incidentally, was recognized in the report (dated January 2005) by Lstiburek [4]. It will be a key challenge for the FMA Installation Committee going forward.

Sheathing interface
~230 mm (9")
from the rough
opening

FIG. 15—*FMA/AAMA 200 wall test with unsealed area blocked by clear acrylic sheet and sealed.*

Summary and Conclusions

The assemblies, which were constructed to be in accord with FMA/AAMA 100 and 200 installations, generally met the basic performance criterion set forth in the FMA/AAMA documents. The installation methods evaluated in this investigation incorporate a sill pan system, as recommended by but not required by ASTM E2112-07. They also rely on an air seal around the window perimeter at the interior edge of the window frame. At the window sill, this air seal also serves as a sill pan back dam. The following observations and findings were made:

1.   The sill pan systems were found to be effective. Problematic water penetration between the pan and the window bottom flange (between which there was NOT a continuous seal) was not observed. The sill pan system is designed to manage water intrusion around the perimeter of the window frame and at the interface with the window and wall. It is not designed to manage water that penetrates through the window glazing.

2.   In formation of the air seal at the interior window perimeter, adhesion to the window frame and sill pan is critical. "Adhesive" as well as "chemical" compatibility between the sealant and interfacial materials is important. Leaks were observed in areas where adhesion was not sufficient.

FIG. 16—*FMA/AAMA 200 wall test with full wall exposure, both sealed and unsealed areas (second phase).*

TABLE 4—*Test results for the second assembly assembled in accord with FMA/AAMA 200.*

FMA/AAMA 200 Wall Test Descriptor	Initial ASTM E331 Water Test Results	Comments/Observations
Tested around sealed area of exterior perimeter only	Passed (no leakage observed) at 575 Pascal (12 psf)	Water leakage through window glazing was noted, but not around installation
Tested entire wall	Failed (seepage observed) at 145 pascal (3.13 psf)—14 minutes into test	Water seepage through block was observed in unsealed area

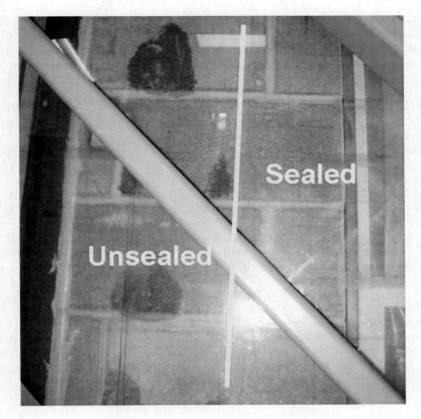

FIG. 17—*FMA/AAMA 200 second phase wall test results—water seepage through the internal portion of the block at unsealed area, but not at in the sealed area.*

3.   The installation methodology detailed in FMA/AAMA 200 for frontal flange windows in a surface barrier concrete block wall system resulted in installations that did not leak at the criterion pressure. An effective seal however between the buck members (used to anchor the window unit) and the surrounding block wall was found to be important. In contrast to the leak resistance of installations that were in accord with FMA/AAMA 200, unsealed portions of the block wall exhibited seepage at the lowest differential pressure included in the test protocol. A "whole wall" approach to water management thus appears necessary.

These test results presented in this paper are preliminary. They are based on testing of assemblies fabricated in a laboratory setting. Tests of field installations are planned.

Acknowledgments

This work represents the efforts of several dedicated people involved in the Fenestration Manufacturers Association (FMA) Installation Committee, which includes representative window and door manufacturers, flashing and sealant manufacturers, installation service providers, and building officials in the Florida region. In particular, the leadership of Mark Daniels of Sika, who originally formed and chaired the committee; Monte Jones from 84 Lumber, Vice Chair of the FMA Installation Committee; Freddie Cole from General Aluminum, President of the FMA; and Dick Wilhelm, Executive Director of FMA is noted. In addition, Barry Hardman from National Building Science was instrumental in developing the content of the installation practices and provided much guidance on wall system testing and evaluation.

This effort also benefited from the collaboration between FMA and AAMA through a joint steering committee, who took an active role in the installations and wall tests reported here. Members of this joint committee include Bill Emley from MI Windows and Doors and President of Southeast AAMA, Larry Livermore, AAMA Technical Standards Manager, Scott Warner from Architectural Testing Institute and Vice President of Southeast AAMA, Sigi Valentin, Southeast AAMA Regional Director, Monte Jones from 84 Lumber and Vice Chair of the FMA Installation Committee, Heath Cobb from WinDoor, Tom Zuppa from Sika, Dennis Chappell from NuAir, Freddie Cole of General Aluminum and President of FMA, and the author.

Expert installation support was provided by Barbara O'Rourke, Senior Research Engineer and Jessica Conlon, Senior R & D Technologist with DuPont Building Innovations.

And finally, the wall tests described in this paper were performed by Architectural Testing Institute, under the direction of Tim McGill and Scott Warner, who sponsored this testing effort. Many of the pictures and observations were taken from reports by Tim McGill.

References

[1]   ASTM Standard E2112-07, "Standard Practice for Installation of Exterior Windows, Doors and Skylights," Vol. 4.12, *Annual Book of ASTM Standards*, ASTM International, West Conshohocken, PA.
[2]   RDH Building Engineering Limited, Vancouver, BC, *Water Penetration Resistance of Windows—Study of Manufacturing, Building Design, Installation and Maintenance Factors*, submitted to Canada Mortgage and Housing Corporation, Ottawa, Ontario, December 2002.
[3]   Partnership for Advancing Technology in Housing (PATH), *Durability by Design, A Guide for Residential Builders and Designers*, NAHB Research Center, Inc., Upper Marlboro, MD., May 2002.
[4]   Lstiburek, J. W., "Rainwater Management Performance of New Constructed Residential Building Enclosures During August and September 2004, Home Builders Association of Metro Orlando and the Florida Home Builders Association Report" Building Science Corporation, www.buildingscience.com, January 2005.
[5]   ASTM, Standard E2266-04, "Standard Guide for Design and Construction of Low-Rise Frame Building Wall Systems to resist Water Intrusion," Vol. 4.12, *Annual Book of ASTM Standards*, ASTM International, West Conshohocken, PA, 2004.
[6]   FMA/AAMA 100-XX, Draft "Standard Practice for the Installation of Windows with Flanges or Mounting Fins in Wood Frame Construction," www.fmausaonline.org,

2007.
[7]   FMA/AAMA 200-XX, Draft "Standard Practice for the Installation of Windows with Frontal Flanges for Surface Barrier Masonry Construction," www.fmausaonline.org, 2007.
[8]   ASTM Standard E331-00, "Standard Test Method for Water Penetration of Exterior Windows, Doors, and Curtain Walls by Uniform Static Air Pressure Difference," Vol. 4.11, *Annual Book of ASTM Standards*, ASTM International, West Conshohocken, PA, 2000.
[9]   ASTM Standard E2264-05, "Standard Practice for Determining the Effect of Temperature Cycling on Fenestration Products," Vol. 4.12, *Annual Book of ASTM Standards*, ASTM International, West Conshohocken, PA.

Reprinted from JAI, Vol. 6, No. 10
doi:10.1520/JAI102695
Available online at www.astm.org/JAI

Jessica S. Conlon,[1] *Barbara K. O'Rourke,*[2] *James D. Katsaros,*[3]
and Theresa A. Weston[4]

A Robust Installation for Brick-Mold Windows and Doors Using Self-Adhered Flashing

ABSTRACT: Current standardized practices for window and door installation methodologies are typically based on fenestration products that feature integral flanges that form a continuous surface to mount and integrate the fenestration product to the water resistive barrier (WRB)/drainage plane of the wall. While these types of units form the majority of fenestration products available, there are several "non-integral" flange type systems that are also utilized in the construction industry. These include "brick-mold" windows and doors, field-applied flange windows, and non-flanged "box" windows. Due to the discontinuity between the mounting system and the window frame, these types of fenestration systems pose special challenges to achieve a robust, continuous, and water-resistant integration between the fenestration product and the wall, which is not adequately addressed by ASTM E2112, "Standard Practice for Installation of Exterior Windows, Doors, and Skylights" or other standardized methods. The paper describes an installation method for windows and doors with factory-applied brick-mold exterior casings and presents the performance characteristics in laboratory testing of units installed using the method.

KEYWORDS: flashing performance, brick-mold window, flanged window, non-integral flanged window, fenestration system, water resistant, moisture intrusion

Manuscript received August 26, 2009; accepted for publication August 28, 2009; published online November 2009.

[1] Senior R&D Technologist, DuPont Building Innovations, Richmond, VA 23261.
[2] Senior Research Engineer, DuPont Building Innovations, Wilmington, DE 19880.
[3] Ph.D., Flashing Systems Development Leader, DuPont Building Innovations, Richmond, VA 23261.
[4] Ph.D., Research Fellow, DuPont Building Innovations, Richmond, VA 23261.

Cite as: Conlon, J. S., O'Rourke, B. K., Katsaros, J. D. and Weston, T. A., "A Robust Installation for Brick-Mold Windows and Doors Using Self-Adhered Flashing," *J. ASTM Intl.*, Vol. 6, No. 10. doi:10.1520/JAI102695.

Introduction

Over the years, solutions have been developed for flashing systems for factory-applied flanged windows using self-adhered flashing systems. Studies have shown that butyl based self-adhered flashing systems are particularly effective and maintain an effective moisture seal through accelerated environmental exposure [1]. Many installation methods using self-adhered flashings have been published [2]. However, effective self-adhered flashing solutions for non-flanged windows and doors, specifically brick-mold and field-applied flanged windows and doors, have remained challenging. In the past, sealants have been used to guard against moisture intrusion issues with these window and door types. However, sealant joints at this interface have been proven ineffective and difficult to maintain, as supported by the Durability by Design guideline published by the Partnership of Advancing Technology in Housing, which reports that "caulks and sealants are generally not a suitable substitute for flashing" [3]. Market trends show an increase in the use of self-adhered flexible flashings. Current standards adequately address the use of self-adhered flexible flashing with integral flanged windows. However, there still exists a need for robust solutions using these products in with windows and doors without integral flanges.

Studies have been conducted to investigate several potential methods for installing fenestration units lacking integral mounting flanges; none of the methods studied previously were found to be effective [4]. In previous laboratory testing, moisture intrusion was observed at brick-mold joint interfaces (where the brick-mold casings joint, and where they interface with the frame of the unit). The previous testing furthermore found that after installed windows were subjected to thermal cycling, the miter joints opened most likely due to changes in moisture content of the wood. Opened joints provide paths for water entry. Although sealant could be used in these applications, this would only be a temporary solution. Over time, with movement of the building coupled with heating and cooling cycles causing expansion and contraction of joints, sealants placed in these areas would be expected to succumb to the repetitive dimensional strains associated with joint movement and to weathering factors such as heat and ultraviolet exposure that result in their chemical degradation.

This paper describes an installation method that relies on use of a specially configured self-adhered flashing to provide a durable and reliable seal around brick-mold windows and doors. The method does not involve the use of sealants. The self-adhering flashing is concealed from exterior view and thus is not exposed to ultraviolet radiation in completed construction.

Development of Improved Installation Methods and Performance Testing

In 2005, AAMA developed a test method to qualify flashing installations [5]. This test method includes the use of water spray concurrent with application of air pressure differential. It also includes thermal cycling and structural testing. It is similar to a protocol for evaluating an installed window/wall system developed by Weston et al. [6]. The protocol developed by Weston et al. [6]was used in the evaluations discussed in this paper. The testing protocol and installation techniques used are described below.

Experimental Method

Flashing and Window Installation Details

The proposed installation methods were evaluated for performance and durability using the protocol outlined in Fig. 1. The fenestration units selected for inclusion in the study were typical commercially available products. Not all products available in the marketplace were included in this investigation. Windows and doors were installed in mock-up wall sections; the installations incorporated the specially configured self-adhering flashing.

Windows were installed in 1.52×2.29 m^2 (60×90 in.^{2}) walls with oriented strand board (OSB) sheathing and wood studs 0.41 m (16 in.) on-center. The brick-mold windows used for this test had factory-installed wood composite brick molding.

Doors were installed in 1.52×2.41 m^2 (60×95 in.^{2}) walls with OSB sheathing and woods studs 0.41 m (16 in.) on-center. The brick-mold doors used for this test had factory-installed primed wood brick molding. Descriptions of the walls tested are shown in Tables 1 and 2.

Walls 21A through 24A all used the new concept of the prefabricated flexible flange self-adhered flashing. The flexible flange self-adhered flashing concept consists of two pieces of non-extendable butyl adhesive flashing that is joined by 25 mm (1 in.) of overlapping butyl adhesive one face up one face down (see Fig. 2).

The water resistive barrier (WRB) and the windows were installed according to the manufacturers' installation guidelines. For walls 21A–24A, the prefabricated flexible flange self-adhered flashing concept was installed at the head on the window such that approximately 25 mm (1 in.) of the flashing was adhered to the back of the brick mold (see Fig. 3).

Walls 5 and 6 also used the new concept of the prefabricated flexible flange self-adhered flashing. The flexible flange self-adhered flashing concept consists of two pieces of non-extendable butyl adhesive flashing that is joined by 25 mm (1 in.) of overlapping butyl adhesive one face up one face down (see Fig. 2).

The WRB and the doors were installed according to the manufacturer's installation guidelines. For walls 5 and 6, the prefabricated flexible flange self-adhered flashing concept was installed at the head on the window such that approximately 25 mm (1 in.) of the flashing was adhered to the back of the brick mold.

Testing Protocol

Air infiltration and exfiltration were tested using the standard ASTM Standard E283, Standard Method for Determining Rate of Air Leakage Through Exterior Windows, Curtain Walls, and Doors Under Specified Pressure Differences

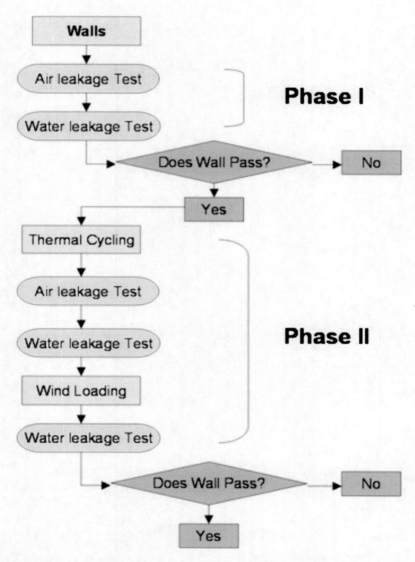

FIG. 1—*Outline of test protocol used to evaluate flashing installation performance and durability. Installations must pass phase I to continue to phase II. Phase II is conducted in its entirety regardless of whether water leakage is observed in the test after thermal cycling and before wind loading.*

Across the Specimen, with pressure differences of 25, 75, and 300 Pa (approximately 0.56, 1.56, and 6.24 psf, respectively) [7]. Air leakage measurements are not necessarily comparable between installations, as leakage through the window-wall interface was not isolated from leakage through the window itself or from leakage through the rest of the wall. Some installations incorporated

TABLE 1—*Window flashing installation details per wall for brick-mold windows.*

Wall Number	Window Type— Description and Size	Installation Order— WRB Before or After Window	Sill Flashing/ Detail	Jamb Flashing/ Detail	Head Flashing/ Detail
21A	Brick-mold window 86.4×101.6 cm^2 (34×40 in.^{2})	WRB prior to window installation	Elastomeric nonwoven composite flashing; adhesive foam tape was installed under flexible flashing as back dam	Flexible flange flashing flange was completed after window installation	Metal drip cap was adhered to the exposed butyl flange corners at the head prior to completing flexible flange, WRB skip taped over drip cap
22A	Brick-mold window 86.4×101.6 cm^2 (34×40 in.^{2})	WRB prior to window installation	Elastomeric nonwoven composite flashing with aluminum angle under flexible flashing as back dam	Flexible flange prefabricated— adhered to back of brick mold, with adhesive attachment extending to unit jambs prior to window installation	Exposed butyl at head was cut away and sealed with 15.2–20.3 cm (6–8 in.) piece of non-extendable butyl flashing no drip cap was used

TABLE 1— (Continued.)

Wall Number	Window Type—Description and Size	Installation Order—WRB Before or After Window	Sill Flashing/Detail	Jamb Flashing/Detail	Head Flashing/Detail
23A	Brick-mold window 86.4 × 101.6 cm² (34 × 40 in.²)	WRB after window installation	Elastomeric nonwoven composite flashing with aluminum angle under flexible flashing as back dam	Flexible flange prefabricated—adhered to back of brick mold, with adhesive attachment extending to unit jambs prior to window installation	Exposed butyl at head was cut away and sealed with 15.2–20.3 cm (6–8 in.) piece of non-extendable butyl flashing metal drip cap then 10.2 cm (4 in.) non-extendable butyl flashing was installed over the cap, WRB skip taped over drip cap

TABLE 1— (Continued.)

Wall Number	Window Type— Description and Size	Installation Order— WRB Before or After Window	Sill Flashing/ Detail	Jamb Flashing/ Detail	Head Flashing/ Detail
24A	Brick-mold window 86.4×101.6 cm² (34×40 in.²)	WRB after window installation	Elastomeric nonwoven composite flashing with aluminum angle under flexible flashing as back dam	Flexible flange prefabricated-installed adhered to back of brick mold, with adhesive attachment extending to unit jambs prior to window installation	The flexible flange was prefabricated in a "T" configuration; the bottom of the T was the width of the window minus the brick mold

TABLE 2—*Door flashing installation details per wall for brick-mold doors.*

Wall Number	Window Type— Description and Size	Installation Order— WRB Before or After Window	Sill Flashing/ Detail	Jamb Flashing/ Detail	Head Flashing/ Detail
5	Brick-mold door 91.4×203.2 cm² (36×80 in.²)	WRB prior to window installation	Vinyl sill pan with sealant	Flexible flange prefabricated— adhered to back of brick mold, with adhesive attachment extending to unit jambs prior to window installation	Flexible flange prefabricated-installed prior to window installation
6	Brick-mold door 91.4×203.2 cm² (36×80 in.²)	WRB prior to window installation	Barrier method using sealant only	Flexible flange prefabricated— adhered to back of brick mold, with adhesive attachment extending to unit jambs prior to window installation	Flexible flange prefabricated-installed prior to window installation

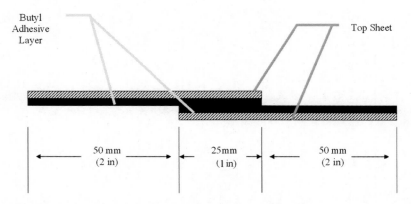

FIG. 2—*Illustration of prefabricated flexible flange concept. (Note: Illustration is not to scale.)*

sill pan flashings with back dams, whereas others did not. Incorporation of a sill pan with a back dam greatly influenced measured air leakage. The air leakage results were mainly used to monitor sealant durability through thermal cycling [6].

After testing the walls for air leakage, ASTM Standard E331, Standard Test Method for Water Penetration of Exterior Windows, Curtain Walls, and Doors by Uniform Static Air Pressure Difference, was used to test for water infiltration [8]. Water infiltration pressures used for testing walls 21A–24A were set at 25 and 75 Pa (approximately 0.56 and 1.56 psf, respectively) for 15-min periods

FIG. 3—*Prefabricated flexible flange in process of being installed behind brick mold.*

TABLE 3—*Water leakage test results (ASTM E 331) at 25 Pa (0.56 psf) for brick-mold windows before and after durability testing.*

Wall Number	Before Thermal Cycling	After Thermal Cycling	After Wind Loading
21A	No leak	No leak	No leak
22A	No leak	No leak	No leak
23A	No leak	No leak	No leak
24A	No leak	No leak	No leak

each, and visual inspections were conducted during the test. Water infiltration pressures used for testing walls 5 and 6 were set at 25, 75, and 300 Pa (approximately 0.56, 1.56, and 6.24 psf, respectively) for 15-min periods each, and visual inspections were conducted during the test. Once the walls were tested for air leakage and water leakage as installed, the walls were thermal cycled to help understand the long-term performance of the walls. Walls were subjected to four 6-h cycles of thermal cycling (−17.8–71.1°C or 0–160°F) per day for 7 days.

After the walls were thermal cycled, they were retested for air leakage and water leakage. Then the walls were subjected to wind loading at 500 Pa (approximately 10.4 psf) according to ASTM Standard E330, Standard Test Method for Structural Performance of Exterior Windows, Curtain Walls, and Doors by Uniform Static Air Pressure Difference, and retested for water leakage using the same pressures set for testing the walls as installed prior to thermal cycling [9]. After the final air, water, and structural testing, the walls were disassembled to better characterize water leakage, which occurred during spray testing, whether or not it was observable in the mock-up in an assembled state.

Experimental Results

Brick-Mold Windows (Walls 21A–24A)

Test results for the windows installed using the method under investigation are provided in Tables 3 and 4. The windows used in this testing had factory-installed brick-mold casings; the casings were painted with primer paint, and the joints in the casings were generally caulked. The primed surfaces of the casings were penetrated by many power-driven fasteners (used to attach the

TABLE 4—*Water leakage test results (ASTM E331) at 75 Pa (1.56 psf) for brick-mold windows before and after durability testing.*

Wall Number	Before Thermal Cycling	After Thermal Cycling	After Wind Loading
21A	No leak	No leak	No leak
22A	No leak	No leak	No leak
23A	No leak	No leak	No leak
24A	No leak	No leak	No leak

FIG. 4—*Illustration of gap in brick-mold frame after thermal cycling.*

casing members to the window frame) and by fasteners used at the top corners of the units to hold mitered casing joints together. Disassembly after phase II testing (which included thermal cycling) commonly revealed gaps at joints between the casing members of the window. These gaps are potential entry points for water in addition to air leakage (see Fig. 4).

Brick-Mold Doors (Walls 5 and 6)

As implied previously, the doors used in this test had factory-installed brick-mold casings. Both the casings and the door jambs were primed with primer paint. As with the exterior casings of the windows included in this investigation, the primed surfaces of the door casings (brick molds) were penetrated by many power-driven fasteners, and gaps were often observed at joints between the casings. The gaps between casing members were potential passageways for water entry as well as for air leakage.

Walls 5 and 6 used the same concept of the prefabricated flexible flange self-adhered flashing as used with the brick-mold window installation.

The only observed leaks occurred at the adjustable threshold of the door (Tables 5 and 6). The type of door included in this investigation is not designed to resist water leakage at the threshold at the default water spray rate of ASTM Standard E331 concurrent with 300 Pa (6.24 psf) (or more) of simulated wind pressure. This suggests the importance of a properly designed and installed sill pan, in conjunction with a functional flashing installation method. No leaks were observed on the head or jambs of the rough opening either during the testing or upon disassembly.

TABLE 5—*Water leakage test results (ASTM E331) at 75 Pa (1.56 psf) for brick-mold doors before and after durability testing.*

Wall Number	Before Thermal Cycling	After Thermal Cycling	After Wind Loading
5	No leak	No leak	Door threshold leak
6	No leak	No leak	Door threshold leak

Conclusions and Recommendations

System Water Management Performance

All variations in the prefabricated flexible flange self-adhered flashing concept used on the jambs and head of the brick-mold window and door installations performed well. It is evident, based on the water intrusion results for the doors evaluated, that leakage at entry door thresholds is a significant potential problem. An appropriately designed and installed sill pan is a potential way to address this problem, and in many cases may be the preferred solution to it.

Brick-mold window and door designs are challenging to install in such a manner that objectionable water penetration around their perimeters is avoided. It is important to protect the rough opening because it is reasonable to assume that eventually the window will leak and water will infiltrate the rough opening space. The sill should be flashed with an elastomeric self-adhered flashing or properly designed and installed sill pan.

In the testing performed for this study, a prefabricated flexible flange self-adhered flashing that consisted of a double-sided butyl adhesive proved effective at providing a seal at the head and jambs of windows and doors with factory-applied exterior brick-mold casings. The flexible flange self-adhered flashing is installed as three separate pieces that integrate with each other in a shingle-lap manner. The first piece is installed on the back of the brick-mold casing at the head of the unit and, subsequently, pieces are installed on the back of the casings at the jambs of the window or door prior to the installation of the window or door into the rough opening (see Fig. 5). As the flashing pieces are installed on the backs of the casing members, this order of installation is necessary to provide shingle-lapping of the flashing pieces. Each piece of self-adhering flashing is extended from the casing to the frame of the window; this forms a watertight seal between the casing members and the frame. After the unit (door or window) is installed, the flexible flange is integrated with the WRB. It is important that the WRB be shingled over the head flashing (see Fig. 6).

TABLE 6—*Water leakage test results (ASTM E331) at 300 Pa (6.24 psf) for brick-mold doors before and after durability testing.*

Wall Number	Before Thermal Cycling	After Thermal Cycling	After Wind Loading
5	Door threshold leak	Door threshold leak	Door threshold leak
6	Door threshold leak	Door threshold leak	Door threshold leak

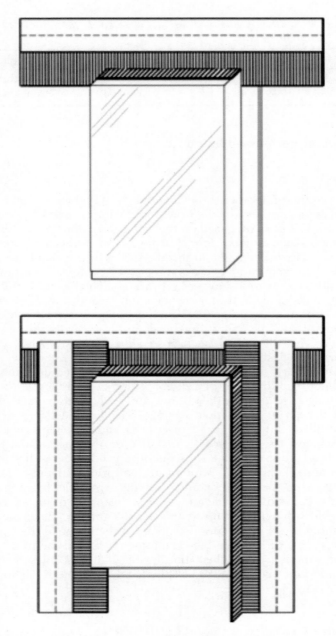

FIG. 5—*Illustration of how to install prefabricated flexible flange to back of window/ door. (Note: Illustration not to scale.)*

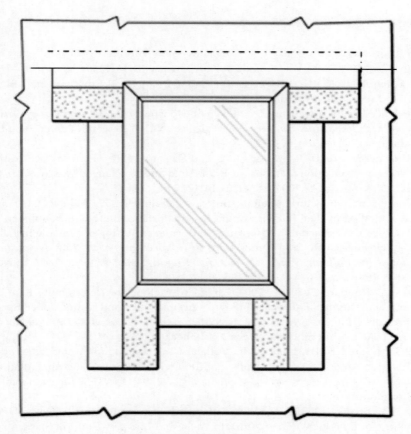

FIG. 6—*Completed installation of prefabricated flexible flange with integration to WRB.* (*Note: Illustration not to scale.*)

It is recommended that testing be conducted to investigate the installation of other types of windows using the self-adhered flashing flexible flange concept addressed in this paper. This flashing material concept may be applicable in the installation of windows with field-applied flanges and in the installation of windows with damaged integral flanges.

Testing a wall system as a whole is important. It is critical to test an integrated system in order to understand the performance of the system. A system should be tested as installed and also tested for durability in order to understand how all products may perform in the field over time. It is also important to understand how various installations perform with different types of windows and to understand that different installation methods or different products may be necessary for different styles of windows.

References

[1]   Katsaros, J. D., "Adhesive Characterization and Durability of Self-Adhered Flash-
        ings," *J. ASTM Int.*, Vol. 2, issue 10, 2002, paper ID JAI12494.
[2]   Lstiburek, J. W., *Water Management Guide*, Energy and Environmental Building
        Association, Eden Prairie, MN, 2006.
[3]   Partnership for Advancing Technology in Housing (PATH), *Durability by Design, A
        Guide for Residential Builders and Designers*, NAHB Research Center, Inc., Upper
        Marlboro, MD, May 2002.
[4]   Crowder-Moore, B. J., Weston, T. A., and Katsaros, J. D., "Performance Testing of
        Flashing Installation Methods for Brick Mold and Nonflanged Windows," *J. ASTM
        Int.*, Vol. 3, issue 1, 2006, paper ID JAI12490.
[5]   American Architectural Manufacturers Association 504-05, "Voluntary Laboratory
        Test Method to Qualify Fenestration Installation Procedures," Schaumburg, IL.
[6]   Weston, T. A., Pascual, X., Herrin, J."Performance Testing of Window Installation
        and Flashing in Hot and Humid Climates," *Proceedings of the 13th Symposium on
        Improving Building Systems in Hot and Humid Climates*, Texas A&M University,
        2002, Houston, TX.
[7]   ASTM Standard E283–04, 2004, "Standard Method for Determining Rate of Air
        Leakage Through Exterior Windows, Curtain Walls, and Doors Under Specified
        Pressure Differences Across the Specimen," *Annual Book of ASTM Standards*, Vol.
        04.11, ASTM International, West Conshohocken, PA.
[8]   ASTM Standard E331–00, 2000, "Standard Test Method for Water Penetration of
        Exterior Windows, Curtain Walls, and Doors by Uniform Static Air Pressure Dif-
        ference," *Annual Book of ASTM Standards*, Vol. 04.11, ASTM International, West
        Conshohocken, PA.
[9]   ASTM Standard E330–02, 2002, "Standard Test Method for Structural Perfor-
        mance of Exterior Windows, Curtain Walls, and Doors by Uniform Static Air Pres-
        sure Difference," *Annual Book of ASTM Standards*, Vol. 04.11, ASTM International,
        West Conshohocken, PA.

Reprinted from JAI, Vol. 6, No. 8
doi:10.1520/JAI101428
Available online at www.astm.org/JAI

M. A. Lacasse,[1] *M. Rousseau,*[2] *S. M. Cornick,*[2] *M. Armstrong,*[2] *G. Ganapathy,*[2] *M. Nicholls,*[2] *and M. F. Williams*[3]

Laboratory Tests of Water Penetration through Wall-Window Interfaces Based on U.S. Residential Window Installation Practice

ABSTRACT: Inadequate detailing practice and defective installation of windows has accounted for a significant number of premature failures of the building envelope. This has spurred the development of alternative construction details to manage water intrusion at the wall-window interface. Laboratory investigations focused on assessing the effectiveness of wall-window interface details to manage rainwater intrusion in the wall assembly have provided an effective way to obtain useful information on the varying performance of different interface details. Previous studies undertaken to investigate the effectiveness of details typically used in wood frame low-rise wall assemblies have shown the degree to which different details manage rainwater intrusion and the extent of fault tolerance of such systems. This paper reports on results obtained from laboratory testing of two sets of wall-window interface details and variations on their implementation, that are representative of residential and light commercial window installation practice in the

Manuscript received September 7, 2007; accepted for publication June 30, 2009; published online September 2009.
[1] Institute for Research in Construction, National Research Council Canada, 1200 Montreal Rd., Building M-20, Ottawa, ON, K1A 0R6, Canada, e-mail: Michael.Lacasse@nrc-cnrc.gc.ca
[2] Institute for Research in Construction, National Research Council Canada, 1200 Montreal Rd., Building M-24, Ottawa, ON, K1A 0R6, Canada.
[3] Building Diagnostics Technology, Maple Glen, PA, 19002-2312.

Cite as: Lacasse, M. A., Rousseau, M., Cornick, S. M., Armstrong, M., Ganapathy, G., Nicholls, M. and Williams, M. F., "Laboratory Tests of Water Penetration through Wall-Window Interfaces Based on U.S. Residential Window Installation Practice," *J. ASTM Intl.*, Vol. 6, No. 8. doi:10.1520/JAI101428.

United States. Results from these tests indicate that the window installations details of the type assessed in this study are adequate to manage even the most significant rainfall events as might occur in North America. It was also demonstrated that window installation designs that do not permit drainage from the sill are vulnerable to excessive water retention during significant wind-driven rain events. Additionally, critical elements for achieving functional window installation details included: Sill-pan flashing with watertight corners; openings along the interface between the sill and window flange to permit water drainage; and continuity of the air barrier system at the interface with the window frame and window. Such designs could be adopted for climate zones having heightened wind-driven rain loads such as the coastal areas of the United States subjected to severe storm events. The work is limited to evaluating the response of wall-window interface details to simulated wind-driven rain and water penetration; it does not address hygrothermal effects.

KEYWORDS: laboratory tests, rainwater intrusion, wall-window interface, watertightness, window installation details, wind-driven rain, nail-flange windows

Introduction

A key functional requirement for exterior walls is, evidently, the control of rain penetration. To effectively control penetration the appropriate design and installation of components is important. The lack of attention to either the detailing of components or their installation may result in the premature deterioration of wall elements. Inadequate detailing and defective installation of windows has accounted for a significant number of premature failures of the building envelope as has been evident across North America in recent years [1–4]. For example, a survey of building envelope failures in the coastal region of British Columbia indicated that 25 % of the moisture problems associated with water ingress into wall assemblies were directly attributed to penetration through windows or the wall-window interface [1]. However, the issue of building envelope failure is not one that is limited to coastal climates given the concern evident throughout North America.

For example, the issue of premature failure of the building envelope has been apparent in the state of Minnesota [3], where it is reported by the building inspection division of the town of Woodbury that homes built since 1990 were experiencing major durability problems. Specifically, 276 of 670 stucco homes built in Woodbury in 1999 had failed (ca. 41 %); the primary cause for failure were window leaks, lack of kickout flashing, and improper deck flashing above the wood framing [3].

The state of California has taken interest in understanding the level of risk afforded by different window installation methods and has recently reported on a test program to evaluate the performance of different window installation details [4]. The overall goal was to perform a systematic laboratory evaluation of specifically identified conventional and innovative residential building materials, assemblies, and construction practices. The laboratory evaluations were designed to provide experimental evidence of moisture loading, propensity for mold formation, and potential performance improvements associated with innovative building assemblies and construction practices.

Clearly the problem of water penetration at window openings persists and not only in coastal areas for which the perception is that climate loads are very severe. Although coastal climates may indeed be severe, details that promote the entrapment of water and that are not fault tolerant are likewise susceptible to premature deterioration, even in areas of apparently reduced "climate loads." Carll [5] made the point regarding the need for additional information related to moisture loads on buildings and the need to characterize the degree of water entry in relation to such loads.

The vulnerability of the wall-window interface to water entry was identified in two recent studies [6,7], which were conducted on behalf of the Canada Mortgage and Housing Corporation. Although a wide range of factors was found to contribute to water leakage, the principal paths for leakage were those associated with the wall-window interface. Two common leakage paths were identified: (1) Through the window assembly extending into the adjacent wall assembly; and (2) through the window to wall interface extending into the adjacent wall assembly. The criteria for water penetration control found in CSA A440 B rating performance [6] do not identify leakage associated with either of these leakage paths. Moreover, testing of the installed window assembly is not a requirement of the standard.

There appears to be considerable concern for more in depth understanding of the behavior of window installation methods over a range of climate loads. To this end, a laboratory investigation was undertaken by the Institute for Research in Construction to evaluate different wall-window interface details and their ability to manage rainwater entry. The approach adopted in the "wall-window interface" consortium project provided a means of assessing the robustness of specified window installation details by considering what occurs when, for example, the jointing product fails, the window leaks, or the assembly has reduced airtightness. Selected results from an initial phase of the project that focused on Canadian window installation practice were reported in [8] and [9].

In this paper, results from a subsequent phase are presented that focus on the evaluation of window installation practice for low-rise wood frame construction in the United States. Specifically, results are given from a laboratory evaluation of the air and watertightness of a select set of wall-window interface details. The details were based on variations of a method for installing windows with mounting flanges that is outlined in ASTM E2112 [10].

An overview of the experimental approach is provided that includes a generic description of the test specimen, a summary description of the test facility, and a brief outline of the test protocol. Thereafter, installation details, and variations thereof, are given specifically to the wall for which results are reported in this paper.

Water entry characteristics for the different wall-window interface configurations are presented, and the effectiveness of the different details is discussed. Insights are offered into the relative importance in respect to air and watertightness afforded the different components incorporated in the various installation methods.

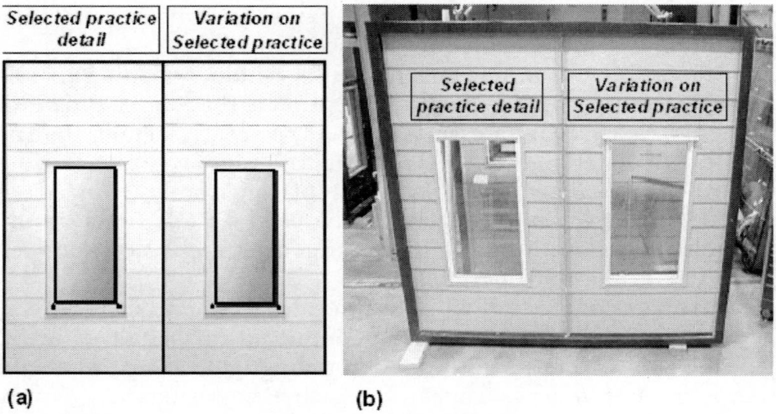

FIG. 1—(a) Schematic of front elevation of 2.44 m by 2.44 m (8 ft by 8 ft) specimen showing location of 600 mm by 1200 mm (2 ft by 4 ft) windows; one-half of specimen might be representative of installation details used in current practice whereas the other one-half a variation on that practice; (b) photo of a completed specimen clad with hardboard siding.

Experimental Approach to Evaluating Water Management of Window Interface Details

The experimental approach adopted for evaluating these sets of window interface details has been previously developed by Lacasse and coworkers in [8] and [9] and was based on similar water penetration tests undertaken on different wall assemblies as described in [11]. Although watertightness evaluations determined from laboratory tests simulating wind-driven rain events do not directly relate to expected long-term performance of the assemblies, these can provide a linkage to the response of assemblies to specific rain events for which the recurrence period is known. Establishing the response of wall assemblies to simulated events is an indirect means of determining the likely risk of water entry over a given period for a specific climate region. Such type of evaluations may also provide some measure of the expected risk to water entry and fault tolerance of different installation methods in extreme conditions [12].

In the context of evaluating the watertightness of wall-window interface installation details, the ability of specific details to manage rainwater is determined on the basis of air leakage and water penetration tests and the response of the respective details, and details incorporating deficiencies, when subjected to simulated conditions of wind-driven rain.

Generic Description of Test Specimen

Wall specimens were designed to permit side-by-side comparison of two wall-window interfaces (Fig. 1). The wall specimens were intended to be the representative of low-rise residential and light commercial construction except that they used clear materials in place of interior gypsum board or wood-based sheathing. The specimens consisted of 38 by 138 mm (nominal 2 in. by 4 in.) wood studs, transparent acrylic sheet installed against the inside surfaces of the studs [in place of gypsum board, and serving as the principal element of the air barrier system (ABS)], acrylic sheets installed against the exterior surfaces of the studs (in place of plywood or oriented strandboard sheathing), a sheathing membrane [also known as a water resistive barrier (WRB)], and exterior horizontal lap siding. The siding was installed either directly against the WRB or against a drainage medium [proprietary drainage mat (PDM) or a proprietary WRB with attached drainage strips]. The clear acrylic sheets permitted observation of water penetration past the WRB. The acrylic sheets that served as sheathing had a 3 mm (1/8 in.) horizontal joint at mid height; this was consistent with the manner in which 2.4 m (48 in.) wide wood-based sheathing panels are usually installed (where the long dimension of panels is perpendicular to the studs).

Each wall specimen included two openings of 635 mm by 1245 mm (25 in. by 4 ft 1 in.); in each opening, a 600 mm by 1200 mm window (nominal size: 2 ft by 4 ft) was installed. Wall-window interface details at the window head, jambs, and sill differed. One of the windows was installed as a "selected practice detail," and the other as a variation on the selected practice detail. In one of the test specimens, the selected practice detail was representative of a common current practice (it was consistent with an installation method outlined in ASTM E2112 [10] for flanged windows).

The windows were fixed (non-operable) windows, made of either wood or polyvinyl chloride (PVC), with integral mounting flanges. The windows were fabricated in Canada; windows having the same (or appreciably similar) configuration and style are commonly used in new residential construction across North America.

The entry of water around either window opening was collected in troughs located beneath the respective sills. Water was also collected at the base of the wall behind the cladding. Additional details regarding the test specimen configuration specific to the results reported are provided below.

Description of Test Apparatus—Dynamic Wind and Wall Test Facility (DWTF)

The dynamic wind and wall test facility (DWTF), previously used to subject similar specimens to simulated wind-driven rain conditions [11], was utilized for the investigations reported in this manuscript. The facility is capable of subjecting full-scale test specimens (nominal size 2.44 m by 2.44 m; 8 ft by 8 ft) to both static or dynamic pressure fluctuations of over 2 kPa [41.8 psf (pounds/ft^2)][4] and water spray rates ranging between 0.8 and 8 L/min·m^2 (1.2 and 12 gal/ft^2·h). The dynamic (wind pulsing) capabilities of the facility were not used in the investigations reported in this manuscript; static pressure conditions were instead investigated in this study. The facility provided a means to assess the air leakage characteristics of the specimens. Its pressure regulated water spray system was used in each of two formats. For one of the test speci-

---

[4]Equivalents in Imperial units are provided at least once on a page, but not in every instance.

mens, water was applied in full-spray format, (where the water was deposited evenly across the front of the specimen through an array of spray nozzles). For the other test specimens, water was applied at the top of the specimen from a water header pipe, having the capacity of the entire array of nozzles, and from which the lower portions of the specimen were wetted by the downward flow of water.

Summary of Test Protocol

The test protocol was adapted from previous work [11] and a review of wind-driven rain loads as might be experienced across North America [13,14], that also took into consideration existing North American water penetration test standards such as ASTM E331 [15] (Standard test method for water penetration of exterior windows) and CSA A440.4 [16]. The protocol involved spray exposure at a series of spray rates (water deposition rates), and at each spray rate over a series of air pressure differentials across the assembly [13]. A more detailed description of the protocol is provided in Refs 8 and 9 but the essential elements are:

1. Characterization of air leakage and pressure equalization potential of the wall assembly—Air leakage characterization was completed for two nominal air leakage conditions: 0.3 $L/s \cdot m^2$ (at 75 Pa pressure differential) and 0.8 $L/s \cdot m^2$; these are referred to as the 0.3 ABS and 0.8 ABS conditions, respectively. Description regarding how the specified air leakage rates of the ABSs were attained is provided in a subsequent section.

2. Water penetration without deficiency in static mode at specified spray rates of 0.8, 1.6, and 3.4 $L/min \cdot m^2$ (1.2, 2.4, 5 $gal/ft^2 \cdot h$) with pressure variations from 0 to 700 Pa (14.6 psf) and nominal ABS leakage of 0.3 and 0.8 L/s-m^2 at 75 Pa (0.06 and 0.16 cfm/ft^2 at 1.57 psf).

3. Water entry with deficiency in static mode at spray rates varying from 0.8 to 3.4 $L/min \cdot m^2$ (1.2 to 5 $gal/ft^2 \cdot h$) and pressure variations from 0 to 700 Pa (14.6 psf) and nominal ABS leakage of 0.3 and 0.8 $L/s \cdot m^2$ at 75 Pa (0.06 and 0.16 cfm/ft^2 at 1.57 psf).

Specimens were thus subjected to simulated wind-driven rain conditions for specified periods of time; these conditions replicated the main features of rain events. Rates of water entry at the subsill and behind the cladding were determined by measuring the rate of water collected from these locations as well as that portion that entered the window at the interface between the window lite and the frame. The use of the facility together with the test protocol permitted comparisons of water entry results among the different wall-window interface details.

Selection of Wall-Window Detailing

This manuscript reports on the middle phase of a three-phase project involving evaluation of wall-window interfaces. This phase of the project was designated phase B. It addressed installation methodology that is employed, or might be employed in low-rise, residential, and wood frame construction in the United States.

More specifically, this manuscript concerns evaluation of two wall test specimens, each clad with hardboard lap siding and each with two identical flanged windows. The first of these specimens, designated B-W1, featured an installation that was in accord with method A1 of ASTM E2112 [10], and an alternative installation method that incorporated a sill pan and provision for drainage between the sheathing and the siding. As will be discussed later, the test results for test specimen B-W1 suggested that the alternate installation method had advantages relative to the ASTM E2112 A1 method.

The results of tests on a similar test specimen (designated B-W2), which for reasons of brevity are not reported in this manuscript, likewise suggested that installation methodology that incorporated a sill pan and provision for drainage between the cladding and the siding was advantageous. Based on these observations, a third specimen, designated B-W3, was constructed and tested. Each window in specimen B-W3 was installed with a sill pan and included provision for drainage between the cladding and the siding.

Descriptions of the test specimens addressed in this manuscript are summarized in Table 1. Additional details for the respective wall specimens are provided in subsequent sections.

For both sides of each of the specimens, the hardboard siding was installed with a 3 mm gap between the siding and the window; no j-channel receptor was used. In all cases, non-operable (fixed) flanged windows of the same size (600 mm by 1200 mm, as indicated previously) were used; two identical metal-clad wood windows were used in specimen B-W1, while two identical PVC windows were used in specimen B-W3. There were no staple penetrations through the outer surface of the WRB membrane, (as the acrylic sheathing was not a suitable staple-base).

As indicated in Table 1, this phase of the project included evaluation of a drainage medium (either a mat or a WRB with attached strips that provided drainage channels between the strips). There was particular interest in the degree to which the different approaches would provide drainage of the subsill area, and the degree to which the mounting flanges would restrict drainage from the subsill.

In respect to ensuring the continuity of airtightness at the window frame perimeter, the window "tie-ins" for the test specimens were not completed using aerosol foam or backer rod and sealant as might typically be used in practice. Given that the interior finish was acrylic sheet, "return" sections of acrylic sheet were also used to provide the interface to the window. Tape was used to seal the window frame perimeter to the acrylic sheet return sections, and likewise between the return sections and the acrylic sheet used as interior finish. For the period of testing, the tape effectively sealed the window perimeter thus making the airtightness of the installations dependent on the airtightness of the interior acrylic sheets.

Specimen B-W1—Wall-Window Details

A conceptual sketch of specimen B-W1 configuration, is shown in Fig. 2(*a*). As indicated in Table 1, the B-side of B-W1 incorporated a proprietary pre-

TABLE 1—*Wall-window combinations selected for testing.*

Specimen	Description	
	B-Side	A-Side
B-W1	• WRB (non-woven polypropylene with microporous coating) installed before window in single-piece (slightly larger than the test specimen) and wrapped around end studs, into window rough openings, and around top and bottom plates; i.e., no lap joints in WRB; • Sill-pan, proprietary pre-fabricated flashing product (fabricated of HDPE[a] components and self-adhesive sheets); Window flanges not bedded in sealant; nails used to anchor window flange along flange at window head and vertical flanges; metal clips used to secure underside of flange at sill; and • Drainage mat; proprietary product (10 mm plastic filament with reticulated drainage channels) installed after setting window.	• ASTM E2112 method A1; • WRB (non-woven polypropylene microporous coating) installed before window in single-piece (slightly larger than the test specimen) and wrapped around end studs, into window rough openings, and around top and bottom plates; i.e., no lap joints in WRB; • No sill-pan; • Window flanges (including bottom flange) bedded in sealant; • Nails used to anchor window flange along perimeter of opening; and • Siding not spaced (neither furring strips nor drainage mat).

TABLE 1— (Continued.)

Specimen	Description	
	B-Side	A-Side
B-W3	• WRB installed before window; WRB includes two (2) sheets of 1.22 m (4 ft) wide WRB installed over entire wall surface and overlapped by 152 mm (6 in.); • Integral furring strips attached to WRB (closed-cell foam strips—1 3/4 in. wide; 1/4 in. thick—spaced 203 mm (8 in.) apart); • Sloped sill pan fabricated of proprietary pre-fabricated components and self-adhesive sheets; nominally provides drainage from sill; installed over sill flashing membrane; • Window flanges not bedded in sealant; and • Nails used to anchor window flange along flange at window head and vertical flanges; metal clips used to secure underside of flange at sill.	• WRB installed after setting window; • WRB (same as B-side) applied in two (2) layers; • Integral furring strips attached to WRB (same as B-side); • Sloped sill pan fabricated of proprietary pre-fabricated components and self-adhesive sheets (same as B-side); • Window flanges not bedded in sealant; and • Nails used to anchor window flange along flange at window head and vertical flanges; metal clips used to secure underside of flange at sill.

[a]HDPE—high density polyethylene.

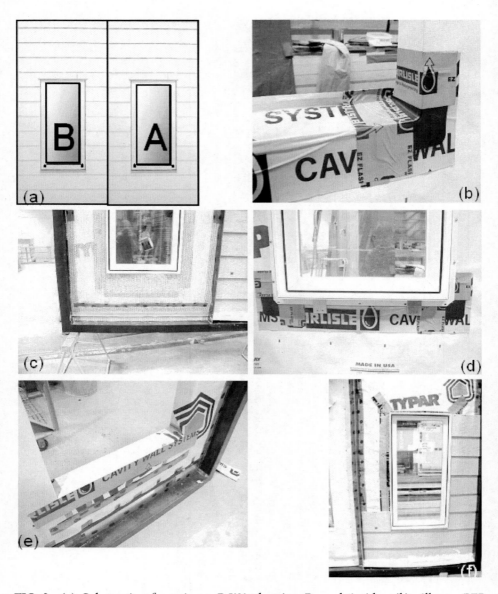

FIG. 2—(a) Schematic of specimen B-W1 showing B- and A-sides; (b) sill pan PFP method B-side; (c) propriety drainage mat for B-side; (d) lower portion of window on B-side prior to installation of drainage mat, cladding; metal clips support lower window flange; (e) installation of WRB in the rough opening of A-side prior to installation of the window; shows lower portion next to sill; and (f) A-side showing exterior cladding, and self-adhering flashing sheets at head (largely covered by flap in the WRB) and along one of the jambs.

fabricated sill-pan flashing product (S-PFP) and a PDM behind the siding. An illustration of the S-PFP is given in Fig. 2(b). Figure 2(c) is a photo of the drainage mat used on the B-side of the specimen. In Fig. 2(d) the lower portion of the window on the B-side is shown prior to the installation of the drainage mat and cladding. The two (2) clips located beneath the window flange support the lower flange and provide an opening through which water might drain from the sill area.

As indicated in Table 1, the A-side of specimen B-W1 was built in accord with method A-1 of section 8.1 of ASTM E2112. Figure 2(e) shows the installation of the WRB in the rough opening of the specimen prior to the installation of the window. Figure 2(f) shows the A-side of the specimen in a stage nearing completion (with the exterior cladding partially installed).

Specimen B-W3—Wall-Window Details

The objective in testing specimen B-W3 was to compare the response of two appreciably similar window interface details. The details each incorporated a WRB with integral drainage strips, but the details differed with regard to sequencing of window installation relative to the placement of the WRB. As indicated in Table 1, on one side of the specimen the WRB was installed prior to setting the window, whereas on the other side of the specimen the WRB was installed after setting the window.

The WRB used on specimen B-W3 incorporated strips that provided drainage channels (Fig. 3). The strips, composed of closed-cell polyethylene foam, were 45 mm wide by 6 mm thick (1 3/4 in. by 1/4 in.), and were spaced 203 mm (8 in.) apart. The strips were attached to either side of the WRB and were thus considered as integral with the WRB. The WRB incorporating the foam strips was installed in two layers, with the upper layer overlapping the lower. On one edge of the WRB first installed at the base of the specimen, the strips were held back by 200 mm (8 in.) thus permitting a 200 mm overlap to the adjoining WRB [Fig. 3(a)]. Figure 3(b) shows the WRB installed on the B-side of the wall assembly; at the window opening the WRB has been cut and the individual foam strips can be seen on either side of the WRB membrane. Figure 3(c) shows the full view of B-side of the specimen as observed from the exterior side of the WRB prior to the WRB being cut at the window opening [this photo was taken before the photo shown in Fig. 3(b)]. Figure 3(d) shows the full view of the B-side of the specimen, at the same stage as shown in Fig. 3(c), but viewed from the opposite side of the specimen; the foam strips on the inner face of the WRB membrane can be seen through the window opening (where sheathing is absent) and through the transparent acrylic sheathing panels above, below, and to the sides of the window opening.

Vertical sectional views and related photographs of the A-side of the specimen (window set before installation of WRB) are given in Fig. 4. Horizontal sectional views (at the jambs) of the A- and B-sides are provided in Fig. 5(a) and Fig. 5(b), respectively. The sketches of the windows provided in Figs. 4 and 5 are stylized (simplified), and are provided for the purpose of showing the details of the interface and collection troughs. Apart from the information provided in Table 1, additional details regarding the installation of this specimen focus on

FIG. 3—(a) *Installation of WRB with integral closed-cell polyethylene foam strips; (b) view showing WRB installed on wall and at window rough opening; (c) B-side of specimen B-W3 with WRB installed on wall; and (d) B-side of specimens from opposite face showing vertical foam strips on inside of WRB.*

the protection of the rough opening and the manner in which the window was tied-in to the window at the exterior and interior of the assembly, specifically

- Protection at rough sill of rough opening: 152 mm (6 in.) strip of self-adhered flashing membrane wrapped onto the sloped sill, 51 mm (2 in.) on the sill and 102 mm (4 in.) on the face of the WRB; 76 mm (3 in.) wide strips of self-adhered flashing membrane secured the sill pan to jambs;
- Window exterior tie-in: Two metal brackets at the base of the window created a small gap behind the window flange and supported the window during installation
- Window flange at the sill is not taped to ensure adequate drainage;
- No caulking or J-trim used between cladding and window frame (1/4 in. butt joint); and
- No drip cap head flashing.
- Window interior tie-in: Sheets of clear acrylic were used as interior fin-

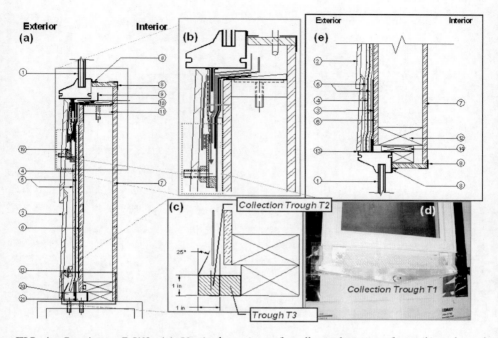

FIG. 4—*Specimen B-W3:* (a) *Vertical section of wall-window interface;* (b) *enlarged detail of sectional view at sill left side;* (c) *enlarged detail on left side showing collection troughs at the base of wall;* (d) *yellow mesh (photo), allows air to pass freely in behind plastic, creates path for water flow between plastic and flashing; path of water drainage (blue line) from sill pan to collection trough T1 shown in* (b); *and* (e) *vertical section at head for both sides of the test specimen.*

ish that would be butted against the window frame and thereafter sealed with adhesive tape of the type typically used to seal the WRB.

Measurement and Observation

A measurement was devised for water that penetrated into the test specimen by collection in troughs located, as shown in Figs. 6 and 7.[5] Figure 6 offers an illustration of the trough locations both in elevation and section views showing a collection trough at the window (W), beneath and collecting water draining from sill (T1), and another located between the backside of the cladding and the WRB at the base of specimen (T2). A variation of this arrangement is given in Fig. 7 that in addition shows the location of a subsill collection tray (ss) only used in Test trial 4 on the A-side of specimen B-W1.

---

[5]These figures do not provide all interface details as these have already been offered in Figs. 4 and 5. Primarily, the information provided relates to the location of water collection troughs.

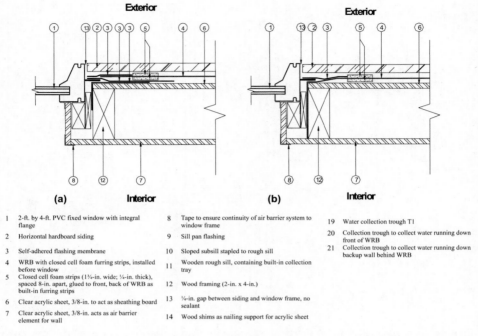

FIG. 5—*Specimen B-W3: Horizontal section of wall-window interface at jamb for* (a) *A-side;* (b) *B-side.*

1	2-ft. by 4-ft. PVC fixed window with integral flange	8	Tape to ensure continuity of air barrier system to window frame
2	Horizontal hardboard siding	9	Sill pan flashing
3	Self-adhered flashing membrane	10	Sloped subsill stapled to rough sill
4	WRB with closed cell foam furring strips, installed before window	11	Wooden rough sill, containing built-in collection tray
5	Closed cell foam strips (1¼-in. wide; ¼-in. thick), spaced 8-in. apart, glued to front, back of WRB as built-in furring strips	12	Wood framing (2-in. x 4-in.)
6	Clear acrylic sheet, 3/8-in. to act as sheathing board	13	¼-in. gap between siding and window frame, no sealant
7	Clear acrylic sheet, 3/8-in. acts as air barrier element for wall	14	Wood shims as nailing support for acrylic sheet

19	Water collection trough T1
20	Collection trough to collect water running down front of WRB
21	Collection trough to collect water running down backup wall behind WRB

Water accumulating and drained from the sill could be collected in collection trough T1; water finding its way behind the cladding and water running down the face of the WRB would be collected near the base of the wall in trough T2. In the case of specimen B-W3 an additional trough was included to collect water that might penetrate behind both the cladding and the WRB and thereafter run down the face of the back-up wall (acrylic sheathing) to collect near the base of the wall in trough T3 [Fig. 4(c)].

Nominally, the use of troughs permitted quantifying the amount and rate of water entry along different paths and differentiating the significance of these paths given different test conditions. Water collection rates in the respective troughs were calculated in mL/min and the results presented in the different figures relating to the nominal rates of collection obtained in the various test trials are also provided in gallons per hour (gph).

As indicated previously, the use of acrylic sheet as interior and exterior sheathing permitted the observation of water intrusion. It also allowed personnel conducting the tests to see where water that penetrated the specimen was directed. Throughout the testing, no permeation of the WRB membrane was observed, and because there were no staple penetrations; breach of the WRB at locations removed from the window perimeter was never observed.

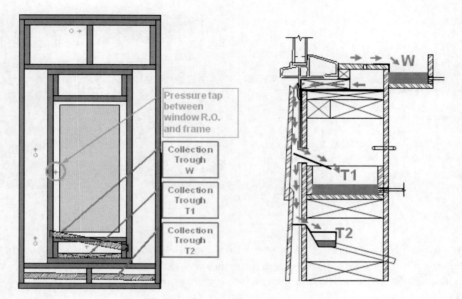

FIG. 6—*Notional sketch of collection trough locations showing collection trough at window (W), beneath and collecting water draining from sill (T1), between backside of cladding and back-up wall at base of wall (T2). The location of pressure taps are shown in elevation sketch as (+—located in stud cavity) and (o—located behind cladding (T2).*

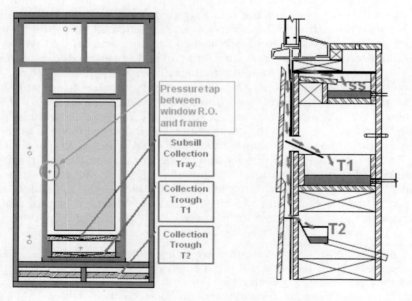

FIG. 7—*Notional location of collection trough with subsill (ss) water collection tray.*

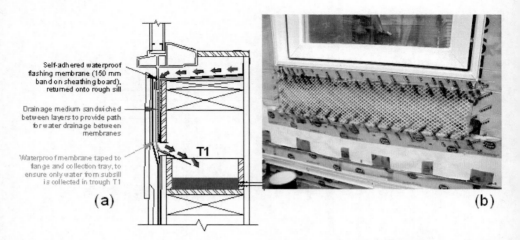

FIG. 8—(a) *Vertical sectional view of the installation on the B-side of specimen B-W1 showing path of supposed water drainage from sill to collection trough T1; (b) photo of the B-side of specimen B-W1 showing assembly prior to installation of drainage mat.*

Penetrating Water

Measurement was made of water collected from the rough opening (below the unit sill) and also from the base of the wall behind the siding. As is more fully described later, a series of four test trials was performed on specimen B-W1 and a series of two test trials was performed on specimen B-W3. In some of the test trials of specimen B-W1, and in both of the test trials of specimen B-W3, the joint between the window and the siding was left open (i.e., not caulked). Water entry between the siding and the window was anticipated when the joint was left open, and was considered possible when the joint was caulked. Water that was to the exterior of the window's bottom flange was assumed to have entered below the window's sill and not to have entered the rough opening. Efforts were taken to separate water on opposite sides of the window's bottom flange.

The means to accomplish this differed for specimens B-W1 and B-W3. For specimen B-W1, a drainage medium of similar thickness as the window flange was used,[6] and was placed in the plane of the flange, located below it. A vertical sectional view of the installation on the B-side of specimen B-W1, at the sill, is shown in Fig. 8(a). A frontal photograph of the installation (taken at a moderately advanced stage of fabrication) is shown in Fig. 8(b). The photo shows the section of drainage medium that was used to direct water that might drain from the sill to the collection trough (T1) and the interface of this drainage medium with the lower (sill) flange of the window. The expected path of water

---

[6]This drainage medium was for measurement purposes and was present on both the A-side and the B-side of specimen B-W1; it is purposely not shown in Figs. 6 and 7. This drainage medium, being roughly the thickness of the window flange, was considerably thinner than the drainage mat incorporated, as a construction feature, of side B of specimen B-W1.

drainage from the sill to the water collection trough (T1) beneath the sill is depicted in Fig. 8(a). The sketch shows that the section of drainage medium extended through a slot in the sheathing to collection trough T1, which was located inside the wall.

As will be discussed later in this manuscript, four test trials were conducted on specimen B-W1. For the last of these, the A-side of this specimen was altered to include a sub-sill collection trough (Fig. 7). The purpose of the sub-sill collection trough was to estimate the amount of water that, during a previous test trial, penetrated into the rough opening and failed to drain from it. Stated in a different way, the use of the sub-sill permitted estimating the amount of water that accumulated at the sill and thus could not be collected in trough T1 from prior testing without the sub-sill.

For each window installation of specimen B-W3, the collection troughs for water entering the subsill area were located in the space between the sheathing and the siding, as shown in Fig. 4(a), 4(b), and 4(d).

Air Pressure Differential

The risk of water entry can be inferred from the knowledge of the degree of pressure drop across a supposed plane of water tightness, the presence of water at that plane, and openings through which water can pass. Measuring the pressure drop in these test trials thus provided a means to infer the risk to water entry to the rough opening along the periphery of the wall-window interface given openings through which water could pass. Air pressure differential was monitored at various locations across the test specimen; the location points for monitoring of differential pressure are provided in the elevations sketches of Figs. 6 and 7. The location of the pressure tap between the window rough opening and the window frame is also shown; measurements from this location permitted determining the pressure difference across the window flange. As indicated previously, Figs. 6 and 7 relate to the A-side of specimen B-W1; differential air pressure measurements were made in similar locations on the B-side of specimen B-W1, and on either side of specimen B-W3. Pressure differential between the exterior surface the surface being sprayed and various framing cavities was measured, with the pressure differential between the exterior and the rough opening airspace (the "perimeter cavity") being of particular interest (Figs. 6 and 7). The window flanges provided an evident barrier between the exterior and the rough opening airspace. Differential pressure between the exterior and the rough opening airspace was thus considered as largely characterizing the wall-window interface. For the A-side of test specimens B-W1 and B-W3 the location point for this measurement can be identified in the elevation sketches in Figs. 6 and 7, i.e., along the window framing stud on the left side of the rough opening at mid height; whereas, for the B-side, this point was on the right side of the rough opening at mid height.

Variations in Air Leakage of the Air Barrier System

The primary plain of air tightness of the test specimens was the acrylic sheet referred to as the ABS. The airtightness of the ABS was controlled at the nominal leakage rate by cutting holes in the acrylic sheet (in a distributed manner) on the interior surface of the wall (where gypsum board would normally be used as interior finish). Thus a series of holes provided an air leakage rate of 0.8 L/s·m² at a pressure differential of 75 Pa across the specimen. The 0.3 ABS condition was obtained by closing the holes with tape, as many as needed to reach the target nominal air leakage rate at 75 Pa pressure differential.

Test Trials and Deficiencies

Test specimen B-W1 was subjected to four test trials, as outlined in Table 2. It should be noted that for all trials, a sequence of tests were performed at a series of three water spray rates, and at any single water spray rate, differential air pressure across the wall was stepped through a series of pressures ranging from 0 to 700 Pa.

For the first set of test trials, the wall was tested in a relatively airtight condition (nominal leakage rate 0.3 L/s·m² at 75 Pa.) and thereafter in a less airtight condition (nominal leakage rate 0.8 L/s·m² at 75 Pa). As indicated in Table 2, for the second, third, and fourth series of trials, specimen B-W1 was tested in the nominal 0.8 ABS condition only. As also indicated in the table, the first test trial was conducted without an exterior perimeter seal, whereas for the subsequent three test trials the gap between the window frame and the cladding was sealed (by use of backer rod and elastomeric sealant). The intent in this instance was to determine the influence of sealing the perimeter gap on water penetration into the rough opening.

Deficiencies were not included in the first two test trials whereas the contribution of water entry through small openings in the window corners was estimated from results of the final two test trials; a description of the deficiency in the window corner for B-W1 is given in a subsequent section (see Deficiencies).

Test specimen B-W3 was subjected to two test trials, as outlined in Table 3. The different trials permitted estimating the effect of including a deficiency in the window corners on the water entry to and subsequent drainage from the sill.

Deficiencies—the locations of deficiencies in the respective windows for either side of wall specimen B-W1 or B-W3 are given in Fig. 9. The intent of including deficiencies in the window components was to simulate conditions of a prematurely failed window or of a window that had deteriorated over time; either would be expected to result in water penetration into the sill space of the rough opening. Performing trials with deficiencies permitted determination of the robustness of the flashing details and allowed observation of the manner in which penetrating water was managed.

As can be seen in Fig. 9(a), the deficiencies are located at the lower and opposing corners of each window. For specimen B-W1 [Fig. 9(b)] the deficiencies were approximately 1 mm in diameter. These openings were sealed with elastomeric sealant for those test trials in which no deficiencies were being tested, as shown in Fig. 9(c). Similar size openings were placed at the lower corner of the windows of specimen B-W3, as shown in Fig. 9(d). When speci-

TABLE 2—*Test trials and parameters for specimen B-W1.*

Test Trial	Description	Exterior Perimeter Seal	Deficiencies	ABS[a]	Spray Rates L/min·m² (gal/hr·ft²)
1	As constructed—intent: To determine the effect of ABS leakage rate on water entry	No	None	0.3	0.8, 1.6, 3.4 cascade, (1.2, 2.4, 5)
		No	None	0.8	Same as above
2	Sealant and backer rod added between window frame and cladding, full perimeter—intent: Compare with results of Trial 1 at 0.8 ABS condition to characterize the influence of the exterior perimeter seal	Yes	None	0.8	Same as above
3	Un-plug small openings in window corners—effect of deficiencies on water entry to sill area of rough opening	Yes	Present	0.8	Same as above
4	Same as Trial 3, except with a subsill collector trough added to A-side of specimen to estimate rate of accumulation at sill	Yes	Present	0.8	Same as above

[a]Air barrier system—ABS leakage rates of 0.3 and 0.8 L/s·m² (0.06 and 0.16 cfm/ft²).

TABLE 3—Test trials and parameters for specimen B-W3.

Test trial	Description	Deficiency	ABS[a]	Spray Rates L/min·m² (gal/h·ft²)
1	As constructed	No	0.3	0.8, 1.6, 3.4 full spray (1.2, 2.4, 5)
		No	0.8	Same as above
2	Deficiency at each lower window corner (Fig. 9)	Yes	0.3	Same as above
		Yes	0.8	Same as above

[a]ABS—air barrier system; 0.3 ABS—ABS leakage of 0.3 L/s·m² (0.06 cfm/ft²); 0.8 ABS—0.8 L/s·m² (0.16 cfm/ft²).

FIG. 9—(a) *Pictorial representation showing front elevation of test specimen (cladding exterior) and nominal location of deficiencies at the lower corners of windows; (b) photo of specimen B-W1 of deficiency (ca. 1 mm diameter) at the lower right corner of window; (c) photo of specimen B-W1 showing lower right hand corner with deficiency "plugged" with sealant; and (d) specimen B-W3 showing the "un-plugged" lower right corner of window.*

men B-W3 was tested with no deficiencies (i.e., B-W3 Test trial 1 "as constructed"), these openings were likewise sealed with caulking as was done with the other specimen.

Selected Results from Tests on B-W1

In the test trials reported for this test specimen, water spray was applied in the cascade format at three different spray rates, and with air pressure differential at each spray rate stepped through seven different levels. Results are reported in terms of water collection rates as related to spray rates and to air pressure

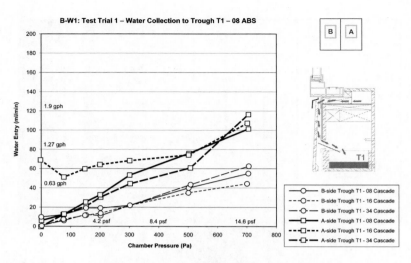

FIG. 10—*B-W1 Test Trial 1—water collection rates to trough T1 in relation to applied pressure differential at 08 ABS for rates of water spray of 0.8, 1.6, and 3.4 L/min·m².*

differential across the specimen. The rates of collection are given in mL/min. Equivalent rates expressed in gph, are not provided in the text, but are (at selected values) shown graphically in the respective figures.[7]

Test Trial 1 (Comparison of 03 and 08 Air Barrier System Leakage Conditions; No Caulking or Backer Rod at Window Perimeter)

As expected, increasing the nominal air leakage rate of the wall (by unplugging holes in the interior ABS) resulted in exertion of a greater proportion of the pressure differential across the window-wall interface. At either ABS condition, the proportion of the pressure differential across the wall exerted on the window-wall interface was greater on the A-side of the specimen (~11 % for the 0.3 ABS condition and <85 % for the 0.8 ABS condition) than on the B-side of the specimen (<3 % for the 0.3 ABS condition and <45 % for the 0.8 ABS condition) at all pressure levels to which the specimens were subjected.

Water collection rates in trough T1 at the 0.3 ABS leakage condition was as great as 20 mL/min at the highest water deposition rate. Rates of collection were highly dependent on the pressure difference across the assembly and not dependent on the water spray rate applied onto the cladding. Rates of collection were both greater and increased more significantly from an increased ABS leakage on the A-side (ASTM) side as compared to the B-side; increases in maximum rates from the 0.3 to the 0.8 ABS condition ranged from 30 mL/min to 116 mL/min, and 7 mL/min to 63 mL/min for the A-side and B-side, respec-

---

[7]Water collection rates in gph are obtained by multiplying mL/min by 0.016; e.g., 20mL/min: 0.32 gph; e.g., in Fig. 10, rates of collection of 40, 80, and 120 mL/min are given as 0.63, 1.27, and 1.9 gph, respectively.

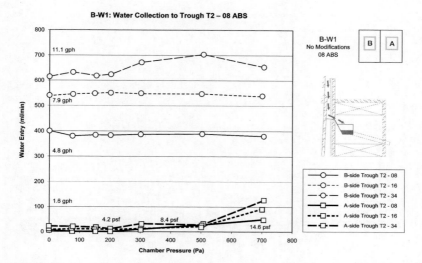

FIG. 11—*B-W1 Test trial 1—water collection rates to trough T2 in relation to applied pressure differential at 08 ABS.*

tively. As shown in Fig. 10, at the 0.8 ABS air leakage condition and the highest applied differential pressure, rates of up to 110 mL/min and 60 mL/min were obtained on the A-side (ASTM) and B-sides, respectively.

The water collection rate to trough T2 (Fig. 11) was very high, (up to 700 mL/min) on the side of the wall where the cladding was spaced and installed over a drainage mat (the B-side). Rates of collection were dependent on cascade rate and were relatively constant across the full range of chamber pressure conditions, increasing from ~400 mL/min at the 0.8 L/min·m^2 (1.2 gal/ft^2·h) cascade rate, to ~650 mL/min at a cascade rate of 3.4 L/min·m^2 (5 gal/ft^2·h). Water collection at trough T2 was lower on the A-side (ASTM); it was below 100 mL/min for the majority of test conditions. Water collection rates at T2 on this side of the wall was less than 20 mL/min at low pressure differentials, and increased with progressively higher differential pressure to a maximum of 126 mL/min at 700 Pa. Trends in collection rates at T2 at the 0.8 ABS condition were similar to those observed at the lower ABS leakage rate (0.3 ABS).

Test Trial 2 (Window Perimeter Sealed with Caulking)

As previously indicated (Table 3), in this test trial, a caulk seal (consisting of backer rod and sealant) was applied between the window frame and cladding. With the perimeter joints along the window frame sealed, water collection rates to trough T2, located at the base of the wall, were reduced significantly (Fig. 12). The B-side showed a significant decrease from 703 mL/min (in Test trial 1) to 18 mL/min (in this trial). On the A-side (ASTM), collection rate at T2 decreased from a high of 126 mL/min to no water collection. Collection rates to trough T1 also decreased although less significantly. On the B-side the maxi-

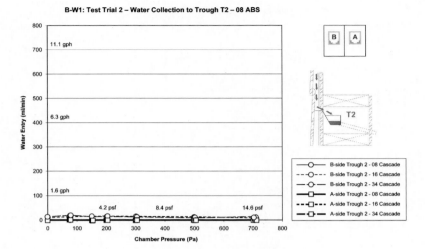

FIG. 12—*B-W1 Test Trial 2 (window perimeter sealed with caulking)—water collection rates to trough T2 in relation to applied pressure differential at 08 ABS.*

mum rate at T1 decreased modestly (63 mL/min in Trial 1 versus 55 mL/min in Trial 2). On the A-side (ASTM) the maximum rate at T1 decreased appreciably, (116 mL/min in Trial 1 versus 35 mL/min in Trial 2); the decrease at T1 was nonetheless of lesser degree that at T2.

Test Trial 3 (Window Perimeter Sealed and Deficiencies at Window Corners)

Collection rates with deficiencies at the window corners (leakage paths though holes in the window frames) were very similar to those in the previous trial (when leakage paths through the frames were plugged). Corner deficiencies appeared to have little to no effect on rates of collection on the B-side (Fig. 13); rates of water collection in trough T1 increased very modestly (from 55 to 67 mL/min) at the highest spray rate (3.4 L/min·m²). On the A-side (ASTM) at pressure differentials above 300 Pa (6.3 psf), water drainage to collection trough T1 dropped off. At test pressures above this level, water was observed to be collecting on the rough sill indicating that drainage from the sill area of the rough opening was not effective. In contrast on the B-side of the specimen, water drained to trough T1 at all levels of applied pressure differential.

Test Trial 4 (Window Perimeter Sealed, Deficiencies at Window Corners, Subsill Collection Tray)

The subsill collection tray that was added to the A-side of the specimen confirmed that the drop-off in collection at T1 that was observed in the third trial at higher differential pressures for the window installed in accord with ASTM E2112 was not reflective of a decrease in water entry into the sill area of the

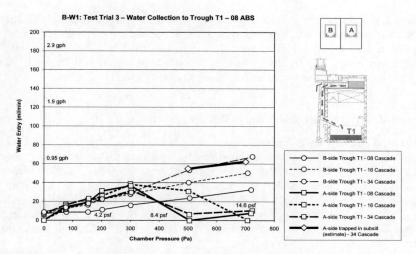

FIG. 13—*B-W1 Test trial 3 (sealed perimeter with caulking removed in corners)—water collection rates to trough T1 in relation to applied pressure differential at 0.8 ABS.*

rough opening, but instead was because water that entered this subsill region was unable to drain from the region at the higher levels of pressure differential (Fig. 14).

Recalling the results of Test trial 3, water was observed to collect in trough T1 on the A-side (ASTM) up to a differential pressure of 300 Pa (6.3 psf), after which collection in the trough decreased. A plausible explanation for this observation is that at pressures in excess of 300 Pa, pathways that permitted

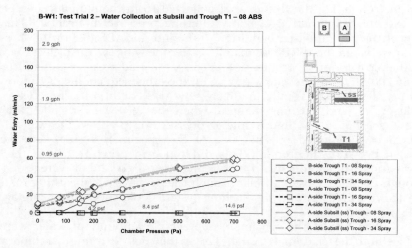

FIG. 14—*B-W1 Test Trial 4 (sealed perimeter with caulking removed in corners) collection rates to trough T1 in relation to differential pressure across specimen at 0.8 ABS. Subsill collection tray on A-side (ASTM).*

drainage from the subsill area were restricted. In the fourth trial, the rates of collection at subsill collection tray up to 300 Pa pressure differential were similar to the rates of collection in trough T1 in the third trial. This suggests that substantial drainage from the subsill area occurred up to 300 Pa, but that beyond this level drainage became increasingly restricted.

Selected Results from Tests on B-W3

As indicated previously in Table 3, specimen B-W3 was subjected to two (2) test trials, and in each of these trials the spray format was full spray (as opposed to cascade format). Although the spray format was different than in the trials conducted on specimen B-W1, specimen B-W3 was prepared to the same ABS leakage conditions (0.3 and 0.8 ABS) as specimen B-W1. In addition, the series of spray rates and pressure differentials followed in the two trials conducted on this specimen (B-W3) were the same as those followed in the trials conducted on the other specimen (B-W1).

The configuration of collection troughs in this specimen was, (as can be seen by comparing Fig. 4 with Figs. 6–8), different than in specimen B-W1. Results are reported in terms of the maximum rates of water collection in the various collection troughs (Table 4), with collection amounts identified by specimen side, ABS leakage condition during test, and presence or absence of window deficiencies during test. Collection rates in trough T1, which collected drainage from the sill-pan, are plotted in Fig. 15.

Results for Test Trial Set 1—No Deficiencies in the Wall

Table 4 indicates that when the WRB was installed before the window, and the window did not have deficiencies, very little water (<10 mL/min) was collected in trough T1 (the trough that collected from the sill-pan), even at the most extreme combination of spray rate and pressure differential. This was moreover the case at either condition of the interior ABS (0.3 or 0.8 L/s·m^2). In contrast, when the WRB was installed after the window, the collection rate at T1 at the most extreme combination of spray rate and pressure differential was roughly 200 mL/min (the rate was, as with the other sequencing of window and WRB installation, apparently unaffected by ABS condition). There were multiple layers of jamb flashing material when the WRB was installed after the window (see Fig. 5). A slightly higher pressure drop across the wall-window interface was observed on this side of the specimen at the same across-specimen pressure differential. This difference in pressure across the wall-window interface could explain the greater measured rate of water entry into the rough opening. Observations through the transparent sheathing materials suggested however that the pan flashing system could successfully manage this degree of water entry.

On either side of the specimen, appreciable amounts of water were collected behind the cladding (trough T2) at the most extreme combination of spray rate and differential pressure (Table 4). For each installation, the collection rates were somewhat higher when the ABS condition was relatively tight. Conversely, at the same sets of ABS condition, the collection rate in T2 was

TABLE 4—*Test Trial Sets 1 and 2—threshold conditions for water entry.*

| | | | Maximum Rate of Water Collection in Respective Troughs (mL/min) | | | | | |
| | | | WRB Set-Up After Window Installed (i.e., Window Installed Before WRB) | | | WRB Set-Up Before Window Installed (i.e., Window Installed After WRB) | | |
Test Trial	ABS Leakage	Deficiency	T1	T2	T3	T1	T2	T3
1	0.3ABS	No	215	704	Nil	8	995	Nil
	0.8ABS	No	197	509	Nil	7	705	Nil
2	0.3ABS	With	120	1139	Nil	39	931	Nil
	0.8ABS	With	328	1013	Nil	99	1130	Nil

T1—Window sill reservoir; T2—Behind siding; T3—Behind WRB

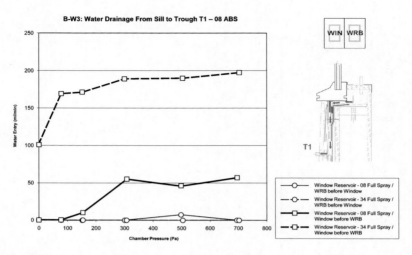

FIG. 15—*B-W3—water collection rate (T1) in relation to pressure difference across wall at 08 ABS air leakage.*

somewhat higher for the side of the specimen where the window was installed after the WRB (705 and 995 mL/min for 0.3 and 0.8 ABS conditions respectively versus 509 to 704 mL/min at the same set of ABS conditions). These differences are of modest relative magnitude; they are essentially unimportant, inasmuch as the collection rate values at T2 (at the most extreme combination of spray rate and pressure differential) exceed 500 mL/min. These high rates reflect the fact that the joint between the cladding and the window frame was neither caulked nor had J-trim been used to complete the joint along this interface. Hence water had a ready entry path along the gap between the cladding and the window. No water was collected behind the WRB indicating that the overlapping details for the WRB effectively restricted water entry. In the installation where the window was installed before WRB, water was observed to occasionally intrude behind the WRB through the layers of flashing (Figs. 16 and 17). It was never of sufficient quantity however to find its way to collection trough T3 [Fig. 5(c)].

Discussion

Test results relating to specimen B-W1 are discussed first, followed by discussion of results relating to specimen B-W3.

Results from Tests on Specimen B-W1

Pressure Differential between the Exterior and the Rough Opening— Throughout the tests, this pressure differential, (which we consider to be the pressure across the wall-window interface), was higher on the A-side (ASTM) than on the B-side of the specimen. The A-side incorporated a bead of sealant

FIG. 16—*B-W3—observed water leak behind WRB at the bottom corner of the window flashing; window installed before WRB; testing with no deficiencies.*

behind all flanges of the window (a continuous bead at jamb and head flanges and a discontinuous bead at the sill flange). The sealant was intended to seal the flange to the WRB. In contrast, the window installed on of the B-side of the

FIG. 17—*B-W3—observed water leak behind WRB at the bottom corner of the window flashing; window installed before WRB; testing with deficiencies.*

specimen did not have this seal. The likely cause of this higher pressure drop was the restriction of air movement across the wall-window interface when the window flanges are bedded in sealant; the restriction of air movement evidently increased the pressure differential across the plane of the seal.

Wall-Window Interface Water Entry—Collection to Trough T1—The method of window installation for the A-side (ASTM) of the wall is intended to prevent water from attaining the subsill area whereas the B-side (S-PFP) details are intended to manage water that penetrates the wall-window interface by collection at and drainage from the sill. Because of these fundamental differences in rainwater management strategy, two distinct results would be expected between these two approaches to window installation practice.

Twice as much water collection in trough T1 (drainage from the sill) occurred on the A-side as compared to the B-side even though neither window had evident deficiencies. The efforts to block water entry through a sealed interface were evidently ineffective. Leakage paths were assumed to be blocked by sealant, and the windows contained no known leakage paths, but water nonetheless entered the rough opening.

In the installation on the A-side of the specimen, self-adhering flashing membrane was applied over the jamb flanges, this presumably added another layer of protection from water entry (in addition to the sealant behind the flange). However in locations where the self-adhering flashing failed to adhere to the window flange or to the WRB, the non-adhered areas could provide paths for water entry. With the removal of the lap siding from the specimen following completion of the test trials, it was found that the self-adhered flashing had lost adhesion to the WRB in certain locations. This created openings sometimes called "fish mouths" (Fig. 18). The fish mouths proved to be leakage paths. Several "pour test" into these openings located along the jambs showed that water that entered at these locations reached collection trough T1.

Given that openings for water entry exist, the presence of water at these locations combined with a pressure differential necessarily brings about water penetration. As previously mentioned, at the same differential pressure across the assembly, the pressure drop across the A-side was greater than the B-side. This evidently raised the potential for water entry. This is almost certainly the reason why greater amounts of water accumulated at the sill on the A-side of this specimen than on the B-side.

This explanation for water entry is furthermore supported by the observation (reported previously) that water collection to trough T1 for either side of the specimen showed a high dependence on pressure differential across the specimen and no dependence on the water deposition rate on the cladding. This would be indicative of water occluding small openings and being driven through these openings at rates of penetration dependent on the capacity of the openings to admit water and the pressure difference across them.

Water collection to trough T1 on the A-side was greater than that of the B-side despite the absence on the A-side of the specimen of a direct drainage path between the sill area of the rough opening and trough T1. An explanation for this seemingly counter-intuitive observation was that water that pooled at the subsill could reach trough T1 by passage through joints between rough

FIG. 18—*Location of Fish Mouths on the B-side (left) and V-side (right) of B-W1.*

opening framing members and through joints that framing members made with the acrylic sheets that were used instead of gypsum board and wood-based sheathing (as shown by the red arrows in Fig. 19).

Collection to Trough T2 (Base of Wall behind Cladding)—A comparison of Figs. 10 and 11 indicates that rates of collection to trough T2 on the B-side were

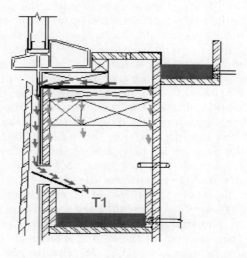

FIG. 19—*Water entry path from subsill to collection trough T1 (A-side).*

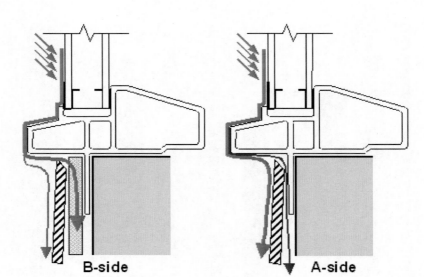

FIG. 20—*Water path at the sill behind the siding for B- and A-side of test specimen.*

significant in relation to the collection rates of the other troughs (up to 700 mL/min). Water collection on the B-side showed no dependence on pressure differential across the assembly and increased with an increase in water deposition rate (Fig. 11). There was evidently little restriction to water drainage behind the siding on the B-side, likely attributable to the proprietary drainage mat. In contrast, on the A-side (ASTM), the rates of collection were much lower and showed a greater dependence on differential pressure (Fig. 11), with the highest collection rate being observed at the highest applied pressure. As discussed in greater detail in the following paragraph, the configuration on the A-side apparently resulted in lesser amounts of water penetration behind the siding. This, in addition to restricted drainage of water that did penetrate behind the siding, explains the relatively low collection rates at trough T2 that were observed on the A-side of this specimen.

Certain features of the configuration on the A-side are apparent that would reduce the likelihood of water finding its way to the base of the wall and trough T2. The cladding on this side of the specimen was directly affixed to the back-up wall and at this location, rested on the window flange. On the B-side, in contrast, the cladding was installed over the drainage mat and thus, its outer face was closer to the exterior leading edge of the windowsill (Fig. 20). The inadvertent entry of water through a gap is necessarily complicated and in these tests, no direct visual observation of the cladding exterior was possible during testing. It is supposed that this feature contributed to the increased likelihood that water flowing over the sill edge would find its way to the gap between the cladding and underside of the sill. The increased likelihood of water entry behind the cladding for the B- and A-sides of the specimen at the interface is depicted schematically in Fig. 20. The supposed paths for water migration and entry are evident and differing line sizes mark the relative im-

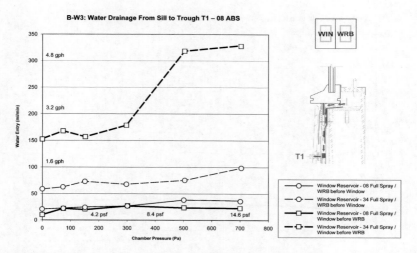

FIG. 21—*B-W3: Results from Test Trial 2, with deficiency—water drainage from sill to trough T1 at 08 ABS.*

portance of competing paths.

Throughout these tests, the B-side tended to adequately drain water from the subsill area and direct it to a location where its management would be likely. The A-side in contrast, was vulnerable to water entry into the sill area of the rough opening, even at lower driving pressures, and showed little or no drainage from this area, particularly at higher driving pressures.

Results from Tests on Specimen B-W3: Test Trial Set 2—Wall with Deficiencies in Window Corners

Pressure drops—Very small pressure drops (PDs) were observed across the wall-window interface for either of the windows in this specimen. This was the case even when the condition of the ABS was far from being airtight; the pressure differential between the exterior and the rough opening space was less than 5 % of the across-wall pressure differential at the 0.8 ABS condition. The largest PD in this specimen occurred across the acrylic sheet used in lieu of gypsum board, well away from wetted surfaces. PDs between the exterior and the rough opening space were slightly higher for the window that had been installed before the WRB. This may explain why more water entry to the sill area was observed for this window than for the one installed after the WRB.

Wall-Window Interface Water Entry—As indicated previously, the introduction (unplugging) of deficiencies in the corners of the window frames was what distinguished second trial from the first trial performed on this specimen (Table 3). The introduction of deficiencies necessarily resulted in greater rates of water entry to the sill area. Figure 21 shows water collection rates to trough T1 (drainage from sill) in relation to the applied pressure across the wall assembly for the 0.8 ABS air leakage condition, and with deficiencies present (un-

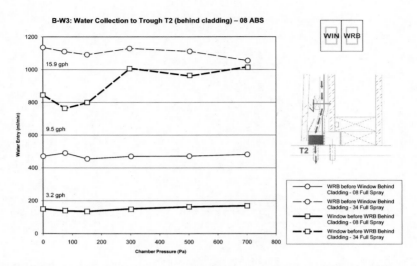

FIG. 22—*B-W3 with deficiency—water collection to trough T2 (behind cladding) at 08 ABS.*

plugged). At this ABS condition, the maximum collection rates to trough T1 for the window that was installed before the WRB, increased from 197 mL/min (with deficiencies plugged) to 324 mL/min (with deficiencies unplugged). For the window that was installed after the WRB, the corresponding maximum rates increased from 7 mL/min to 99 mL/min. Even with deficiencies present and high collection rates at trough T1, no water was observed to pool on the rough sill. Water that entered the sill space (most of which entered through the deficiencies) drained successfully from the sill-pan.

In each of the test trials performed on this specimen, large amounts of water passed behind the cladding and ran down the face of the WRB to collection trough T2. The amounts collected in T2 during the second trial are shown in Fig. 22. The figure indicates that water entry behind the cladding was predominantly dependent on water spray rate. At the highest spray rate (3.4 L/s·m^2) water collection rates to trough T2 often exceeded 1000 mL/min. As indicated previously, this was evidently due to the unsealed gap between the siding and the window frame. However, there was no large driving force for water entry across the membrane since PDs across it were low. Indeed, no water was collected behind the WRB (in trough T3) on either one-half of the wall assembly.

However, and as was the case for Test trial 1 of B-W3, on the side of the specimen where the window was installed before WRB, water was observed to occasionally intrude behind the WRB through the layers of jamb flashing, (Fig. 17). As indicated previously in the Results section of this manuscript, the amount of water that entered through the layers of jamb flashing was of insufficient quantity to reach collection trough 3.

Summary

This manuscript presents selected results relating to watertightness and water management as observed in laboratory spray testing of four wall-window interface details. The details were fabricated in a manner consistent with construction practices in North America for low-rise residential and light commercial buildings. The installation details included an approach outlined in ASTM E2112 and three alternate approaches. All of the alternate approaches incorporated a sill pan in the rough opening and a drainage medium between the cladding and the sheathing. All the installations were of windows with mounting flanges. The test specimens were clad with hardboard lap siding and they incorporated a non-woven polymer-based membrane as weather resistive barrier. Each specimen was tested in a condition where the window itself did not leak, and also in a condition where the window leaked.

The three window installation details that incorporated a sill pan and a means for drainage between the cladding and sheathing appeared capable of managing the most significant rainfall events that may be anticipated in North America. In contrast, the window installation that did not incorporate a means to drain the rough opening space was found vulnerable to problematic water entry when it was exposed to combinations of water spray and differential air pressure that simulated significant wind-driven rain loads. The installation details that performed effectively included three essential features: (1) A sill-pan flashing with watertight corners and an integral back dam; (2) a drainage path behind the bottom flange of the window; and (3) an uninterrupted ABS at the interface of the window frame and the window opening, located toward the interior of the assembly, and well away from wetted surfaces.

This manuscript addresses water entry into the envelope components; it considers rainwater penetration, at the wall-window interface. It does not address hygrothermal phenomena related to the movement of water vapor that may occur as a result of temperature and humidity difference across the assembly. Additionally, it does not address the potential reduction in thermal performance associated with providing an open drainage space around the perimeter of the window. If details for providing this space are not carefully implemented, cold air may be present around the perimeter of the window; this can diminish the overall thermal performance of the installed window, and condensation on the window frame and on surrounding components may occur.

Acknowledgments

The writers are indebted to Mr. C. Carll for his sustained efforts for providing a thorough review of this paper and his many helpful suggestions for its improvement. In addition, the writers gratefully acknowledge the support for this work provided by Building Diagnostics Technology, DuPont Weatherization Systems, the Canada Mortgage and Housing Corporation, Public Works and Government Services Canada and the collaboration between the National Research Council Canada and consortium partners for the completion of this project.

References

[1]   Morrison Hershfield Limited, "Survey of Building Envelope Failures in the Coastal Climate of British Columbia," *Report to Canada Mortgage and Housing Corporation* (CIDN 1569 0300001), Ottawa, Canada, 1996, 43 pp.

[2]   Building Envelope Engineering, "Wall Moisture Problems in Alberta Dwellings," *Report to Canada Mortgage and Housing Corporation*, Ottawa, Canada, 1999, 60 pp.

[3]   Building Inspection Division, "Stucco in Residential Construction," *Report to the City of Woodbury (MN)*, February 2005.

[4]   Leslie, N., "Window Installation Methods Test Results-Task 3.3 Report," *Report to the California Energy Commission*, (Contract No. 500–03–013), Gas Technology Institute (Project No. 15485), Des Plaines, IL, 2006, 38 pp.

[5]   Carll, C., "Rainwater Intrusion in Light-Frame Building Walls," *Proceedings of the 2nd Annual Conference on Durability and Disaster Mitigation in Wood-Frame Housing*, 2001, pp. 33–40.

[6]   Ricketts, D. R., "Water Penetration Resistance of Windows: Study of Manufacturing, Building Design, Installation, and Maintenance Factors," *Report to Canada Mortgage and Housing Corporation*, Ottawa, Canada, December 2002, 86 pp.

[7]   Ricketts, D. R., "Water Penetration Resistance of Windows: Study of Codes, Standards, Testing and Certification," *Report to Canada Mortgage and Housing Corporation*, Ottawa, December 2002.

[8]   Lacasse, M. A., Rousseau, M., Cornick, S. M., and Plescia, S., Assessing the Effectiveness of Wall-Window Interface Details to Manage Rainwater, *10th Canadian Conference on Building Science and Technology*, 2005, pp. 127–138.

[9]   Lacasse, M. A., Manning, M. M., Rousseau, M. Z., Cornick, S. M., Plescia, S., Nicholls, M., and Nunes, S. C., "Results on Assessing the Effectiveness of Wall-Window Interface Details to Manage Rainwater," *11th Canadian Conference on Building Science and Technology*, 2007, pp. 1–14.

[10] ASTM E2112-07, 2001, "Standard Practice for Installation of Exterior Windows, Doors and Skylights," *Annual Book of ASTM Standards*, ASTM International, West Conshohocken, PA.

[11] Lacasse, M. A., O'Connor, T. J., Nunes, S., and Beaulieu, P., "Report from Task 6 of MEWS Project Experimental Assessment of Water Penetration and Entry into Wood-Frame Wall Specimens, Final Report," *Report No. 133*, Institute for Research in Construction, National Research Council Canada, February 2003.

[12] Lacasse, M. A., "Durability and Performance of Building Envelopes," *BSI 2003 Proceedings*, 2003, pp. 1–6.

[13] Cornick, S. M. and M. A. Lacasse, "A Review of Climate Loads Relevant to Assessing the Watertightness Performance of Walls, Windows, and Wall-Window Interfaces," *J. ASTM Int.*, Vol. 2, No. 10, 2005, pp. 1–16.

[14] Cornick, S. M. and Lacasse, M. A., "An Investigation of Climate Loads on Building Façades for Selected Locations in the US," *J. ASTM Int.*, Vol. 6(2), 2009, pp. 1–17.

[15] ASTM E331-00, 2000, "Standard Test Method for Water Penetration of Exterior Windows, Skylights, Doors, and Curtain Walls by Uniform Static Air Pressure Difference," *Annual Book of ASTM Standards*, Vol. 04.11, ASTM International, West Conshohocken, PA, pp. 1–7.

[16] CAN/CSA A440.4, 1998, "Window and Door Installation," Canadian Standards Association, Mississauga, Canada.

Reprinted from JAI, Vol. 6, No. 9
doi:10.1520/JAI101270
Available online at www.astm.org/JAI

M. A. Lacasse,[1] *M. Armstrong,*[1] *G. Ganapathy,*[1] *M. Rousseau,*[1]
S. M. Cornick,[1] *D. Bibee,*[2] *D. Shuler,*[3] *and A. Hoffee*[4]

Assessing the Effectiveness of Wall-Window Interface Details to Manage Rainwater— Selected Results from Window Installation to a Wall Sheathed in Extruded Polystyrene

ABSTRACT: The detailing of wall-window interfaces and the consequences of defective installation of windows are an on-going concern in North America. This paper concerns laboratory evaluation of the water leakage performance of a select set of window-wall interface details. The details were for windows with mounting flanges installed in wood-frame walls sheathed with rigid extruded polystyrene foam. The tests were performed on a single full-scale test assembly in which two identical windows were installed by two similar but nonetheless different means. Each detail included a sill pan intended to collect water that gained entry into the assembly and thus was designed to be robust (tolerant of flaws). Tests were performed over a series of different water loading (spray) rates and over a series of different air pressure differentials at each spray rate. Air leakage rates through the window opening were monitored; they were controlled by a unique methodology. Leakage paths were introduced in the window frames, and these paths were

Manuscript received June 15, 2007; accepted for publication July 28, 2009; published online September 2009.
[1] Institute for Research in Construction, National Research Council Canada, 1200 Montreal Rd., Building M-20, Ottawa, ON K1A 0R6, Canada.
[2] The Dow Chemical Company, 2878 Canyon Rd., Granville, OH 43023.
[3] Owens Corning, One Owens Corning Parkway, Toledo, OH 43659.
[4] Pactiv Building Products, 2100 River Edge Pkwy., Suite 175, Atlanta, GA 30328.

Cite as: Lacasse, M. A., Armstrong, M., Ganapathy, G., Rousseau, M., Cornick, S. M., Bibee, D., Shuler, D. and Hoffee, A., "Assessing the Effectiveness of Wall-Window Interface Details to Manage Rainwater—Selected Results from Window Installation to a Wall Sheathed in Extruded Polystyrene," *J. ASTM Intl.*, Vol. 6, No. 9. doi:10.1520/JAI101270.

alternatively blocked or opened to permit evaluation of the performance of the installation details under two different assumed conditions of window leakage. Air pressure distribution within the assemblies was monitored during spray testing. The wall assembly was designed to permit observation of water entry in it and to allow measurement of water entry to, or drainage from, various locations within the assembly. Results on water entry and management for the two wall-window interface configurations are given, and effectiveness of the details is discussed.

KEYWORDS: laboratory tests, rainwater intrusion, wall-window interface, watertightness, window installation details, wind-driven rain, extruded polystyrene foam sheathing, flashing

Introduction

The control of rain penetration is evidently a key functional requirement for exterior walls. Lack of attention to either the selection of wall components or to their installation and detailing may result in the premature deterioration of wall elements. Deficient installation and detailing of windows have accounted for a significant number of premature failures of building envelopes in recent years [1–4]. A survey of building envelope failures in the coastal region of British Columbia indicated that 25 % of the moisture problems associated with water ingress into wall assemblies were directly attributed to penetration through the windows or the window-wall interface [1]. The issue of building envelope failure associated with deficient installation of windows is not limited to coastal climates

For example, numerous recent failures of newly constructed building envelopes have occurred in the state of Minnesota [3]. The Building Inspection Division of the town of Woodbury has reported that an appreciable number of homes built since 1990 have experienced major durability problems. Specifically, 276 of 670 stucco homes built in Woodbury in 1999 (~41 %) experienced severe within-wall damage within 6 years. The primary causes for failure were window leaks, lack of kick out flashing at eave ends of roof-to-wall junctures, and improper deck flashing [3]. Cautley [5] also found that water intrusion associated with windows can occur in contemporary residential buildings in an upper midwestern state. Cautley's study involved instrumentation of walls in a newly constructed home in Wisconsin. The instrumentation detected several episodes of wetting of wall framing below windows, each of which was preceded by a rainstorm.

The State of California has taken interest in understanding the level of risk associated with different window installation methods and has recently sponsored a test program to evaluate the performance of different window installation details [4].

Clearly the problem of water penetration at window openings persists and not only in coastal areas for which the perception is that climate loads are severe. Although coastal climates may indeed be severe, details that promote the entrapment of water and that are not fault tolerant are likewise susceptible to premature deterioration, even in areas of apparently reduced "climate loads." Carll [6] made the point regarding the need for additional information related to moisture loads on buildings and the need to characterize the degree of water entry in relation to such loads.

Two studies that addressed the watertightness of windows and the wall-window interface were conducted by Ricketts [7,8] on behalf of the Canada Mortgage and Housing Corporation. A wide range of factors was found to contribute to water leakage, but the principal paths for leakage were those associated with the wall-window interface. The two principal paths were (1) through the window assembly (extending into the adjacent wall assembly) and (2) through the window to wall interface (extending into the adjacent wall assembly). The investigator found that for the most part, the criteria for water penetration control cited in standard specification Canadian Standards Association (CSA) A440 [9] do not address leakage associated with these two paths. The CSA standard concerns selection of window units and does not address installed performance; it does not require testing of installed assemblies. Finally, it was noted that the specification [9] does not consider local exposure conditions as would be affected by local topography or by building features such as overhang protection.

There is widespread interest in obtaining a better understanding of the comportment of different window installation methods over a range of climate loads. To this end, laboratory investigations have been undertaken by the Institute for Research in Construction (IRC) to evaluate different wall-window interface details and their ability to manage rainwater entry. The investigations have focused on assessing the robustness of specified window installation details. They have addressed what occurs, for example, when sealant ("caulking") joints around window perimeters fail or when window units develop leaks. They have also addressed the influence of airtightness of installations on their resistance to water leakage. Results of IRC studies relating to window installation practice in Canada are reported National Research Council of Canada publications [10,11]. Results relating to installation practice in the United States are reported in the Journal of ASTM International [12].

This paper concerns laboratory evaluation of the watertightness of a select set of wall-window interface details. The details are for windows with mounting flanges installed in wood-frame walls sheathed with rigid extruded polystyrene (XPS) foam. The use of XPS sheathing in low-rise wood-frame homes typically results in lesser energy expenditure for space conditioning [13,14]. XPS sheathing can shed water and is not prone to deterioration due to moisture uptake.[5] These characteristics can allow XPS to be used as a wall's concealed water-resistive barrier (WRB).

Window installation details for flanged windows installed in walls with XPS sheathing have been suggested in the Energy and Environmental Building Association Water Management Guide [15]. Some of the details described in the Guide may not, however, be practical to implement, and the Guide does not indicate whether the details it suggests have been evaluated by testing.

A set of two wall-window interface details and variations in their implementation were evaluated in the investigation reported in this paper. The de-

---

[5]XPS does not readily absorb moisture (<0.3 wt % following ASTM C578-06*).

tails were for fixed polyvinyl chloride (PVC) windows incorporating mounting flanges. Results on water entry for the different wall-window interface configurations are given, and the effectiveness of different details is discussed.

Experimental Approach to Evaluating Water Management of Window Interface Details

Although watertightness studies undertaken in the laboratory do not directly relate to expected long-term performance, the laboratory tests can identify the response of wall assemblies to specific exposures that simulate rain events. Laboratory exposures can be selected to simulate the most extreme storm at a specified locale that would be expected to occur over a specified recurrence period. In this way, establishing the response of wall assemblies to simulated events is an indirect means of determining the likely risk of water entry over a given period for a specific climate region. Laboratory testing may also provide a measure of the expected risk of water entry associated with different installations methods and their relative fault tolerances [16,17].

The investigation described in this paper followed that used in previous studies [10–12]; the ability of different wall-window installation details to manage rainwater was determined on the basis of laboratory watertightness testing. The testing characterized the response of different interface details to simulated conditions of wind-driven rain (WDR).

Description of Test Apparatus

The Dynamic Wind and Wall Test Facility used to subject similar specimens to simulated WDR conditions in previous studies [10–12,16] was used in this investigation. The facility is capable of subjecting full-scale test specimens (nominal size of 2.44×2.44 m^2) to static levels of air pressure differential or to air pressure differentials that fluctuate dynamically; the dynamic pressure fluctuation capabilities of the facility were not, however, used in this investigation. The facility provides a means to assess the air leakage characteristics of test specimens; this capability was utilized in this investigation. The apparatus contains a pressure regulated water spray system that simulates the action of rain deposition on the cladding surface. Water can be applied at a specified rate to the front face of the specimen through an array of spray nozzles.

Summary of Test Protocol

The test protocol was adapted from previous work [16] and a review of WDR loads as might be experienced across North America [18,19]. The protocol was patterned in part on existing North American water penetration standard test methods such as ASTM E331-00, "Standard Test Method for Water Penetration of Exterior Windows, Skylights, Doors, and Curtain Walls by Uniform Static Air Pressure Difference [20]." The protocol consisted of three stages:

(1) Stage 1: The air leakage characteristics of the wall assembly were determined at this stage, as was pressure distribution across the wall assembly. In this investigation, the air leakage characteristics of the test

wall sections were adjusted by the method described in Lacasse et al. [21] to have nominal air leakage rates of 0.3 or 0.8 L/(s m²) at 75 Pa air pressure differential across the test specimen. As described in Lacasse et al. [21], the adjustment was made by either plugging or unplugging holes in a rigid acrylic sheet situated as an interior rebate return on the interior surface of the test specimen. The number of holes and their arrangement sufficient to yield the 0.3 and 0.8 L/(s m²) conditions at 75 Pa were determined during this stage of the test protocol.

(2) Stage 2: Water spray testing was conducted at this stage, and at this stage test specimens did not contain any known deficiencies through which water entry might be anticipated. Testing was performed over a series of spray rates and over a series of differential pressures at each spray rate. The series of spray rates was 0.8, 1.6, and 3.4 L/(min m²), and differential pressure at each spray rate ranged from 0 to 700 Pa. Testing over the full series of spray rates was conducted with the specimen adjusted to the condition that corresponded with the 0.3 L/(s m²) air leakage condition. The specimen was then adjusted to the 0.8 L/(s m²) air leakage condition and re-tested over the full series of spray rates.

(3) Stage 3: Water spray testing was again conducted at this stage but this time with known deficiencies in the specimen through which water entry was expected. Testing was performed over the same series of spray rates and differential pressures as in stage 2, with the specimen adjusted to each of the air leakage conditions described above.The objective of first test stage of the protocol was to assure that spray tests on different specimens would nominally be conducted at or near the same air leakage rate. As indicated previously, information was also gathered at this stage on the pressure distribution across the wall, in particular in locations at or near water collection points. This identified the approximate air pressure differential across different elements in the wall when the wall was subsequently exposed to water spray. The desired nominal air leakage rates through the air barrier system (ABS) were achieved (as indicated previously) by the method described by Lacasse et al. [21]

The water penetration tests conducted during stage 2 were to simulate an installation, carefully assembled from components without flaws under favorable working conditions, and in "new" condition. The ability of the wall-window interface details to manage water given a deficiency along one of the interfaces was assessed in stage 3. Deficiencies purposely introduced in the specimens consisted of small openings that perforated the window frame at the lower corners of the window. Such deficiencies might simulate the failure of corner joints brought about by the effects of aging or the imperfect jointing that is apparent in certain windows. In this situation, the sensitivity of water penetration through relatively larger deficiencies to the rate of water impinging on the façade can be evaluated. Deficiencies introduced in the first line of defense against water entry provide a path for water entry behind the face of the window. This, in turn, permits evaluating the ability of the wall-window interface detail to collect and evacuate water to the exterior of the assembly. Introduction

FIG. 1—(*a*) *Schematic of front elevation of* 2.44×2.44 m² (8×8 ft²) *specimen show-ing location of* 600×1200 mm² (2×4 ft²) *windows and adjacent wood framing studs. Detail "B" might be representative of installation details used in current practice, whereas detail "V" a variation of that practice. (b) Photo of a completed specimen clad with hardboard siding.*

of deficiencies may also permit replicating imperfect installation workmanship and thus helps determine the fault tolerance of the installation detail with re-spect to water management.

Specimens were thus subjected to simulated WDR conditions for specified periods of time; these conditions replicated the main features of rain events. Rates of water drainage from the sill area of the rough opening and from be-hind the cladding (at the base of the wall) were determined by measuring the rate of water collected from these locations. The test protocol permitted com-parisons of water entry results among the different wall-window interface de-tails with regard to water entry and with regard to how that water was man-aged.

Generic Description of Test Specimen

Test specimens were of 2.44×2.44 m² (8×8 ft²) dimension. A test specimen contained two windows, each measuring 600×1200 mm² (nominal size: 2 ×4 ft²), installed in an opening measuring 625×1250 mm² (Fig. 1). Installa-tion details for the window on the left side of a test specimen differed in one regard from the installation details for the window on the right side of the specimen. Entry of water around either window opening was collected in troughs located beneath the respective sill areas of the openings. Water was also collected at the base of the wall behind the cladding. The window-wall combinations evaluated were determined by the interests of an industry group. Additional details regarding the test specimen configuration are provided below.

A number of different wall assemblies were evaluated; these varied in a number of different ways. For brevity, one type of wall assembly is, however, described here. The wall assembly was intended to be representative of low-rise residential construction, except that clear acrylic sheet was used in lieu of interior gypsum wallboard. Each specimen consisted of 38×138 mm^2 (nominal 2×4 in.^{2}) wood studs, transparent acrylic sheet attached to the inside of the wood frame (serving as the principal element of the ABS), XPS foam installed on the exterior of the wood frame (serving as a sheathing board and a WRB), and horizontal lap hardboard siding installed directly over the XPS sheathing (not on furring strips). The clear acrylic sheet used in lieu of gypsum wallboard allowed observation of water penetration into the rough opening or into stud cavities. The expectation was that the location and timing of water ingress could readily be observed using this technique.

Wall-Window Details for Test Specimen

Test results for a selected test specimen, designated specimen W3, are discussed in this paper. Each of the windows in this specimen was installed in an opening that included a sloped sill pan flashing nominally capable of drainage. The basic issue under investigation in this specimen was the influence of incorporating a non-hardening sealant behind the mounting flanges at the head and jambs of the window. Hence the window on the "B-side" (base-case side) of the specimen was installed with sealant applied behind the head and jamb flanges, whereas the window on the "V-side" (variation case side) did not have sealant behind its flanges.

A summary of the construction details for both sides of specimen W3 is presented in Table 1. A vertical sectional view of the V-side of the specimen (without sealant behind flange) is given in Fig. 2. Horizontal sectional views of the B- and V-sides are provided in Figs. 3 and 4, respectively. Of note is that no sheathing membrane is used in either assembly; the 25 mm (1 in.) thick XPS foam board acts as the WRB.

Of interest as well is the use of cap nails, as can be seen in Fig. 2, to create a gap behind the window mounting flange along the sill such that drainage from the sloped sill can readily be accommodated. Also, no sealant was applied at this location. Following installation of the window, a self-adhered 200 mm (4 in.) wide flashing membrane was used to seal the fastener heads and flange ends at the head and along the jambs.

Description of Test Trials and Deficiencies Incorporated in Cladding

Four (4) sets of test trials were undertaken as follows.

(1) Trial 1: Specimen nominally in "as is" condition
(2) Trial 2: With a rubber gasket inserted at the head and jambs at the cladding to window frame interface
(3) Trial 3: With gasket from trial 2 removed and an interior air seal, consisting of spray polyurethane foam, at the interface between the rough opening and the interior edges of the window frame
(4) Trial 4: With foam interior air seal (as in trial 3) and with drip cap flashing added at the head of the windowA schematic representation of

each of the four test trials is given in Fig. 5. All four sets of trials included tests undertaken with deficiencies incorporated at the lower corners of the windows as shown in Fig. 5(b). These deficiencies were approximately 1 mm (0.039 in.)

TABLE 1—*Summary of construction details for specimen W3.*

Item	V-Side Without Sealant	B-Side With Sealant
Interior surface	Acrylic sheet	Same
Framing	2×4 in.^{2} wood studs	Same
Insulation in stud cavity	None	Same
Sheathing board	1 in. (25 mm) XPS foam	Same
Sheathing membrane	None	Same
Window	Fixed solid PVC windows with integral flange; 600×1200 mm^2 (2 ft wide $\times$ 4 ft high) CSA ratings: Air leakage: 0.25 m^3/h m; water resistance: B7; wind load resistance: C4	Same
Siding	Horizontal hardboard siding installed directly over the XPS sheathing and terminated at the window sill and jambs with J-channel trim; no trim used at head	Same
Wall/Window Interface: Window anchoring	XPS foam sheathing extended under the flange up to the framing around the window, and fasteners were placed through the foam into the framing	Same
Sill of R.O.	Sloped (by placing a tapered piece of wood over the rough sill)	Same
Protective treatment of R.O. frame	Drained pan flashing placed over the sloped sill surface; pan flashing sealed to the rough jambs	Same
Joint between window frame and cladding system	3 mm (1/8 in.) gap between J-trim and perimeter of window frame without use of backer rod or sealant; Test trial set 2: Rubber gasket introduced in this joint for test trials	Same

TABLE 1— (*Continued.*)

Item	V-Side Without Sealant	B-Side With Sealant
Joint between the window flange and the backup wall	Shingle-lapped pieces of 200 mm (4 in.) self-adhered flashing membrane sealed to outside face of window flange at jambs and head and on face of XPS at sill; *without sealant* applied to back of window flange; shingle-lapping of flashing sheets and the way they interfaced with window flanges concurred with ASTM E2112 method A-1	Same except: *Sealant applied* to back of window flange at head and jambs (sill left open for drainage)
Joint between window frame and rough opening	Test trial set 3: Spray-in-place polyurethane foam applied from the interior along head and jambs; this changed the air leakage characteristics of the assembly, making the assembly essentially airtight around the window perimeter	Same
Joint between window frame and interior layers	Construction tape and/or sealant joins window frame to interior sheet of acrylic, creating plane of airtightness	Same
Drip cap head flashing	Test trial set 4: Drip cap installed	Same

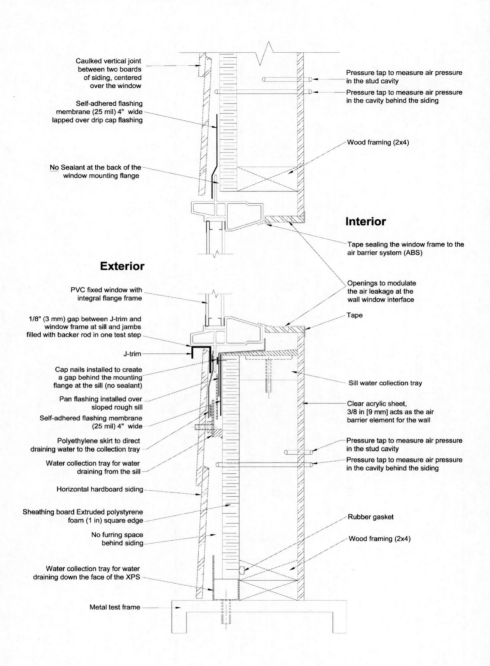

Caulked vertical joint between two boards of siding, centered over the window

Self-adhered flashing membrane (25 mil) 4" wide lapped over drip cap flashing

No Sealant at the back of the window mounting flange

Pressure tap to measure air pressure in the stud cavity

Pressure tap to measure air pressure in the cavity behind the siding

Wood framing (2x4)

Interior

Tape sealing the window frame to the air barrier system (ABS)

Exterior

PVC fixed window with integral flange frame

1/8" (3 mm) gap between J-trim and window frame at sill and jambs filled with backer rod in one test step

J-trim

Cap nails installed to create a gap behind the mounting flange at the sill (no sealant)

Pan flashing installed over sloped rough sill

Self-adhered flashing membrane (25 mil) 4" wide

Polyethylene skirt to direct draining water to the collection tray

Water collection tray for water draining from the sill

Horizontal hardboard siding

Sheathing board Extruded polystyrene foam (1 in) square edge

No furring space behind siding

Water collection tray for water draining down the face of the XPS

Metal test frame

Openings to modulate the air leakage at the wall window interface

Tape

Sill water collection tray

Clear acrylic sheet, 3/8 in [9 mm] acts as the air barrier element for the wall

Pressure tap to measure air pressure in the stud cavity

Pressure tap to measure air pressure in the cavity behind the siding

Rubber gasket

Wood framing (2x4)

FIG. 2—*Schematic drawing of XPSA W3 V-side Vertical Wall Section: Without sealant behind the window flange. Note that the drawings are not accurate with regard to depth details of the components, i.e., the size and spacing between components have in some places been modified to better depict individual items, e.g., the thickness and configuration of the siding edges have been modified as its location in relation to the WRB.*

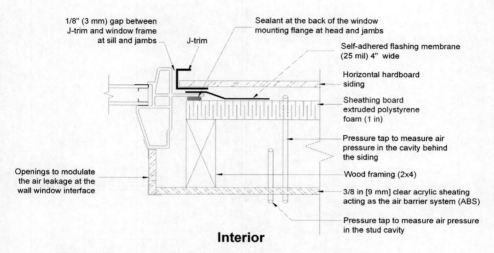

FIG. 3—*XPSA W3 B-side horizontal wall section with sealant behind the window flange.*

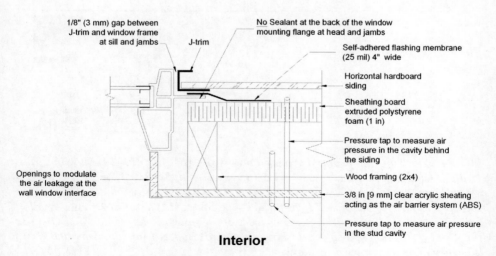

FIG. 4—*XPSA W3 V-side horizontal wall section without sealant behind window flange.*

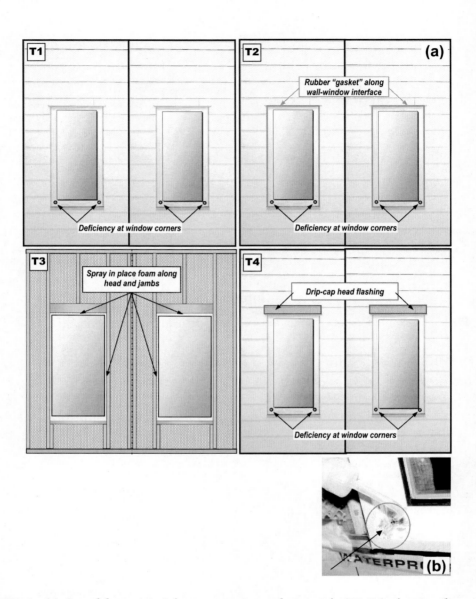

FIG. 5—(a) Set of four pictorial representations of test trials (T1–T4) showing front elevation (cladding exterior) of 2.44 × 2.44 m² specimen (8 × 8 ft²) for T1, T2, and T4 and specimen interior of T3. Location of deficiencies at corners of windows is given on respective exterior elevations. (T1) Test trial 1—test as is; (T2) test trial 2 shows location of rubber gasket; (T3) test trial 3 shows location of spray-in-place foam; and (T4) test trial 4 shows location of drip cap flashing. (b) Approximately 1 mm diameter (0.039 in.) deficiency at lower corner of window.

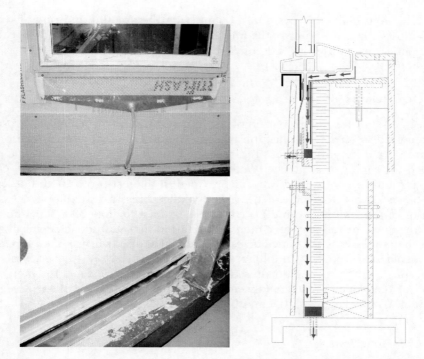

FIG. 6—*Photos and related pictorials of collection troughs.* (a) *Trough for collection of water that drains from sill and* (b) *trough for collection of water behind cladding at base of wall.*

in diameter and were sealed with a sealing compound for those test sequences in which no deficiencies were being tested.

As well, tests were conducted at two nominal ABS leakage rates, 0.3 and 0.8 L/(s m²), respectively (referred to as the 03 ABS and the 08 ABS conditions, respectively), as previously described in the test protocol. Finally, tests were also conducted at three (3) different spray rates (0.8, 1.6, and 3.4 L/(min m²)), the highest spray rate being the default rate specified in ASTM E331-00. For each test sequence, at a given water spray rate and ABS leakage, results were obtained at pressures varying between 0 and 700 Pa (2.81 in. of water; 14.6 psf).

Water Collection Troughs—Two sets of water collection troughs were used to obtain a measure of water entry behind the cladding and in the sub-sill area: (i) Water accumulating in and draining from the sill space was collected in a trough (shown in Fig. 6(a)) and (ii) water draining to the base of the wall was collected in a separate trough (shown in Fig. 6(b)). The intent of the placing a collection trough at the base of the wall was to collect water that may have passed the cladding and found its way to the WRB and thereafter the base of the wall. Nominally, this permitted quantifying the amount and rate of water entry along these different paths and differentiating the significance between these paths given different test conditions.

Selected Results

A selected set of results from each of the four test trials is provided. The results are reported in terms of collection rates in the different troughs in relation to the pressure differential across the specimen for specified test conditions prescribed for each test sequence. Water spray was deposited over the wall cladding at the three prescribed rates as provided in the test protocol and description of test trials; for each of these spray rates pressure was applied to the exterior of the wall at seven different levels: 0, 75, 100, 200, 300, 500, and 700 Pa. During each trail set, specimens were tested first with deficiencies absent from the windows (with deficiencies plugged). The trial set was then repeated with deficiencies present (unplugged). Within each trial set, the series of test conditions (spray rate and air pressure differential) was repeated for each condition of deficiency presence (absent or present) and at each of the levels of nominal ABS leakage (i.e., 0.3 and 0.8 $L/(s\ m^2)$).

Results for Test Trial Set T1

Collection of Water Behind Cladding—Significant quantities of water evidently passed behind the cladding during this trial (when there were open joints between the cladding system and the window). Significantly greater rates of water collection are observed at the base of the wall than at the trough that collected water from the sill pan. Figure 7 indicates that water collection rates ranged from 170 to 1000 mL/min at the wall base; these rates were higher than collection rates from the trough that collected water from the sill pan even when defects were present in the window frames.

Drainage from the Sill Pan—No Deficiencies—Smaller rates of water collection (<20 mL/min) were evident for the trough accommodating drainage from the sill pan as compared to rates obtained at the base of the wall behind the cladding (Fig. 8; no deficiency and 03 ABS). Rates of drainage from the sill pan on the B-side (with sealant behind flanges) were greater than those of the V-side (without sealant). This was the case even when the installations were adjusted to the relatively restrictive air leakage condition (03 ABS) and when no differential air pressure was exerted across the specimen (0 Pa). At the less restrictive air leakage condition (Fig. 9; no deficiency and 08 ABS), both sides showed small increases in rates of collection of water draining from the sill pan (<20 mL/min).

Water leakage at the window head on the V-side of the specimen (no sealant behind jamb or head flanges) was observed at 700 Pa air pressure level at any of the three spray rates (0.8, 1.6, and 3.4 $L/(min\ m^2)$).

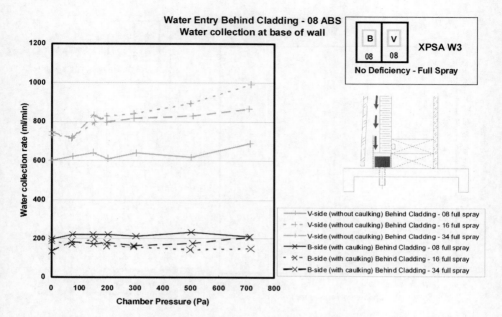

FIG. 7—*Water collection rates at base of wall (behind cladding). Trial T1—no deficiency and 08 ABS.*

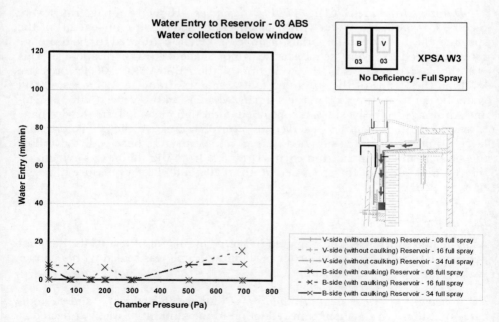

FIG. 8—*Water collection rates from sill pan. Trial T1—no deficiency and 03 ABS.*

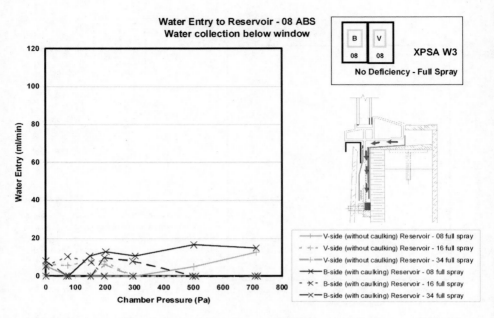

FIG. 9—*Water collection rates from sill pan. Trial T1—no deficiency and 08 ABS.*

Drainage from the Sill Pan—with Deficiencies—Higher drainage rates were recorded on both the B-side (with sealant) and V-side (without sealant) of the specimen at pressure differentials of up to 300 Pa as compared to the drainage rates recorded from test sequences with no deficiency (Figs. 10 and 11). This was the case regardless of the condition of the ABS. At the 500 Pa pressure level, on the B-side of the specimen (with sealant), drainage was arrested and water began to accumulate in the sill pan, whereas on the V-side (without sealant), drainage from the sill pan continued (although in some tests the drainage rate was less than the rates observed at lower pressures). At the 700 Pa pressure level, drainage on either side had ceased, and water was observed to overflow the sill pan and enter the stud cavity. Drainage from the sill on was evident on the B- and V-sides of the specimen at up to 200 and 300 Pa pressure differentials, respectively.

Results for Test Trial Set T2

As indicated previously and depicted in Fig. 5, in this set of test trials, the joint between the cladding and the exterior window frame was sealed with a rubber gasket along the head and jambs.

Collection of Water Behind Cladding—Comparison of Figs. 7 and 12 indicates that there was a significant reduction in the amount of water collected at the base of the wall behind the cladding with the gasket in place. On either side

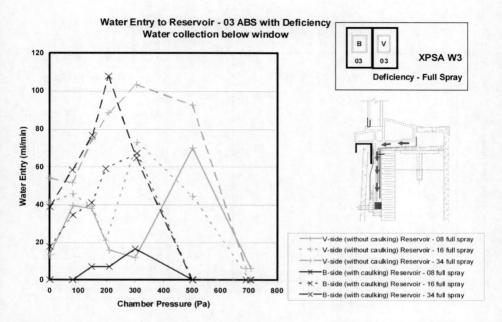

FIG. 10—*Water collection rates from sill pan. Trial T1—deficiency at window corners and 03 ABS.*

of the specimen, the rate of water collection was reduced to ~10 % of the rate collected prior to sealing the head and jambs with the gasket.

Drainage from the Sill Pan—There was little change in the amount of water reaching the sill pan and which subsequently drained to the collection trough in this trial set as compared to test trial set T1. Collection rates and visual observations closely resembled those from trial set T1 (for which the rubber gasket was not present). Without deficiencies (Fig. 13) very small rates of water were collected (<20 mL/min) in the trough that collected water from the sill pan. However, with deficiencies at the window corners (Fig. 14), water readily penetrated to the sill pan; pan drainage at a rate of up to 71 mL/min (B-side at 03 ABS) was recorded. At pressures levels above 300 Pa (6.27 psf), drainage rates diminished, and water was seen to accumulate in the sill pan. At 700 Pa (14.62 psf), drainage was completely arrested and eventually water completely filled the pan. Once filled, additional water that entered the sill pan spilled over its back dam into the stud cavity. As was the case for test trial set T1, for this test trial, drainage from the sill was evident at pressures differentials of up to 200 Pa (4.18 psf) on the B-side and up to 300 Pa (6.27 psf) for drainage of the sill on the V-side.

Water Entry at Window Head—No water entry was observed at the head on either side of the specimen even at the highest pressure differential. This contrasted with what was observed during trial set 1 (where water entry had been observed on the V-side at 700 Pa differential).

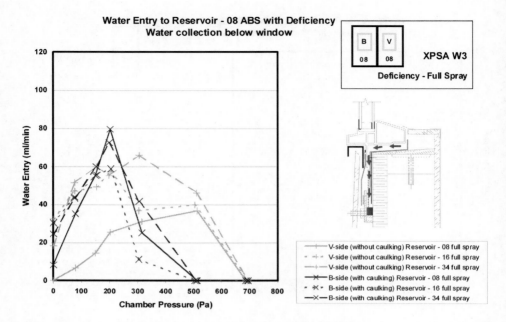

FIG. 11—*Water collection rates from sill pan. Trial T1—deficiency at window corners and 08 ABS.*

Results for Test Trial Set T3

In this test trial, spray-in-place polyurethane foam was placed between the rough opening and the window frame to nominally provide a heightened degree of airtightness at the interior of the window assembly. As indicated previously, the rubber gaskets used in test trial set T2 were removed, thus providing an open perimeter joint between the cladding and the exterior surfaces of the window frame. As regards the specimen's exterior surfaces, essentially the same conditions were in effect during this test trail set as during test trial set T1.

Collection of Water Behind Cladding—As was the case in test trial set 1, significant amounts of water passed behind the cladding to the collection trough at the base of the wall (Fig. 15). Rates of water collection were slightly higher than those of test trial set T1. Interestingly, water entry behind the cladding showed a higher degree of dependence on water spray rate than had been observed during test trial set T1.

Drainage from the Sill Pan—Little or no water was collected at the trough servicing the sill pan when no deficiencies were present at the windows (Fig. 16), whereas with deficiencies, water evidently was introduced to the sill pan (Fig. 17). The maximum drainage collection rate in this instance was ~110 mL/min. Rates of water collection from the sill pan were comparatively higher than the base condition (without foam), particularly at higher pressure levels. Visual observations for both sides of the wall also showed that the sill pan

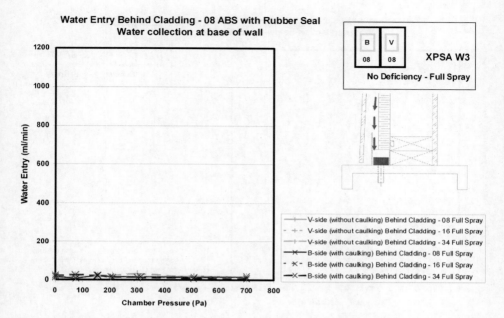

FIG. 12—*Water collection rates at base of wall (behind cladding). Trial T2—with rubber gasket, no deficiency, and 08 ABS.*

overflowed after only a few minutes at the 500 Pa (10.44 psf) pressure level (08 ABS leakage condition), indicating a higher rate of water entry than in the original trials. As in previous trials, sill pan drainage was almost completely arrested at the 700 Pa (14.62 psf) pressure level, whereas drainage from the sill pan was evident at pressures differentials of up to 300 Pa (6.27 psf).

Water Entry at Window Head—No water leakage was observed at the head on the V-side (without sealant) of the window even at the highest applied pressure (700 Pa and 14.62 psf) (as was observed in test trial set T1). This is a similar result to that obtained for test trial set T2.

Results for Test Trial Set T4

The specimen was modified to include drip cap flashing at the head of both sides of the specimen. The foam used to form an air seal between the rough opening and the interior perimeter of the window frame for test trial set 3 was left in place for most of test trial set 4; the foam was removed for testing at the highest spray rate.

Collection of Water Behind Cladding—The amount of water collected at the base of the wall behind the cladding remained high despite the installation of the drip cap flashing (Fig. 18). Addition of the drip cap flashing evidently did not reduce the amount of water that penetrated behind the cladding.

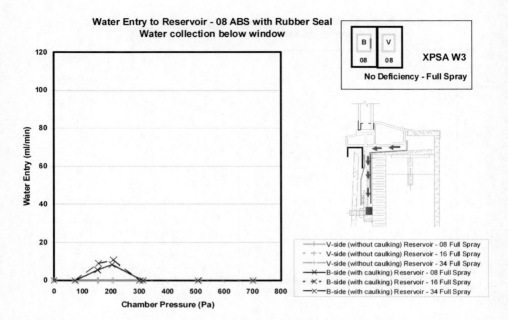

FIG. 13—*Water collection rates from sill pan. Trial 2 with rubber gasket—no deficiency and 08 ABS.*

Drainage from the Sill Pan—Addition of the drip cap (trial set T4) to specimens that incorporated perimeter foam air seals (trial set T3) had no apparent influence on collection rates at troughs collecting water from the sill pans. As would be intuitively expected for specimens with an interior air seal, collection rates from sill spaces were dominated by presence or absence of deficiencies at window corners. A comparison of Figs. 16 and 19 shows that (with deficiencies absent and a perimeter interior foam air seal present) collection rates at the sill were always low; the presence or absence of the drip cap had no obvious effect on collection rate. A comparison of Figs. 17 and 20 with Figs. 16 and 19 indicates that when corner deficiencies were added to specimens incorporating an interior perimeter air seal, collection rates increased substantially. In a similar manner that Figs. 16 and 19 indicate for specimens with perimeter air seals but with corner deficiencies absent, Figs. 17 and 20 indicate that for specimens incorporating both interior perimeter air seals and corner deficiencies, the addition of a drip cap had no apparent influence on collection rates at troughs servicing the sill pans

Water Entry at Window Head—No water was observed at the head on either side of the test specimen even when the interior foam seal (which had been installed for test trial set 3) was removed. It thus appears that addition of the drip cap helped prevent water entry at this location on the V-side.

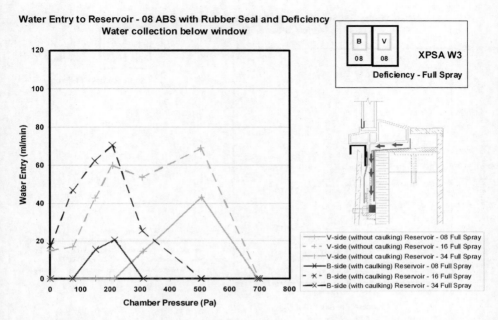

FIG. 14—*Water collection rates from sill pan. Trial 2 with rubber gasket, deficiency at window corners, and 08 ABS.*

Discussion

A brief discussion on the results derived from tests follows in the same order as was previously presented, and relevant implications are considered in respect to the design, installation, and testing of assemblies.

Collection of Water Behind Cladding

The specimen configuration that incorporated the rubber gasket between the window perimeter and the cladding system (the configuration for test trial set 2) showed the least amounts of water entry behind the cladding. Open joints, which were present in the other three specimen configurations, permitted water entry behind the cladding. The addition of the drip cap head flashing resulted in essentially no reduction in the measured rates of water collection at the base of the wall from behind the siding. This suggests that a good portion of the water collected at this location probably entered through the horizontal joint beneath the window (between the cladding and the window frame). Further water penetration tests would be needed to confirm this assumption.

The amounts of water collected from the sill pan area were essentially unrelated to the amounts collected at the base of the wall behind the cladding. Although it would be desirable to limit the amounts of water that get behind the cladding, the test specimen showed an ability to drain water from behind the cladding, down the face of the foam sheathing board. Drainage via this path was appreciable even though the cladding was not spaced from the sheathing.

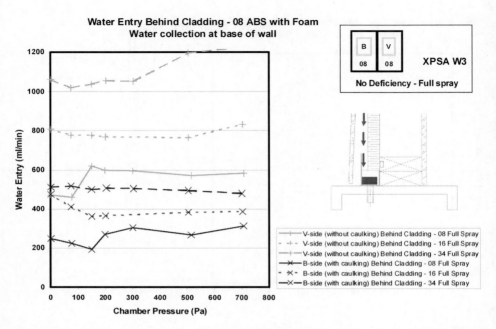

FIG. 15—*Water collection rates at base of wall (behind cladding). Trial 3—with foam, no deficiency, and 08 ABS.*

No water penetration through the XPS sheathing was observed, although it should be noted that the foam sheathing was continuous (it did not include any joints).

Implication—In the test specimen evaluated, sealing of joints between the cladding and the window frame did not appear to be absolutely necessary, owing to the drainage capabilities of the cladding system. The drainage capabilities of the cladding system, combined with the water penetration resistance of the XPS sheathing, prevented water that penetrated behind the cladding from entering wall framing cavities. However, the ability of the cladding system to itself tolerate substantial and chronic water penetration without deterioration is in doubt. Limiting water penetration past the cladding system would also limit the likelihood of water leakage through deficiencies in XPS sheathing board that acts as WRB.

Open joints would likely be less of an issue for cladding placed on furring strips or hollow-backed vinyl siding, as water entry behind the cladding would drain even more freely to the base of the wall than was the case in the specimen tested in this investigation.

Hollow-backed vinyl siding is typically installed with open joints and J-trim at the window interface. The use of J-trim with lap siding, as in the specimen tested, is not common but has advantages. The J-trim made it possible to use preformed gasketing as a perimeter seal between the window and the lap siding

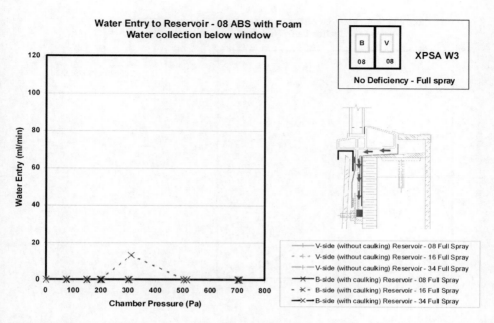

FIG. 16—*Water collection rates from sill pan. Trial T3—with foam, no deficiency, and 08 ABS.*

(which has a stepped profile between siding courses). Preformed gasketing is simpler to install than are sealant joints; joints made with gasketing are also more convenient to maintain.

Drainage from the Sill Pan

Protection of the rough sill and the adjacent jambs with a sill pan will help ensure the long-term performance of the window installation, provided that drainage occurs from the sill pan. A functional sill pan will protect the framing members if at some point over the life of the assembly water entry to the rough opening occurs.

Test results from the four trials, with the windows configured to contain deficiencies (Table 2), indicate that water entry around (or more likely through) the window was less on the V-side of the specimen (where sealant behind the jamb and head flanges was omitted) than on the B-side of the specimen (where there was sealant behind the jamb and head flanges). The table indicates that at test pressures of up to and including 200 Pa, rates of collection from the sill pan on the V-side of the specimen were consistently less than on the B-side of the specimen.

Additionally, at higher pressure levels (i.e., >200 Pa and 4.2 psf), significant accumulation of water in the sill pan was observed on the B-side of the specimen. The accumulation was brought about by both increased water entry to the sill area and reduced drainage from the pan (given that pressure differentials were present across the drainage path from the pan and were in a di-

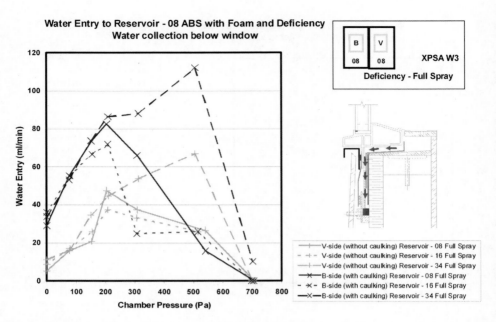

FIG. 17—*Water collection rates from sill pan. Trial T3—with foam, deficiency at window corners, and 08 ABS.*

rection that would oppose drainage). Nonetheless, drainage from the sill pan occurred on both sides of the specimens up to 300 Pa (6.27 psf) pressure differential. When accumulation was observed, water was seen to "bubble" in the sill pan area as a consequence of air flow through the drainage opening through the same tube from which water would drain but in the direction opposite to that of drainage. At heightened pressure levels (i.e., 500 and 700 Pa and 10.44 and 14.62 psf), accumulation in the sill pan in some instances exceeded pan capacity, resulting in pan overflow and thereafter spillage into the stud cavity. Visual observations relating to accumulation and bubbling of water in the sill pan are presented in Table 3.

During test trial set T1, the response was essentially the same on either side of the test specimen; on the V-side of the specimen water penetration around the window head was observed, which appeared to find its way to the sill pan. During test trial sets T2, T3, and T4, pan overflow occurred on the B-side of the specimen, with the spray and pressure levels at which overflow occurred varying between trial sets. In contrast, pan overflow was not observed on the V-side of the specimen during test trial sets T2, T3, or T4 regardless of spray rate or air pressure differential (although "bubbling" was sometimes observed).

The heightened vulnerability of the B-side of the specimen to overflow of the sill pan may be explained in part by the pressure differentials that arise in the window rough opening when the specimen is tested in wet conditions. When subjected to air pressure differential in a dry condition, B-side as well as the V-side of the specimen showed similar pressure drops at the window interface (Figs. 21 and 22), although the pressure drops were slightly higher on the

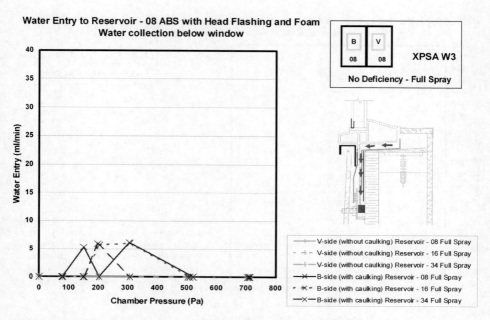

FIG. 18—*Water collection rates at base of wall (behind cladding). Trial T4—with foam and drip cap head flashing, no deficiency, and 08 ABS.*

B-side. In these figures, the pressure drops at the window interface in relation to the pressure across the specimen are given for both ABS leakage conditions (03 and 08 ABS).

In Figs. 21 and 22 the solid lines indicate trends in pressure drop across the window flanges with the specimen at the more restrictive (03) ABS condition, while the dotted lines indicate the corresponding trends at the less restrictive (08) ABS condition. At a chamber pressure of 700 Pa (14.62 psf), the pressure drop values at the 03 ABS condition on the B-side of the specimen ranged from 117 to 212 Pa, while the corresponding values at the 08 ABS condition ranged from 297 and 584 Pa (Table 4). At a lower ABS leakage condition, the pressure drops across the window flanges were obviously lower. These phenomena are apparent for the B- and V-sides, although as indicated previously the pressure drops were slightly higher on the B-side of the specimen (Table 4).

When tested in a wet condition, pressure drops across the window flanges increased in relation to those recorded under dry conditions (Figs. 23 and 24). The largest relative increases in pressure drop across the window flanges, between dry and wet conditions, were recorded on the B-side of the specimen when the installation was in the more restrictive (03) ABS condition (Table 4). Although the pressure drops across the window flanges with the specimens in a wet condition are not drastically higher on the B-side, they nonetheless are higher than on the V-side of the specimen. Higher pressure drops provide for a greater driving force for water entry across the flanges and a greater resistance to drainage from the sill pan.

It is thought that sealant application behind the window flanges blocks the

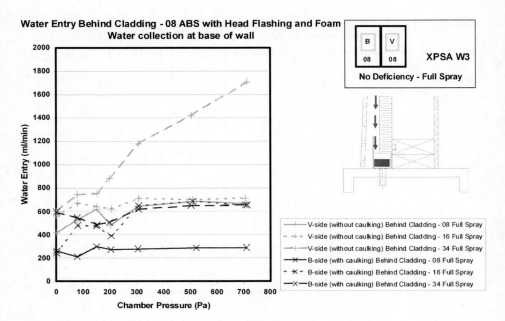

FIG. 19—*Water collection rates from sill pan. Trial T4—with foam and drip cap head flashing, no deficiency, and 08 ABS.*

larger air leakage paths, and the smaller paths that remain are easily occluded by water once the assembly becomes wet. Once occlusion of the small pathways by water occurs, the pressure drops across them (and any other remaining passageways) are increased; this can in turn cause greater amounts of water entry to the sill.

Water Entry at Window Head

Water entry at the head of the V-side was only observed for test trial set T1 and only at the 700 Pa pressure level. Reducing the water loading in the proximity of the head flange, as was achieved by the placement of a rubber gasket (in test trial set 2) or by restricting the number of openings through which air and water could pass, as was accomplished by the use of spray-in-place polyurethane foam around the interior perimeter of the window (in test trial set 3), reduced the likelihood of water entry. In both trails leakage at the head flange was in fact eliminated.

Over the course of installing the drip cap for test trial set 4, a minute (barely perceptible) discontinuity was found at the intersection between two of the self-adhered flashing sheets (between one of the jamb sheets and the head sheet), in other words, near an upper window corner. It is supposed that this deficiency permitted entry of water behind the flange during extreme test conditions. That such a deficiency was evident even though care and attention was brought to the installation process suggests that many such occurrences are likely in the field; the evidence of water entry at window penetrations bears this

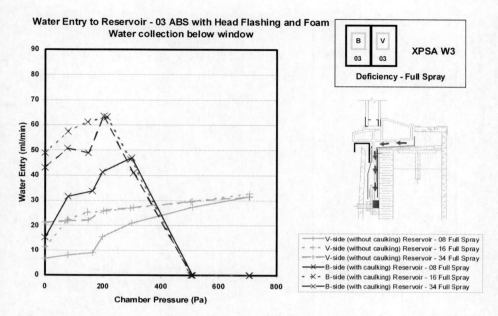

FIG. 20—*Water collection rates from sill pan. Trial T4—with foam and drip cap head flashing, deficiency at window corners, and 03 ABS.*

out. The installation of a drip cap flashing was shown to solve this problem, provided the installation is itself correctly done. Methods other than the use of a drip cap flashing at the head should also be investigated as possible solutions to reducing the likelihood of water entry at this vulnerable location.

Implications—Should a window be installed without application of a sealant behind the mounting flange, measures ought to be taken to ensure that a robust water management design is afforded not only at the sill but at the head of the window as well. This may evidently be accomplished by the installation of a drip cap flashing.

Although a wind pressure of 700 Pa (14.62 psf) coincident with rain is rarely encountered even in climates subject to tropical storms, tests undertaken in such extreme conditions often reveal weak links in the wall system.

Relating Test Conditions to Weather Parameters

A summary of extreme WDR conditions over a range of return periods (in years) is provided in Table 5 for five different locations across the United States [19]. Information on rates of WDR deposition ($L/(min\ m^2)$) and driving rain wind pressures (DRWPs) are given as average extreme hourly values. The DRWP is the velocity pressure (Pa) exerted on a surface (e.g., wall) normal to the wind direction during rain. A word of caution is justified; the WDR and DRWP values listed in Table 5 for Miami are probably over-estimates for the shorter return periods (i.e., ≤ 10 years) and under estimates for the longer

TABLE 2—*Water collection rates (mL/min) from sill pan in relation to nominal pressure levels (Pa) for walls with deficiencies at window corners and tested at a water spray rate of 3.4 L/min m² and 03 ABS leakage.*

Test Trial Set	Water Collection Rates (mL/min) B-Side (Sealant) at Nominal Test Pressure Levels (Pa)				Water Collection Rates (mL/min) V-Side (Without Sealant) at Nominal Test Pressure Levels (Pa)			
	0	75	150	200	0	75	100	200
T1	39	59	77	108	54	52	75	89
T2	32	49	54	72	0	7	9	9
T3	23	59	56	69	0	10	35	40
T4	43	51	49	63	21	22	22	26

TABLE 3—*Visual observations of water in sill pan for walls with deficiencies at window corners and tested at O3 ABS leakage.*

Test Trial Set	B-Side (Sealant)	V-Side (Without Sealant)
T1	Water in sill pan "bubbled" but did not "overflow" the pan; occurred only at 700 Pa and 3.4 L/(min m^2) water spray rate	Water in sill pan bubbled but did not overflow pan; condition occurred only at 700 Pa for all water spray rates (water from head likely increased amount of water to sill pan)
T2	Water "overflowed" only at 700 Pa and 3.4 L/(min m^2) water spray rate	Water bubbled but did not overflow the pan; bubbling at >300 Pa at all water spray rates
T3	Water bubbled and overflowed to rough sill at 500 Pa; condition similar for all water spray rates	At a water spray rate of 3.4 L/(min m^2) and pressure levels >300 Pa, some bubbling but no overflow occurred; at lower water spray rates, little water was visible in the pan
T4	Water bubbled at 500 Pa and overflowed to rough sill at 700 Pa; condition similar for all water spray rates	No bubbling and no overflow, even at 700 Pa; condition unaffected by water spray rate

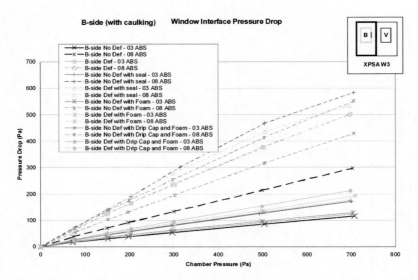

FIG. 21—*Pressure drops for XPSA W3 B-side (with sealant) wall/window interface when dry.*

return periods (≥20 years). The extent of under- or over-estimation has not yet been determined, as this would require a more detailed analysis of the recurrence and intensity of tropical cyclonic storms in the location.

In the United States, design wind pressures are derived from information based on a 1 in 50 year return period [22]. With reference to this return period,

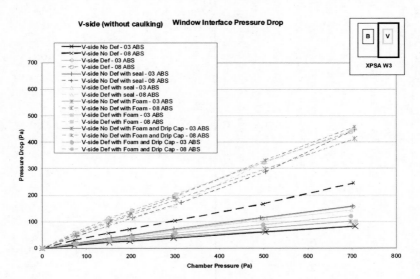

FIG. 22—*Pressure drops for XPSA W3 V-side (without sealant) wall/window interface when dry.*

TABLE 4—*Ranges in window interface pressure drops (Pa) at 500 Pa chamber pressure at different ABS leakage conditions for the B- and V-sides when tested under dry or wet condition.*

Leakage Condition	B-Side (With Sealant)		V-Side (Without Sealant)	
	Dry	Wet	Dry	Wet
03 ABS	86–154 (68)	84–481 (397)	61–114 (53)	66–300 (234)
08 ABS	214–467 (253)	240–504 (264)	167–332 (165)	398–490 (92)

extreme driving rain conditions for Miami, FL, would be simulated with a water deposition rate of 3.9 L/(min m^2) and a DRWP of 553 Pa (11.6 psf). In comparison, extreme driving rain conditions for Seattle, WA, would be simulated with a water deposition rate of 0.3 L/(min m^2) and a DRWP of 198 Pa (4.1 psf). It should be emphasized that these values represent extreme values associated with each individual driving rain parameter and are unlikely to occur coincidentally. This implies that testing at conditions in which both extremes are used would subject a specimen to an event that would have a much heighten return period as compared to the return period associated with a particular extreme WDR parameter. Typically, for non-tropical cyclonic events, at heightened rates of WDR, the corresponding DRWPs are lower than those of the extreme values shown in Table 5, and likewise, rates of WDR are lower when extreme values of DRWP are evident.

However, what is evident from this information is that tests undertaken at

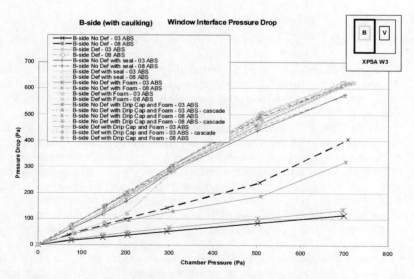

FIG. 23—*Pressure drops for XPSA W3 B-side (with sealant) wall-window interface when wet; 3.4 spray rate.*

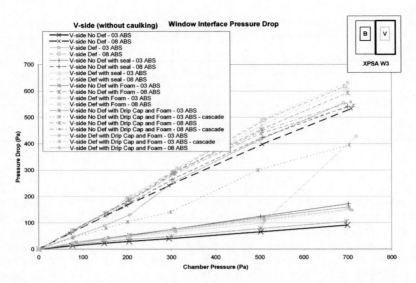

FIG. 24—*Pressure drops (Pa) for XPSA W3 V-side (without sealant) at wall-window interface when wet.*

the 700 Pa (14.62 psf) level and 3.4 L/(min m^2) could be considered as roughly representative of the expected extremes occurring over longer return periods in Miami.

Conclusions

The laboratory test results reported in this paper help support the following findings.

- Water that enters the sill area, either through deficiencies in the window or those due to imperfect installation, can under all most conditions be collected and drained from the area with an appropriately installed pan flashing.
- When the "plane" of airtightness (greatest pressure drop) was located to the interior side of the wall assembly and furthest away from locations of potential water entry, water entry into the assembly was lessened.
- With respect to window installations for flanged windows and the degree of pressure difference across the flange at the interface with the wall assembly, those details that reduce the degree of airtightness at the window-wall interface lessen the risk of water entry. Conversely, those that increase the pressure difference at this location raise the risk of water entry.
  - Applying sealant to seal the joint between the flange and sheathing board tends to increase the pressure difference at these locations.
  - The omission of sealant between the window flange and the sheathing board reduces the degree of airtightness at the window-wall in-

TABLE 5—*Summary of extreme WDR values.*

Location	BOS		MIA		MSP		PHL		SEA	
Return Period	WDR, L/m^2 min	DRWP, Pa	WDR, L/m^2 min	DRWP, Pa	WDR, L/m^2 min	DRWP, Pa	WDR, L/m^2 min	DRWP, Pa	WDR, L/m^2 min	DRWP, Pa
2	0.40	197	0.883	121	0.45	105	0.466	122	0.167	109
5	0.483	247	1.85	259	0.633	134	0.6	172	0.2	137
10	0.55	280	2.48	351	0.766	153	0.7	206	0.233	156
20	0.617	311	3.1	439	0.883	171	0.783	238	0.266	174
30	0.65	329	3.45	490	0.95	182	0.85	256	0.266	185
50	0.70	352	3.88	553	1.033	195	0.9	279	0.3	198
100	0.75	383	4.483	638	1.15	212	1	310	0.316	216

Note: BOS = Boston, MA; MIA = Miami, FL; MSP = Minneapolis, MN; PHL = Philadelphia, PA; and SEA = Seattle, WA.

terface, thereby tending to decrease pressure differential across the window flanges.

- Appling spacers behind the sill (bottom) flange not only reduces the pressure difference at this location but also permits water to drain from the sill area.

- At the 300 Pa pressure level (6.27 psf) and the highest water spray rate (3.4 L/(min m²)), all flashing configurations tested with foam sheathing were successful in draining water from the sill pan that protected the rough opening.

Summary

This paper reports selected results of a series laboratory spray tests of two wall-window interface details for flanged vinyl windows installed in wood-frame walls sheathed with XPS foam insulation board. The two details were similar and were considered representative of selected North American construction practice; they varied with regard to whether or not sealant was used behind the jamb and head flanges (to seal the joint between n the flange and sheathing board). Both details were incorporated in a single full-scale test assembly. The assembly included a cladding system, which was horizontal lap hardboard siding. Leakage paths ("deficiencies") were introduced the window frames, and the paths were alternatively blocked or opened to permit evaluation of the performance of the installation details under two different assumed conditions of window leakage. The test series was also conducted with three modifications made to each installation details. These modifications were the installation of gasketing in perimeter joints between the window and the cladding, the use of spray-in-place polyurethane foam between the window and rough opening on the interior, and the incorporation of drip cap flashing at the window head. Little water entry to the sill area was observed when deficiencies were not present in the windows. With deficiencies present in the windows, considerable water entry to the sill area was apparent, and the entry amounts were greater for the installation in which sealant was used behind the mounting flanges. The sill pans proved capable of managing the amounts of water that entered into the rough opening under all but the most extreme test conditions. Overflow of the pan and spillage to the rough opening were only observed for the installation in which sealant was used behind the window mounting flanges and only when differential pressure across the specimen during spray testing was high (500 Pa or more). Significant amounts of water entry between the windows and the cladding system occurred when the joints between them were open. This water largely drained to the base of the wall, even though the cladding system was not installed over a drainage space; no penetration of this water past the sheathing was observed. It should however be noted that the drainage distance between the joints between the window and the cladding and the base of the wall was modest in the assembly tested, and the extruded foam that served as a WRB was continuous (without joints) over that distance.

Acknowledgments

The writers are indebted to Mr. Charles Carll for his thorough review of, many useful suggestions for, and keen effort in the preparation of this paper. The writers would also like to gratefully acknowledge support of this work provided by the Extruded Polystyrene Association (XPSA) and the collaboration between the National Research Council Canada and the XPSA for completion of this project.

References

[1]   Morrison Hershfield Limited, *Survey of Building Envelope Failures in the Coastal Climate of British Columbia*, Canada Mortgage and Housing Corporation, Ottawa, 1996.

[2]   Building Envelope Engineering, *Wall Moisture Problems in Alberta Dwellings*, Canada Mortgage and Housing Corporation, Ottawa, 1999.

[3]   Glubka, R., *Stucco in Residential Construction*, Building Inspection Division, Woodbury, MN, February 9, 2005.

[4]   Leslie, N., "Window Installation Methods Test Results," *Task 3.3 Report*, California Energy Commission/Contract No. 500-03-013, *GTI Project No. 15485*, Gas Technology Institute, Des Plaines, IL, 2006, p. 38.

[5]   Cautley, D., "Comparative Measured Moisture Performance of Woodframe Walls," *Proceedings of Conference on Woodframe Housing Durability and Disaster Issues*, Las Vegas, NV, October 4–6, 2004, Forest Products Society, Madison, WI, 2004, pp. 201–209.

[6]   Carll, C., "Rainwater Intrusion in Light-Frame Building Walls," *Proceedings of the Second Annual Conference on Durability and Disaster Mitigation in Wood-Frame Housing*, Madison, WI, November 6–8, 2000, Forest Products Society, Madison, WI, 2001, pp. 33–40.

[7]   Ricketts, D. R., "Water Penetration Resistance of Windows: Study of Manufacturing, Building Design, Installation and Maintenance Factors," *Study 1*, Canada Mortgage and Housing Corporation, Ottawa, December 2002, p. 86.

[8]   Ricketts, D. R., "Water Penetration Resistance of Windows: Study of Codes, Standards, Testing and Certification," *Study 2*, Canada Mortgage and Housing Corporation, Ottawa, December 2002, p. 91.

[9]   CAN/CSA A440, 2000, "Windows," Canadian Standards Association, Mississauga, ON, p. 249.

[10] Lacasse, M. A., Rousseau, M., Cornick, S. M., and Plescia, S., "Assessing the Effectiveness of Wall-Window Interface Details to Manage Rainwater," *Tenth Canadian Conference on Building Science and Technology*, May 12–13, 2005, Ottawa, ON, Building Envelope Council Ottawa Region (BECOR), pp. 127–138 (NRCC-47685).

[11] Lacasse, M. A., Manning, M. M., Rousseau, M. Z., Cornick, S. M., Plescia, S., Nicholls, M., and Nunes, S. C., "Results on Assessing the Effectiveness of Wall-Window Interface Details to Manage Rainwater," *11th Canadian Conference on Building Science and Technology*, March 21–23, 2007, Banff, AB, Alberta Building Envelope Council (South), pp. 1–14 (NRCC-49201).

[12] Lacasse, M. A., Rousseau, M., Cornick, S. M., Manning, M. M., Ganapathy, G., Nicholls, M., and Williams, M. F., "Laboratory Tests of Water Penetration Through Wall-Window Interfaces Based on U.S. Residential Window Installation Practice,"

J. ASTM Int., Vol. 6, No. 8, 2009, Paper ID JAI101428.

[13]   McBride, M. F., "Energy and Environmental Benefits of Extruded Polystyrene Foam and Fiberglass Insulation Products in U.S. Residential and Commercial Building," *15th Annual Earth Technologies Forum (Earth Tech Forum 2004)*, Washington, D.C., April 13–15, 2004, Alliance for Responsible Atmospheric Policy (ARAP) and Environmental Protection Agency (EPA), 2004.

[14]   Franklin Associates, *Plastics Energy and Greenhouse Gas Savings Using Rigid Foam Sheathing Applied to Exterior Walls of Single-Family Residential Housing in the U.S. and Canada—A Case Study*, September 2000, p. 34.

[15]   Lstiburek, J. W., *Water Management Guide*, 2nd ed., Energy & Environmental Building Association, Minneapolis, MN, 2002, pp. 2002–2004.

[16]   Lacasse, M. A., O'Connor, T. J., Nunes, S., and Beaulieu, P., "Report from Task 6 of MEWS Project Experimental Assessment of Water Penetration and Entry into Wood-Frame Wall Specimens, Final Report," *Research Report No. 133*, Institute for Research in Construction, National Research Council Canada, February 2003, p. 133 (IRC-RR-133).

[17]   Lacasse, M. A., "Durability and Performance of Building Envelopes," *BSI 2003 Proceedings*, October 7, 2003, Institute for Research in Construction, National Research Council, Ottawa, 6 p. (NRCC-46888).

[18]   Cornick, S. M. and M. A. Lacasse, "A Review of Climate Loads Relevant to Assessing the Watertightness Performance of Walls, Windows, and Wall-Window Interfaces," *J. ASTM Int.*, Vol. 2, No. 10, 2005, Paper ID JAI12505 (NRCC-47645).

[19]   Cornick, S. M. and Lacasse, M. A., "An Investigation of Climate Loads on Building Facades for Selected Locations in the U.S.," *J. ASTM Int.*, Vol. 6, No. 2, 2009, Paper ID JAI101210.

[20]   ASTM E331-00, 2009, "Standard Test Method for Water Penetration of Exterior Windows, Skylights, Doors, and Curtain Walls by Uniform Static Air Pressure Difference," *Annual Book of ASTM Standards*, Vol. 04.11, ASTM International, West Conshohocken, PA.

[21]   Lacasse, M. A., Cornick, S. M., Rousseau, M., Armstrong, M., Ganapathy, G., Nicholls, M., and Plescia, S., "Towards Development of a Performance Standard for Assessing the Effectiveness of Wall-Window Interface Details to Manage Rainwater Intrusion," *J. ASTM Int.*, Vol. 6, 2009, Paper ID 102048.

[22]   Mehta, K. C. and Delahay, J. M., *Guide to the Use of the Wind Load Provisions of ASCE 7-02*, American Society of Civil Engineers (ASCE) Press, Reston, VA, January 2004, p. 142.